GW00870069

Touching the Past

Jean Wheeler

authorHOUSE®

AuthorHouse™ UK Ltd.
500 Avebury Boulevard
Central Milton Keynes, MK9 2BE
www.authorhouse.co.uk
Phone: 08001974150

© 2010 Jean Wheeler. All rights reserved.

No part of this book may be reproduced, stored in a retrieval system, or transmitted by any means without the written permission of the author.

First published by AuthorHouse 3/15/2010

ISBN: 978-1-4389-7408-8 (sc)

This book is printed on acid-free paper.

Acknowledgements

Thanks to Paul Abbott of the Isle of Wight Lavender Farm

for all his help in the early stages of this book,

for his sustained interest and for the inspiration

I derived from the work of the Farm

&

To my husband, Ray, for his support
and encouragement

With love to all the family

Chronological History of Bridge Farm

Romans

850 AD	**Monastery – land farmed by monks**
	Civil War
1-1558	**Henry VIII**
1536-1549	**Dissolution of the Monasteries**
1539	**Land given to Francis Courtney (later Sir Francis) aged 44**
1542	**Manor House built.**
1539-1564	**Francis Courtney died 1564 aged 70 (1494-1564)**
	Survived by wife and son William who inherited aged 32
1-1600	**William Courtney died aged 58 (1532-1600)**
	Survived by wife and son Thomas who inherited aged 26
1600-1635	**Thomas Courtney died aged 61 (1574-1635)**
	Survived by daughter Elizabeth who inherited aged 39.
	1624 Married John Hampton, silversmith who died 1650

	Had a son Bevis – father Walter Tanner
1635-1688	Elizabeth Hampton died aged 92 (1596-1688).
	Survived by Bevis Hampton who inherited aged 64
1-1706	Bevis Hampton a spendthrift.
	House sold to John Herbert, farmer age 38.
1706-1750	John Herbert died aged 82 (1668-1750)
	Survived by sons, the eldest Walter who inherited aged 61
1750-1752	Walter Herbert died aged 63 (1689-1752)
	Not married. Survived by brother Thomas who inherited aged 59
1752-1764	Thomas Herbert died aged 71 (1689-1752)
	House sold, purchased by Cedric Morey aged 42
1764-1788	Cedric Morey died aged 66 (1722-1788)
	Survived by daughter Agnes, inheriting aged 44
1788-1815	Agnes Lafolley (nee Morey) died aged 71 (1744-1815)
	Married Matthew Lafolley 1765. Matthew died 1800
	Survived by son Patrick inheriting aged 50
1815-1831	Patrick Lafolley died aged 66 (1765-1831). Married Margaret 1788.

	Survived by son Walter aged 41.
1831-1870	Walter Lafolley died aged 80 (1790-1870)
	Survived by son Stephen inheriting aged 46
1870-1875	Stephen Lafolley died aged 51 (1824-1875)
	Survived by son Bernard aged 17
1875-1905	Bernard Lafolley died aged 47 (1858-1905)
	PROPERTY PUT ON THE MARKET
1905	Property bought by David Harris senior (Pa Harris)
1957	Transferred to David Harris junior (Dave Harris)
1987	Dave Harris dies – property purchased by Joanna and Seth Short

KICK START

1

The black plastic bag bounced down the stairs. 'I hope it doesn't split' said Sarah to herself. The bag was joining six others that had been filled with Aunt Grace's clothes, they were piled at the bottom of the stairs and hopefully the Red Cross would be collecting them in the afternoon. Aunt Grace had recently died at the age of ninety one and as the main beneficiary the house was now Sarahs, so she had the thankless task of clearing out all her Aunt's belongings. The dressing table was the last piece of furniture to get her attention. She smiled as she opened the drawers, everything was neatly folded and carefully arranged, just as everything else had been. It was in one of the small top drawers under the handkerchiefs and stockings that Sarah found something rather out of character, a shabby envelope addressed to Miss Grace Bruce, postmarked, Tolford, 28th September 1912. The photograph inside was rather tattered, obviously well handled! It showed a lovely young woman leaning over a bridge and laughing into the camera, in the background was a copse and farm buildings. Sarah's curiosity was aroused. Was this lovely woman the Aunt Grace she had known and had eventually grown to love? If not who was she? Who took the photograph, where and why was it hidden? Sarah put the photograph back in the envelope together with a small sachet of lavender that had fallen out and put them in her bag thinking to herself that she would never know.

The house, apart from a few pieces of antique furniture, which Sarah was still considering whether to keep, was now empty and feeling very strange. Sarah sneezed and it echoed around the emptiness, she gave a little shiver it was as if Aunt Grace was still there, and thinking of the photograph Sarah wondered if she had really known her? She jumped as the doorbell rang, it was the Red Cross, they thanked Sarah for thinking of them, collected the sacks and drove away. Sarah shut the door and looked around, she had a lot to think about, the house was hers, but should she keep it? Could she afford to live in it? At this particular time she managed to pay for her flat and the electricity, but would the fact of having no rent to pay compensate for the Council Tax charges and general maintenance, or, would the bills be more than she could afford? Obviously some sums had to be done and very soon. Sarah suddenly did a 'double-take', she realised she was bored with her present job and what was more important did she want to go on living in a town? Perhaps this was the time to rethink her way of life. She had a little chuckle and wondered if Aunt Grace was trying to tell her something.

She went back to her flat for a meal and a well earned rest. Sitting at the kitchen table with a glass of red wine waiting for the microwave to bleep, she took out the photograph to see if she had missed anything, and found she was just as puzzled, mainly because it had been hidden. Why hide such a lovely photograph? It was so tattered it had obviously been well looked at, and why the lavender? It occurred to her that she had a long weekend off and did not have to go into the library until Tuesday. It was nearly six o'clock so she put the radio on for the weather forecast, 'warm, sunny periods particularly in the South-east. The winds have dropped and the weather seems settled for the next few days.' 'That settles it, I'll go to Tolford and see if I can find out anything. If I don't at least I can have a walk along the estuary and breathe the sea air.' The lasagne was ready and Sarah sat down and enjoyed her meal, the wine tasted good and the tiredness dropped away as she started to plan for her few days of investigation.

'I'll get off early on Saturday morning, find Tolford, I know it is near the coast so it should be a pleasant trip. First of all I will make sure that the bridge is in Tolford, I'll show the photograph to local people and if it is a local bridge ask for directions and go and have a look. Will it tell me anything the photograph doesn't? Return to the village, ask around to see if there is anyone who could possibly help. Then, time permitting, pay them a visit. On Sunday I will follow up any leads, if any and on Monday, if I've got time, I can go the local library to look up old newspapers. I hope it is open on Mondays. That's my plan, but it is a flexible one so could change.'

'What do I need? Petrol, that should be alright, I filled up yesterday. The road map is on the dresser, must remember to put it in the car. Money? A trip to the cashpoint I think. What shall I pack? In order of priority make-up bag, toothbrush, pants, T-shirts, spare pair of jeans, pyjamas, spare jumper, fleece and wellie boots would be a good idea. Another good idea would be somewhere to stay. I'll gamble on that and hope that there is a B and B near the village. One final thing, a phone call to Mum just to let her know that I have not been abducted but I will not be around until Tuesday.'

The weather forecast was right, it was a beautiful autumnal

morning and Sarah felt a frisson of excitement as she got into her car and set off. Driving along the country roads she felt at peace, there was hardly any traffic, such a change from the daily dual carriageway. It occurred to her that it could have been such a morning when the photograph had been taken. After about forty minutes Sarah came across the first signpost with 'Tolford' on it, then a few minutes later one pointing right - 'Tolford 2 miles'.

The village sprawled round a ragged village green, a few oak trees with their bright yellow and orange autumn leaves giving height and colour to the picture. The brash red sign of the Post Office stood out amongst the soft grey stone of the cottages and Sarah finding a parking spot nearby decided that she would start her enquiries there.

The Post Office was at the far end of a general store and Sarah showed the photograph to the assistant behind the counter. 'Well, it certainly looks like our bridge, built by the Romans you know, but who the young woman is, I just cannot tell. 1912 did you say? That was just before World War I so you'll need to speak to one of our old 'uns. Mrs Knight lives at Malt Cottage on the other side of the Green with her daughter Betty, she must be nearly 90 years old. I suggest you call on her, she don't get many visitors so will be pleased to see you. Late afternoon is a good time after she's had her snooze. You can find the bridge by going left, then left again, look for the brown sign saying 'Roman Bridge' then follow the path. Good Luck! '

Sarah bought a packet of sandwiches and a mineral water and set off. She soon found the path by the river. It was a wide path edged with gnarled roots, clumps of tall grasses backed with the skeletal heads of cow parsley and beyond a blackthorn hedge. On the far side of the river there was a rounded copse, the autumn leaves gleaming in the late sunshine. The silvered trunks of graceful birches contrasted with the dark algae covered beeches and oaks, and just upstream over the bend in the river was a bridge. As she rounded the bend the sun flashed into her eyes the water catching its rays and throwing them up to confuse the picture even more, but Sarah felt it was the right place. She shut her eyes 'Please let it be' she whispered and stood quite still for a few seconds, drawing in deep breaths to control her rapidly beating heart.

The double spanned soft grey stone bridge arched comfortably over the river, ducks swam under it dabbling in the weeds for choice morsels. Swifts looped and swooped, feeding on the insects preparing for their long migration. She took the tattered photograph from her bag. It was all there, the bridge, the bank, the copse, the farm, everything but the young woman. Could it have been Aunt Grace? From her Aunt's birth certificate Sarah knew that in 1912 she would have been 20 years old. Had she really been as lovely as the photograph? Who took the photograph? Why was the photograph hidden? Why the lavender?

2

Sarah was five when she was taken to a cold, dark, terraced house in Southampton and introduced to her father's Aunt Grace. She had been told that she was going to meet a beautiful woman, and Sarah could remember quite clearly her initial disappointment. Aunt Grace had faded red hair pinned back into a loose roll, some elusive strands escaping despite the constant attention of arthritic fingers. However, it was her face that Sarah was taken with. There were fine lines everywhere, round her eyes, her mouth and on her neck, more than she had seen on any other face. Faded eyebrows seemed to take the colour out of her cheeks, the lips were very straight, and Sarah wondered if she ever smiled. Suddenly she was aware of two very blue eyes watching her and she blushed as she realised she had been caught staring.

'So this is Sarah, how old are you? - Do you like ginger biscuits? - There are some in the kitchen in a blue biscuit barrel on the dresser, you may have two. Off you go, and say 'Hello' to Matty, she'll be asleep on one of the chairs.' Sarah was not sure what to do, answer the questions or go to the kitchen in search of ginger biscuits and Matty. Her father nodded his head in the direction of the kitchen. She found the biscuits, but only took one, ginger biscuits were not her favourite. Matty turned out to be a beautiful tabby cat, Sarah knelt down by the chair and gently stroked her, the cat responded with a lovely purr. 'You are gorgeous' whispered Sarah as she nibbled her biscuit. She went back to the sitting room and suddenly saw what her father had meant when he said that she would meet a 'beautiful woman'. Aunt Grace had thrown her head back and was laughing at something her father had said and Sarah could see the sparkle that was hidden behind the faded, lined face. Standing on the river bank, looking at the bridge, Sarah remembered that moment and thought that perhaps it really was Aunt Grace in the photo.

A quick look at the photograph and Sarah's imagination went into overdrive. Was this a secret liaison? Was it a lover's tryst? Was it a friend or a relation? Sarah decided she would not know the answer until she found out who the photographer was? Was it someone who lived in the village? She walked across the bridge and leant over as if she was being photographed. It was such a peaceful scene and the late autumn sun was so beautifully warm that Sarah decided it was a good place for lunch. Finding a convenient rock on the bank of the river she sat down and took out her sandwiches and wondered if the girl in the photograph had ever sat there. She pulled off small pieces of crust and threw them to the ducks, laughing as they squabbled for the bread. It was very pleasant sitting there in the warm sunshine, and Sarah drifted off into that state where memories take over and the present has gone.

Sarah could see that the first visit to Aunt Grace had changed her life, from someone she hadn't known to someone who had become an integral and loving part of her life seemed to have been a very short step. Letters came regularly, she had never had letters before and was so thrilled when they arrived. It was the presents however that were so special. Whilst her friends were receiving boxes of hankies, lisle stockings and, if they were lucky chocolates, she had rather special gifts. Bath salts for her twelve birthday and for her thirteenth birthday a lovely deep blue square silk scarf that had come from India. She remembered her Aunt telling her that a small child had probably stitched the rolled hem and Sarah could remember looking at the small even stitches and then trying to copy them on a handkerchief. Aunt Grace had told her that a pure silk scarf should be able to be pulled through a gold wedding ring and brought out her mother's ring to show her it was true. Sitting in the sunshine Sarah shivered as she remembered the sensuous feel of the silk on her neck. Her mother had said it was 'decadent'. 'What's decadent?' Sarah could remember asking.

'Not quite nice dear.'

'Not quite nice? Why Mother it is just beautiful, really nice.' The scarf had long gone but the memory remained.

All changed when Sarah was fourteen. 'Your father has had an accident dear.' Aunt Grace's words filtered through the sunshine.

What a day that was. Spring at its best, a beautiful April morning with the pale sunshine falling gently on the white lilac by the front door, the narcissi round its base perfuming the morning air, she could no longer look at narcissi without thinking of her father. 'What a glorious morning' said Mother as she kissed Father goodbye. An hour later the police arrived with the news that he had been involved in a road accident. Aunt Grace had come immediately, Father was one of her favourites. She was wonderful explaining that death can come at any time and sometimes it is a blessing, no prolonged pain, no more anguish but peace, and for those left sweet blessed memories.

It was memories that Aunt Grace specialised in, she would talk about Sarah's father and tell her stories about the various things they did when he came to stay with her. Now it was Sarah's turn to stay. Her Mother had to work to keep them and because the Summer holidays were long she asked Aunt Grace to help out. At first Sarah had been unhappy at leaving her Mother, but gradually she adapted realising that her Mother was relieved at not having to worry about whether she was happy or not, neither did she have to dash home to cook a meal. It was obvious that she and Aunt Grace got on extremely well and a deep love developed between them, in fact the time spent there was to affect the way Sarah's life would go.

Aunt Grace had an amazing collection of books there were bookshelves in the sitting room, on the landing and in the spare room where Sarah slept. She was encouraged to read and to discuss the books, this giving her an insight into literature well beyond her years. She could still smell the faintly dusty, musty smell that came from the leather binding on some of the older books as she and Aunt Grace dusted and cleaned the shelves and the books. All this learning from and caring for books decided Sarah to become a librarian and pass on her love and knowledge of books to others. As Sarah drowsed she thought about the feelings she'd had when clearing out Aunt Grace's house. Did she need a change of direction?

The squabbling ducks roused Sarah from her reverie she decided to go back to the village, find somewhere to stay then visit Mrs Knight. 'She just might know who the girl is, or can tell me name of someone who does, she might even know the name of the photographer.'

Reaching the main street Sarah got back in her car and set off to circle the Village Green. Consisting of small houses and five or six shops the main street ran down the north side of the green, linking up with South Street which was lined with small cottages, one of which must be Malt Cottage. It was when she had completed the circle of the green that Sarah saw the notice 'Bridge Farm B and B 100 yds on the left'. Having little sense of direction Sarah did not at first connect this farm with the one in the photograph, until pausing at the cattle grid half way up the lane and seeing the river sparkling through the hawthorn hedge with the bridge beyond she realised that it was and decided it was the perfect place to stay.

3

It was quite a long lane up to the farm, the river glinting through on one side and on the other was a field of cattle making gentle mooing noises as they moved towards the barns - obviously it was milking time. There were still some bedraggled blackberries hanging on the brambles and the leaves were beginning to crumple, but the hawthorns were coming into their own the haws taking on the autumnal flush that would liven up the hedgerows until the birds discovered them. Old Man's Beard was thrown along each side giving spiders and other insects sanctuary. Clumps of Angelica proudly stood up amongst brown unidentifiable undergrowth and Sarah drew in deep breaths as she took in the peaceful autumn scene.

She bumped along the lane eventually ending up at the farmhouse, a notice pointed to the right stating 'Car Park'. Sarah dutifully turned in, by this time the cows were really making themselves heard and Sarah could hear a man's voice calling them into the milking parlour, they were so close she could smell their sweet breath and hear them puffing through their nostrils. 'A pity about the other smells' thought Sarah, as the full impact of the farmyard hit her senses.

The farmhouse was a grey stone L-shaped building set at a slight angle to the lane so that it caught the maximum amount of sun, a small paved courtyard in the angle of the L providing a sheltered suntrap. A black Labrador lazily rose and came towards Sarah his tail waving a greeting, he gave a gentle 'woof' and thrust his nose into her outstretched hand. 'Well, hello, you're friendly ' said Sarah rubbing him behind his ears.

'He'll take as much of that as you can give him.' Sarah turned round to find a woman about the same age as herself leaning against the door.

'He's lovely' said Sarah, 'we had a golden Labrador when I was in my teens and he was just as sloppy.'

'Well, I'm sure you didn't come here to talk about dogs' laughed the woman, 'how can I help? '

'I'm Sarah Bruce and I'm looking for Bed and Breakfast actually, do you have a room I could have until Tuesday?'

'I think so, but come in and I'll check in case any bookings have been taken for the weekend whilst I've been out.'

The hall struck slightly chill as Sarah went in and a shiver went down her back, was it because there was no central heating, was it the stone floor or was there something else? The hall was paved with shiny grey flagstones that looked as if they were polished every day, the walls were painted a rich red but covered with so many paintings of flowers and plants that the impression was one of lightness.

'I'm Joanna Short incidentally, my husband is Seth and as I expect you can hear he is doing the milking.' She opened a large diary on the hall table. 'Room until Tuesday? Yes that's fine, there's an en suite one at the side of the house, it looks over the bridge and is very quiet. It's £25.00 per night. The other visitors this weekend are guests at a local wedding, but they have promised to be quiet coming in. You are welcome to an evening meal, but that will be extra. Here's the key, go and have a look. Up the stairs, turn left and it is the second on the right. It is called Grace's room.' Sarah did a double take, could this be a co-incidence? 'I'll be in the kitchen when you come down'.

The room was large, the pine furniture was minimal, a bedside table, a chest of drawers and a small wardrobe. It was all old and beautifully made with a wonderful patina that could only have been the result of loving care.

Dominating the room was the double bed covered with an attractive cream bedspread splattered with honeysuckle. The walls were plain cream and on the polished wood floor were pale green rugs. The lovely colours of the honeysuckle on the bedspread were accentuated by the deep peach of the silky curtains as they blew gently in the afternoon breeze. From the window Sarah found herself looking over the river and the bridge. A narrow road wound round from the farmhouse and across the bridge. 'I wonder where that goes, could it go to the estuary? Something for me to investigate, at this rate the weekend won't be long enough'. She took a quick look at the bathroom and laughed as she saw the bath, an old-fashioned cast iron one with claw feet and brass taps, it was just right fitting in beautifully with the room.

She went down stairs and into the kitchen 'Yes, I would really like to stay please' and smiled at Joanna, 'the bathroom was the clincher. As for dinner, it would be great to have it with you, I would love to hear about this lovely house and learn a little about its history and that of the area.'

Joanna laughed 'That's fine, but you don't know what you are letting yourself in for, local history is one of my husband's hobbies. Dinner is at seven and we eat in here. See you later then. Could you put your name in the Visitor's book please, it's on the hall table.'

As Sarah turned she saw a framed photograph on the wall and stopped short, it could have been the one she had found at her Aunt Grace's except for one important fact, the figure leaning over the bridge was that of a young man!

'Joanna, who is that?' she asked rather sharply. Joanna looked a bit surprised at the question.

'We don't know, the photo was found when we cleaned out Grace's room, the one you are in, after we bought the farm from Dave Harris. It was underneath the lining paper in the top drawer of the chest of drawers. The furniture, apart from the bed, came with the farm. Why are you interested? Do you think you know who it is?'

'It's quite a long story Joanna, can I tell you about it over dinner'

'You've got me really curious now, but that'll be fine, it means we won't be talking about cattle feed all through the meal,' said Joanna as she turned away and started to prepare the vegetables.

4

As Sarah got into her car to drive back to the village a light drizzle of rain began to fall. 'This wasn't forecast' she muttered. By the time Sarah reached the cattle grid the rain had stopped, the raindrops that had been caught in the spiders' webs festooning the hedge began to sparkle in the weak sunshine and the haws glistened as if just polished, Sarah thought how lovely and fresh everything looked as she bumped across the cattle grid and down the lane. Back on the main road she turned into the village, parked by the Post Office and walked across the Village Green to South Street to find Malt Cottage and Mrs Knight.

Most of the cottages were built of grey stone with darker grey tiled roofs that were brightened with splatterings of yellow algae, they sat serenely behind clipped privet hedges and small front gardens, and most of them had net curtains discreetly pulled, Sarah wondered how many would twitch as she walked down the road. Tucked away at the end of South Street was a terrace of six small cottages all painted white with dark red doors. The second one along was Malt Cottage. The wrought iron gate was desperately in need of painting and squeaked in protest as Sarah opened it, disturbing the ginger cat lying in the shade of a lavender bush. The garden was overgrown with marigolds and pansies and Sarah couldn't help noticing that there were masses of weeds. The paint on the front door was flaking and everything seemed to need so much attention that Sarah pulled a wry face as she rang the bell, wondering what she would find inside. Just as she was going to ring the bell again she could hear movement and what sounded like a stick tapping on the floor. The door was opened by a rather plump old lady leaning heavily on a stick. Her white hair was lovely, beautifully cut in a loose bob with just a suggestion of a fringe, framing an old face gently rouged, a few grey hairs sprouted from her chin and a vivid lipstick clashed with the amazing purple jumper that covered her ample bosom. The jumper definitely had a suspicion of dinner down the front. A multicoloured voluminous skirt and a pair of black slippers completed the picture.

'Well?'

'Good afternoon, I'm looking for Mrs Knight.'

'That's me, what do you want?' She looked at Sarah over the top of her spectacles and clasped both hands over the handle of the stick the veins standing out like the gnarled roots of a tree. Not an auspicious start thought Sarah, but decided that perhaps she didn't get many visitors and was therefore a bit defensive. She drew a deep breath and asked if she could talk to her about Bridge Farm. She briefly explained about finding the photograph and how she felt there might be a connection.

'Bridge Farm, well it's a long time since I worked there and a long time since anyone asked me about it. You'd better come in I can't be doing with standing too long.'

The front door opened straight into the sitting room

beyond which Sarah could see the kitchen and some rather steep looking stairs going up on the left. There was a strong smell of overcooked cabbage, reminiscent of her Grandmother's house. The sitting room was shabbily comfortable, two arm chairs that had seen better days sat either side of a prettily tiled Victorian fireplace, the grate was piled with huge fir cones on a bed of red crepe paper. A sideboard facing the door was covered with a lace runner which in turn was covered in various types of cups and saucers, all beautifully arranged. The wallpaper was plain pale blue but with all the lovely china plates on the walls the room did not look cold. One of the chairs was obviously Mrs Knight's as beside it was a small table littered with an ashtray, cigarettes, a spectacle case, an empty cup, papers, books, tissues and a small photograph album. Mrs Knight slowly manoeuvred herself into her chair and lit a cigarette.

'Sit yourself down, and what is your name please?'

'I'm so sorry Mrs Knight, I should have introduced myself, I'm Sarah Bruce and Grace Bruce was my Great-aunt, she died recently and whilst clearing out the house I found this photograph hidden in a drawer, it was in an envelope postmarked Tolford, so I started here and I believe that the bridge in the photo is the Roman bridge near Bridge Farm.'

Mrs Knight took the photograph, changed to her reading spectacles looked at the photo and immediately put her hand to her mouth.

'Mrs Knight, are you alright?'

'Yes thankyou, I just never expected to see that photograph again I can tell you. You say you found it in your Great-aunt's house.'

'Yes, but I am even more curious now, because whilst booking into Bridge Farm for B and B I noticed another photo on the kitchen wall … '

'Another photograph?' interrupted Mrs Knight.

'Yes, just like this one but with a young man leaning over the bridge. I'm sure they must have been taken at the same time. The really strange thing is that this photograph was also hidden, Joanna Short found it under lining paper in a chest of drawers when she was cleaning out Grace's room. Can you throw any light on the subject? Do you know who they were?'

5

'It was a long time ago, 1910 to be exact, when I went to Bridge Farm, it was straight from school and I had no choice in the matter, in those days you went where your parents sent you. My name was Anne Tully before I was married and I would have liked to have been called Anne by the family but Farmer Harris decided that 'Tully' would be more appropriate. I never did find out what he meant by that, but Tully it was and Tully it stayed even after I was married. It was a pleasant enough family to work for, Farmer Harris, Mistress Harris, as she liked to be called, a daughter Edith and two sons Dave and Alan. Alan was adopted, his father had worked on the farm but was killed in a nasty accident with the bull, Alan was about six at the time and left an orphan as his mother had died from TB two years before. Farmer Harris felt responsible for the boy as his father was not only his best friend but was killed on the farm whilst working for him. So Alan was adopted, but he kept his own name Palmer this leading to some speculation amongst the villagers, which was quite unfounded. He was always treated as a son and that is how we thought of him.'

'The work wasn't too bad, I went as a general help which

21

meant I worked in the house making beds, cleaning and polishing, there was a lot of that, preparing vegetables and if needed I would work in the dairy. That was where I met my husband-to-be Ron. He was the dairyman until 1914 when he had to go off to the War. I remember we were all so excited if one of our boyfriends was called up and so proud if they enlisted, little did we think about the horrors they would encounter in the trenches. We were married in 1916 when he came home on leave and Betty was born the following year. Sadly Ron didn't come home from the War like so many others he is buried somewhere in France.'

'To return to Bridge Farm and the early 1900's. Dave worked on the farm becoming his father's righthand man. Alan finished at University, quite unusual for a farmer's son in those days, and landed himself a high powered job with a newspaper in London. Edith by this time had developed a debilitating disease, it was probably what is now known as Multiple Sclerosis. Alan and Edith became very close and in 1911 when Alan was twentyone and Edith was eighteen they were engaged, even though Alan realised the implications of Edith's illness. As they weren't blood relations Farmer Harris raised no objections.'

'As for the photograph the young woman was called Grace, I never knew her surname. Edith had got much worse and needed constant attention, she could walk around the house but needed a wheelchair when she went out. She needed help with bathing and dressing too, so Grace came to look after her, she was about the same age as Edith and from the beginning they got on really well. She was a lovely person, always cheerful, nothing was too much trouble and she wasn't too demanding as far as I was concerned. She was wonderful with Edith finding things that they could do and more important she made her laugh which was great to hear. Grace was so easy to get on with that we all, in our own way, fell in love with her.'

'Without seeing the photograph of the young man I can only hazard a guess, but if it is like this photograph in every other respect, it must be the one of Alan Palmer that I saw many years ago. He worked as a photographic journalist for a newspaper in London coming down most weekends. He had an old wreck of a car and would take Edith and Grace out for short trips. It became obvious that he too was captivated by Grace's charms in spite of being engaged to Edith. They took to going out for walks together on Grace's afternoons off and would walk along Shore Road down to the estuary. It must have been during one of these walks that the photos were taken. The family never knew about them and it was years later that I saw copies of them.'

'Anyhow the war came along, Dave wasn't called up because he was doing work of national importance. Alan wasn't called up either and we never knew why, rumours went round that he was a Conscientious Objector. He was known for his photographic work and it was only after the War we learnt that he had gone to Belgium and France on special missions to take photographs of the war. I always felt that Edith and Grace knew what he was doing as they did not appear concerned, and took no notice of the rumours, but as they both loved him they must have been beside themselves with worry knowing that he was doing very dangerous work.'

'Alan was invalided home in 1916, he had a badly injured leg which left him with a limp Edith was really pleased to see him, she was feeling so much better, and on April 14th 1917 she and Alan were married. Grace was still looking after Edith at this time, but once the wedding was arranged we all noticed that the sparkle left her and before they got back from their honeymoon she had left Bridge Farm, cutting all ties, no one knew where she had gone. Edith was devastated and wanted to know why she had gone, but none of us could tell her, although we suspected it was because of her feelings for Alan but we had no proof so kept quiet, we knew Edith did not have long to live and we wanted her to be happy. She died after childbirth in 1927 and the baby girl died two years later. Alan had given her the name Grace. He was devastated by these events, and after the baby's funeral moved down to Shore Cottage on the estuary, where he lives to this day.'

'After his father died in 1957 Dave Harris and his wife took over the running of the farm, asking me to stay on as Housekeeper so that they could concentrate on the dairy side of the work without having to worry about cleaning and cooking. This suited me fine, when you get on in years it is difficult to find work and I needed the money.'

'During the last years of Farmer Harris's life the farmhouse had become rather neglected, he would not allow me to go into some of the rooms and the attic was out-of-bounds to everyone, he spent hours up there going through papers and writing, though goodness knows what. As he was paying my wages I respected his wishes. When Farmer Dave took over I was told to 'clean from top to bottom', it was during this clean that I found the photos. In a cupboard in the room that had been Alan's I found a box that he had obviously overlooked, it had some photographic equipment in it and at the bottom there was an envelope containing some photos. Some of the photos were of Edith and the farmhouse, but the two that took my attention were one of Grace leaning over the Roman Bridge, the very same as the one you found, and the other one was of Alan leaning over the same bridge with the same pose.

They were lovely photographs they both looked so happy and the bridge and the copses all looked wonderful. Alan had a room in the farmhouse that he used as a darkroom, so I guess he'd developed these particular photos himself and I can only surmise that as he was engaged to Edith neither he nor Grace wanted anyone else seeing them, therefore they hid them. I do wonder why Grace had a photo of herself and Alan had a photo of himself, perhaps it was just to remind each other of a perfect day and if found would not cause any recriminations.'

'Thankyou so much Mrs Knight' said Sarah, 'you have answered so many questions, can I ask you one more?'

'Yes, of course!' snapped Mrs Knight. By this time Sarah had realised that the 'snapping' didn't mean anything, it was just Mrs Knight's way of dealing with an emotional situation, she had obviously been very attached to all the family at the farm.

'You said that Alan Palmer moved to Shore Cottage after Edith died, can you tell me where that is please, I would really love to talk to him about Grace.'

'Well you might want to talk to him, but he might not want to talk to you.'

'Why not? If he loved Grace, as you think he did, he might like to talk about her. I'm sure he would want to know that she had died.'

'Shore Cottage can be found down Shore Road, which is the road that goes round by the farm, then over the bridge and down to the estuary. You will have to knock two or three times on his door, he has become very deaf.'

Sarah felt really excited as Mrs Knight spoke, she was quite sure that Alan would talk to her and that the mystery surrounding the photograph found in Aunt Grace's room would soon be resolved. Everything that Mrs Knight had told her rang true, but she did want to hear it all from Alan.

'What did you do with the box you found in Alan's old room Mrs Knight?'

'I took it down to Shore Cottage. Some of that photographic equipment costs a lot of money, and I thought Alan would be pleased to get it and the photos. Was he pleased? No he was not! I got my head bitten off for going down there, but he took the box. When I thought about it afterwards I decided I had done the right thing, it was his property after all.'

'Can I come and see you again Mrs Knight?'

'If you must, but don't stay for so long next time.' Sarah smiled to herself as she realised that all the talking had been done by Mrs Knight.

'Don't get up Mrs Knight, I'll see myself out' and Sarah walked out into the fresh air.

6

'Hello Jason' said Sarah as the dog woofed a greeting and wagged his tail. She went into the farmhouse and knocked on the kitchen door.

'Come in' said Joanna 'Hi Sarah you're just in time to lay the table for me. There will be eight of us and everything is either in or on the dresser.' Sarah grinned 'Let me put my bag down and draw breath.'

'Sorry, but dinner is almost ready and I didn't think you would mind. Can you pass the plates please. We've got rabbit stew and dumplings, baked potatoes and cabbage, all home grown,' then Joanna laughed as she added, 'organic of course.'

'I don't mind, it all sounds great, smells great too, I haven't had rabbit for years so it'll be a treat. Why did you laugh when you said 'organic of course'?' she said, passing the plates to Joanna.

'We get quite a few city folk coming to stay and more often than not they ask if the food is 'organic'. I always say it is and don't bother to explain that it is only organic as far as possible, honestly if we didn't take some preventative measures the slugs, and we've got some monsters, would decimate the lot they seem to know exactly when the seed is going to sprout. As soon as the veggies have made reasonable growth we don't have a problem, and from then onwards everything is organic.'

'I've never really thought about it before' admitted Sarah, 'except to wonder why the price of organics is higher than that of non organics.'

'Ask Seth, he'll tell you, he has a real bee in his bonnet about it.' Joanna put the lid on the cabbage. 'I'm just going to call everyone for dinner. Keep your eye on the cabbage Sarah please, don't let it boil over.' Joanna whisked out of the back door and soon the clanging of a bell could be heard. Sarah felt very relaxed and content, it was almost as if she was one of the family and she wondered if Fate in the shape of Aunt Grace and the photograph had intended her to find Bridge Farm. There was obviously a link with the farm, Mrs Knight had established that. She lifted the lid on the cabbage, turned the gas down slightly and looked round the kitchen. It was dominated by the large pine dresser that was home to the Portmerion dinner service, several lidded jars, a pile of catalogues, some unopened mail and a small rack of cookery books. The rectangular dining table was capable of seating sixteen to eighteen and Sarah could imagine it being the centre of many a party. At the far end under the window was a built in unit with dishwasher and a sink, a large old fashioned stone one and Sarah wondered if it had come from the old dairy. The unit continued along the left hand wall, incorporating the handsome double cooker which Sarah couldn't help admiring. All the woodwork was pine and the tops of the units were pale green, the pale green being repeated in the colourful geometric pattern of the curtains. A pot of scarlet geraniums brightened up the window sill and was flanked by several pots of herbs.

The door to the hall crashed open and two teenagers ran into the kitchen.

'Whoops, sorry didn't know anyone was here. I'm James and this is Mollie, our parents run the Lavender Farm.' Sarah held out her hand.

'Hello, I'm Sarah, I've just arrived to stay here for a few days. I didn't know there was a Lavender Farm ...' she was interrupted as the back door opened and Joanna and three others came in laughing and chattering.

'Sarah, this is my husband Seth and these two noisy ones are my sister Babs and her husband Ken, I see you've already met their kids.' Sarah found her hand enveloped in Seth's large, brown, rather rough and, to her surprise, very gentle hand.

'Glad to meet you Sarah, I hear you are here for a few days.'

'Yes' said Sarah 'I'm trying to track down the story behind a photo, or now it might be two photos, and hope that you might be able to help. Mrs Knight has been very helpful and there is obviously a link with Bridge Farm.'

Joanna put the dishes of vegetables on the table, got the stew out of the oven and asked Seth to pass the plates.

'Sarah sit next to Seth please and you can tell us all about it while we eat.'

The smell from the casserole was amazing and Sarah realised she was really hungry. Soon she was tucking into one of the best meals she had had for a long time. She turned to Babs 'Mollie and James said you and Ken run a lavender farm, that sounds wonderful, is it part of the farm?'

'Yes, we were looking for somewhere to start up and Joanna and Seth wanted to sell off a piece of land so we stepped in. They agreed to us buying the land and said that we could also have two of the farm cottages to convert into one. It was perfect, the land is just right for lavender it is in a valley facing south with good drainage as we are on a gravel bed. The acreage is just about right too and there is the possibility of buying more land if we need it.'

'We know that the Romans grew lavender here and the monks after them because some archaeologists excavated here several years ago, and amongst other things lavender seeds were found in the soil. We are hoping to call the enterprise 'Roman Lavender'. Planning permission for a distillery, workshops, a cafe and shop has only just been granted so we are still in the early stages of development. Eventually we hope to have fields of lavender, a distillery to produce our own lavender oil, a small workshop where we can make soap and various other toiletries, a shop selling the soaps etc., a cafe serving lavender scones, sponges and anything else in which we can use lavender, and also a nursery where we can sell plants. It is all very exciting and we hope that in two years time we will be up and running and open to the public, albeit in a very small way. The only problem is we will have to talk the Bank Manager into letting us have a substantial loan, but that is our problem.'

'It does sound exciting though … '

'Not as exciting or romantic as your mission sounds' interrupted Seth, 'and if we start Babs on the topic of lavender we will never hear about it, so go ahead Sarah tell us all about it.'

Sarah reached for her bag and took out the tattered envelope and photograph, explaining how she had found them and because they had been hidden how her curiosity had been aroused and how it had been aroused even further when she saw the photo on their kitchen wall. She had come to Tolford because of the postmark. Sarah's photo was passed round the table and after looking at it Seth got up and went to the photo on the kitchen wall, took it down and placed it on the table. He didn't say a word but looked round at everyone. Sarah broke the silence.

'You've obviously seen the similarity, I wonder if any of you know anything about them. I've spoken to Mrs Knight in the village, she worked for Farmer Harris and his wife here at Bridge Farm for a long time and she said my photo was of 'a' Grace who looked after the Harris's daughter, but she didn't know what the surname was. She told me that Alan Palmer, the adopted son, had married Edith even though he was obviously in love with Grace. She said that she had seen two photos, one with Grace and another with Alan, leaning over the bridge.'

Seth leaned back in his chair and drank his beer, looking very closely at the photos. He picked up the one of the young man.

'We found this photo in a room in the farm, but I expect Joanna has already told you that. We framed it and put it on the wall because we liked it and felt it had a place in the house. Looking at the two photos together it seems obvious that they must have been taken at the same time. I'll have a look and see if there is a date or a name on the back of this one.' He took out his penknife and carefully ran it round the tape holding the frame in place.

'There's nothing here Sarah' and he passed it over to her.

'There's nothing mine either,' said Sarah. 'Well, I suppose if he was in love with Grace, but engaged to Edith, he wouldn't want anyone to know.'

Seth looked questioningly at Joanna as he picked up the photo again and she nodded.

'Would you like this photo to keep Sarah? It obviously goes with yours.'

'Would I?' said Sarah, 'that would be marvellous, but how can I find out some more about them?'

'When we bought the farm from Dave Harris we saw that there was some furniture and several boxes in the attic but we didn't look at them properly and quite frankly we have been so busy getting the farm and B and B just as we want it we haven't given them a thought' said Joanna, 'in fact I had forgotten all about them, do you think they would tell us something? There might be some letters about Grace which would positively identify her as your Great Aunt, you know letters about her background before she started to work here, a sort of CV or whatever they had in those days.'

'Mrs Knight said that latterly Farmer Harris worked on some papers up in the attic and no one else was allowed up, that could be what is in the boxes. So perhaps we ought to investigate' said Sarah. 'Mrs Knight told me that she took a box down to Shore Cottage, she found it when clearing out Alan's old room, and that copies of these photos were in there together with some photographic equipment.'

'Of course', said Babs interrupting 'that's the old chap that we see limping through the woods with a dog like Jason.'

'Mrs Knight said he lives as a recluse and it sounds as though he is a bit cantankerous.'

'Why don't you pay him a visit?' said Babs. 'Take both photos and ask him to tell you about them. If he bites your head off, so be it, but if the photo is of Grace Bruce and you can prove to him that you are her niece I'm sure he'll talk to you.'

'Yes, I think you're right, I'll go tomorrow.' Sarah gave a laugh, 'I'm used to dealing with all sorts of characters in the library, I don't forsee any problems, you never know he might be glad to talk about Grace, if indeed it is her.'

'I'll get the boxes down as soon as possible' said Seth, 'I've been meaning to do that for sometime, there must be quite a bit of local history there that I can sort through. I want to write a history of the farm, this is the kickstart I needed and you never know what skeletons we might find.'

'Not too many I hope' laughed Sarah.

7

That night Sarah tucked herself up in Grace's room and felt so comfortable that she couldn't help smiling to herself. She was sure by now that the photo was of her Great Aunt and she almost felt her presence in the room as her mind began to wander. Her thoughts went back to the house in Southampton, should she sell or should she live in it? Did she really want to work in a town for the rest of her life? In fact, although she loved the work, did she want to be a librarian for the rest of her life? She thought about Babs at dinner time and how she had enthused over the lavender farm and wished that she could feel the same way about her life. A thought came to her. Aunt Grace had not only left her the house in Southampton but money as well, approximately £40,100. Suppose she decided to sell the house, she reckoned it would fetch at least £85,000, and offered to invest some of it in the lavender farm? With some quick arithmetic she thought there was just about enough money for her to do that and find a small cottage in the village. She sat bolt upright in bed and clutched the duvet to her face to stop herself crying out. Would Babs and Ken welcome a partner, particularly someone who knew nothing about lavender except that it smelled nice? Surely she had some skills to offer? Sarah got out of bed and went over to the window, there was a sliver of a moon in the sky just above the willows, an owl lazily hooted in the distance, the cows rustled the hay in the barn, the river rippled over the stones. It was all so lovely that Sarah decided if she could become involved with the lavender farm she would, everything seemed to be telling her that she needed a change and Tolford seemed to be the place.

'Yes' she said to herself as she got back into bed, 'I need a change and a challenge, I also need some new friends and I think I have found them here. I certainly haven't laughed so much for a long time.'

Sleep was a long time coming that night, but eventually Sarah fell asleep and dreamed of a sea of lavender waving gently in the breeze.

'Good morning Joanna' she said as she went into the kitchen for breakfast. She noticed the table was laid for one and felt a bit embarrassed.

'Have I slept too long?'

'No' laughed Joanna, 'work on a farm starts really early, we don't expect our guests to get up at an unearthly hour too. Anyway we are always irritable then, so you wouldn't see us at our best. Help yourself to fruit and cereal, would you like bacon and egg and all that goes with it?'

'Yes please, in spite of that lovely meal last night I'm ravenous.'

'Good, sit down and we can chat while I cook. The others will be in shortly for some coffee and biscuits.'

'Joanna, can I ask your advice please?'

'If it is about going down to Shore Cottage, I'll say go.'

'No, it's something quite different.' Sarah told her about

her thoughts during the night and how she was really sure that she needed a change of direction.

'What I am asking you is, do you think Babs and Ken would mind if I approached them? Do they really want a partner? I know it is a bit of a cheek, I hardly know them and they don't know me, but I have such a strange feeling about Bridge Farm and the idea of a lavender farm just tugs at my imagination. To be as enthusiastic as Babs about an enterprise would be wonderful.'

'Well, that is not what I was expecting to hear.' Joanna put the cooked breakfast in front of Sarah, poured herself her a cup of coffee and sat down opposite her.

'You would be prepared to sell the house in Southampton and invest in an enterprise you know little about?'

'Yes' said Sarah 'I would. Of course my accountants would look over the books and investigate the prospects. That is normal practice even when asking for a bank loan, so Babs and Ken should have all the paper work done.'

Joanna drank her coffee, looked at Sarah, smiled and said 'Ask them, here they are.'

'Ask them what?' said Ken. Sarah finished her last piece of toast and marmalade.

'That breakfast was just the best.'

'Glad you enjoyed it' said Joanna, pouring out the coffee. 'Now put these two out of their misery, they really are inquisitive and want to know everything that is going on.' By this time Sarah had learnt that most things Joanna said were accompanied with a laugh, and Joanna drifted off to the sink with her laugh trailing behind her.

'Ditch the dirt Sarah' said Babs.

'Well, I don't think it is dirt.' Sarah asked them straight out if they would like a partner prepared to put some money up front and to take an active part in the running of the lavender farm. Babs' face was a picture, she was obviously stunned by the question and turned to Ken who was equally gob-smacked.

'Gosh! Golly! Plus all the other things I can't think of at the moment. The answer to your question is that we are prepared to think about it, in fact we have been discussing advertising for a partner as the interest on a bank loan would eat up most of our profits.'

'Are you serious about this?' said Ken.

'Yes I am' said Sarah, 'I know that I need a change of direction and I almost feel that here at Bridge Farm I have come home.'

'We have to be realistic about this' said Ken. 'If you are really serious Sarah come and see us before you go, to see what you are letting yourself in for, then if you are still interested would you put something in writing and give us some proof that you have the funds. We don't doubt you, but our solicitors will.'

'I'm going home late Monday afternoon and will make an appointment with my solicitors for Wednesday or Thursday. The one thing I must say to you is that although I know the money and the house are mine probate has not yet been granted, and that can take quite a while.'

'No problem with that, we will need some time and space to work out exactly what it is we want to do and where a partner would fit in. We have plenty of ideas, but must get organised. Seth said you had given him a kickstart into looking at the local history, I think you've given us a kickstart into planning properly.'

Babs went round the table and gave Sarah a big hug 'I think we need you as much as you need us. Oh dear! I think I'm going to cry,' and she promptly burst into tears.

'It's alright' she sobbed, 'I'm just so happy, we haven't known you for a day but I just have a feeling that you are right for us. It's that little inner voice of mine Ken' she said turning to him, 'and you say that it is usually right.'

'True' said Ken, 'but don't get too carried away, let's see if Sarah is still interested after our chat tomorrow. We must check with our solicitors and bank, find out exactly where we stand and go from there.'

'That's fine with me' said Sarah, 'I'll need time anyway because of the probate, then I have to put the house on the market. If, after our chat I am still interested I ought to ask for advice from my solicitors and bank. If the investment goes through I'll have to give in my notice, clear out my flat and find somewhere to live in Tolford. It does sound like a lot of work, but I won't be able to complain about being bored will I?'

'Somewhere to live won't be a problem' said Joanna, 'there's two empty farm labourer's cottages almost next door to where Babs and Ken live, they need a lot of work on them to make them habitable, but I want that done anyway, you might like to rent one of them until you know what you will be doing.'

'I think it's my turn to burst into tears' said Sarah. 'That would be wonderful Joanna, can I look at them tomorrow. You know, we are all talking about this as if it is a fait a complis, but it isn't. I am just hoping nothing goes wrong because I've got a little inner voice too Babs, and it is telling me to go for it.'

'Or,' said Seth looking at the photograph, 'is it your Great Aunt giving you a kickstart?' They all laughed but Sarah did wonder.

'Well there was a lavender sachet with the photo, perhaps that was there for a purpose too. I'm going to try and see Alan Palmer this morning, then roam around the estuary and the bay in the afternoon. It is so lovely being out of town that I want to make the most of my short weekend and get down to the sea and feel the wind in my hair. I shall be around for most of Monday Ken, can I come and have a look at the lavender farm in the morning?'

'Come and have lunch with us' said Babs, 'we'll be having soup and hot rolls so there won't be a problem.'

'Sounds my sort of lunch' said Sarah, and found that once again she was laughing. 'You know, this laughing business is most infectious, I can't remember having laughed so much for a long time. I really am glad that I decided to come to Tolford and that I found Bridge Farm. Here's to my next long weekend.' She raised her glass of apple juice and felt so at home it was unbelievable.

Back in Grace's room Sarah picked up her small rucksack and put in it the two photos, a notebook and her camera. She decided to take the identification card she wore round her neck at work, so that she could prove she really was Sarah Bruce and for good measure her driving licence as well. Sarah filled the bottle she had had the day before with water from the tap and went down to pick up the sandwiches that Joanna was making for her.

In the kitchen Joanna and Seth were talking about the photos, the one thing they couldn't understand was that Sarah had found a girl's photo in her Aunt Grace's house and they had found a young man's photo in the farmhouse.

'You'd have thought it would have been the other way round' said Seth.

'I'm sure there's a good explanation. Let's hope Sarah finds it.' So saying Joanna put the sandwiches in a plastic bag, added an apple and a small packet of biscuits.

'Well, you won't go hungry' grinned Seth as Sarah came

in, 'I think Joanna has done enough sandwiches for you and Alan Palmer.'

'Thankyou so much,' and Sarah packed her lunch into the rucksack, looked at her watch 'it's 10.35 already, I must be off I really would like to see Alan Palmer before his lunchtime.'

'Good luck' said Seth, 'we'll look forward to hearing all about your adventures over dinner tonight.'

'With all the excitement I'd forgotten to ask you to book me in for dinner.'

Joanna laughed 'I've already booked you in. It's roast pork tonight, hope you like it.'

'Something else I don't cook for myself' said Sarah, 'so I'll look forward to it. Plenty of apple sauce please, my Grandfather always said that he had pork with his apple sauce.'

'Don't worry about that, we eat it by the bucketful. Have a good day Sarah ' and Seth went off to carry on with the ploughing.

'Turn right out of the door, follow the path through the garden, you will come to the gate which is very stiff so you will have to push. The footpath bears left and meets up with Shore Road. Wear your wellies, it is very muddy.' Sarah picked up her rucksack and fleece and called out her goodbyes.

'Wish me luck!'

8

It was a beautiful morning, soft sunshine, a bright blue sky and the rooks circling overhead were joined by seagulls that had drifted in on the light breeze. They were obviously going to trail Seth's tractor hoping to find some tasty morsels. Sarah went to her car and changed into her wellies. She looked back at the farmhouse and thought what a beautiful building it was and wondered when it had been built.

'Something else for me to find out, I expect Seth knows.'

The garden had a ragged look, autumn had obviously taken hold, however there was still some colour about. One or two dahlias were still flowering and the rusty red seed heads of the sedums rose up behind the winter flowering heathers. Starlings were noisily fighting each other for some scraps Joanna had put out, a robin was having a bath and some bees were still busy around the heathers. Sarah went down the paved path, managed to open the gate and soon found Shore Road she walked down to the bridge and stopped to watch the ducks. The water was lovely and clear, running quite fast over the large pebbles, turning sharply to the left as it went under the bridge. She walked on and Sarah was glad that Joanna had told her to wear wellies as it really was muddy. There had been a lot of rain just before the weekend and the puddles were deep. The road was very rutted so she walked as far as possible along the grassy edge, but even then occasionally she slipped on the mud.

'I shall end up with a muddy bottom at this rate' said Sarah to herself as she slipped once more, she regained her balance and went on, looking very carefully where she put her feet.

The road went round the edge of a marshy area, following the shape of the estuary. The tide was low, there were large stretches of mud flats either side of the river as it meandered down to the sea, a home for the dozens of birds wading on the mud and Sarah wished she had some binoculars so that she could really see them. There were some pretty little white and black birds rushing around busily digging into the mud, then suddenly they would all fly off, circle round, come back to the mud flats and start searching again, obviously plenty of things to eat. Several black ones with red beaks dashed around, they didn't seem to be doing anything. There was also one large, rather ungainly bird that she decided could only be a heron, it was standing very still at the edge of the river, almost as if superintending the others.

'This is all very strange' said Sarah to herself, 'I feel as if I know this estuary, I'm sure I've seen it in my dreams, and the farm, I seem to know that as well.'

Shore Road led passed trees misshapen by the wind but Sarah thought they were lovely, particularly those that drooped over the flats. Nearly all the leaves had gone from the hedges, but here and there was a bright splash of yellow where the gorse was blooming. On the left hand side of the road were fields, some of them lying fallow but others were being ploughed. Sarah stopped to have a look and watched the rooks and seagulls swooping and swirling as they followed the tractor churning up the rich reddish brown soil. They were very noisy, the rooks cawing and fighting and the seagulls screaming as they came in to land, the sound seemed to echo all round, but they were obviously feeding well.

Back on the road the surface changed into shingle for which Sarah was relieved, it was easier to walk on, even though it did sometimes feel that she took two steps forward and one back. It was much better though, she didn't have to worry about getting muddy.

The river was sweeping round now to join the sea, Sarah could hear the waves and began to have butterflies in her stomach as she realised that very soon she would find Shore Cottage and Alan Palmer. Suddenly there it was, one of several coast guard cottages looking out to sea. The shore was a few yards away from the narrow road, a small wooden jetty ran out into the water, an old boathouse seemed to be home to several small boats, one or two yachts were pulled up on the shingle their metal stays clanging in the breeze. Some lobster pots were propped up against the boat house and a once bright blue rowing boat was upturned beside them. A cormorant was out on the jetty with his wings outstretched to dry, some seagulls were perched along side him, whilst others were riding the blue-green, white flecked waves looking as if they were waiting for dinner to come in on the tide. The road went on round the small bay and down towards the village and Sarah could see two or three bungalows in the distance. Although the sea was sparkling and the sun was shining to Sarah it seemed a very lonely place.

'I wonder if they still have contraband coming in here? Without the coastguards it would be quite easy I should think.' Sarah smiled to herself and hoped that Alan Palmer hadn't become a smuggler in his later life.

There was no bell on the door so Sarah rapped as loudly as she could, Mrs Knight had said that Alan was slightly deaf. A dog barked and Sarah heard a deep but pleasant voice shout 'Quiet Troy'. The door opened and Sarah was immediately jumped on by a black labrador who seemed really pleased to see her.

'Down Troy.'

'Really I don't mind' said Sarah, 'this must be Jason's brother, I've just come from the farm.' She petted the dog who was still making a fuss of her. 'Yes, you are gorgeous, but that is enough.' She told the dog to sit, and to her surprise he did.

'Well he doesn't do that for many people.' Sarah looked up and saw an old man with a mop of white hair, very blue eyes, lots of wrinkles and an obvious limp as he was a bit lopsided and carried a walking stick. He looked very neat in deep plum corduroys, a blue roll necked shirt and a blue fleecy waistcoat.

'Hello! Are you Alan Palmer?'

'Who wants to know?'

'I'm Sarah Bruce, Mrs Knight told me that you lived here and suggested that I look you up. Grace Bruce was my Great Aunt and I believe you knew her, that is if you are Alan Palmer.'

'Yes, I'm Alan Palmer. What is it you want?'

'I'm really pleased to meet you' said Sarah, 'do you think I could come in I have some old photos I would like to ask you about, in fact I have rather a lot to tell you.' Alan looked at her, grunted, opened the door wide and indicated that she should go in. Sarah gave him a smile, took off her boots and went in. The dog made a big fuss of her, jumping up and down, his paws almost reaching her shoulders. Sarah laughed and stroked his back and rubbed behind his ears.

'Down boy, on your mat.'

'I really don't mind, I just love dogs.'

'That's as maybe, but Troy has to do what he's told, Troy on your mat.' The dog looked up at Alan and went to his mat, his tail was still wagging so Sarah knew he wasn't too unhappy. He flopped down, put his head on his paws and stared rather disconcertingly at Sarah.

'Would you like some coffee?' Sarah was quite surprised as she'd had the feeling of not being very welcome.

'Yes please, black with one sugar.'

'Good, just how I like it' and Alan went off to the kitchen where Sarah could hear him banging about and wondered if she ought to offer to help. She decided against it.

The room was quite small and at a first glance seemed to be lacking in colour, everything appeared to be black and white or grey, with just the backs of the books in the large bookcase giving some colour. As she looked round Sarah realised that it was an illusion created by the hundreds of black and white photos covering the walls. She got up to have a closer look. One wall was covered in photos that must have been taken in Flanders in the 1914 -18 War. Another was covered in lovely studies of the estuary and the sea, there was even a photo of the Roman Bridge, no one on it though.

'I hope you don't mind me looking Mr Palmer, but I don't think I have ever seen so many photos displayed in someone's house. They are beautiful.'

'No, I don't suppose you have. Now sit down, have your coffee and tell me all about your photos, and please call me Alan.'

'Thankyou'. Sarah sat in a small chair next to Alan's

armchair. As she sipped her coffee she took in more of the room, her first impression was wrong, there really was a lot of colour, gold curtains complemented and softened the dark green of the loose covers on the chairs. Yellow and orange cushions were large and looked very comfortable. On the polished mahogany table there was a bowl of beautiful bronze chrysanthemums and a bright, small wood fire was burning in the grate. Alan poked it into life and the sparks flew up the chimney, Sarah looked at Alan, smiled and told him that when she was a little girl her Grandfather used to poke his wood fire especially for her and when the sparks flew up the chimney he told her they were the 'fire fairies'.

'But you don't really want to know that' said Sarah, putting down her cup and delving into her rucksack for the photos. 'This is why I've come.' Alan took them and smiled.

'You did know her didn't you?' said Sarah.

'Oh yes, I knew her, Grace Bruce, but it was a long time ago.'

'I'm sorry to have to tell you that she died earlier this year.' Sarah looked at Alan who was looking at her questioningly.

'She was my Great-aunt and as she had never married and had no children she made me her main beneficiary.' Sarah told him that when clearing out the house in Southampton she had found the photo in a drawer and wondered if it was her Great Aunt, and why it had been hidden? She told him that her curiosity had been even more aroused when at Bridge Farm she saw the photo of the young man in exactly the same pose, leaning over the bridge. Strangely it too had been hidden and was only found when the Shorts bought the farm and they were clearing out the rooms.

'Yes, that's Grace Bruce, she was a lovely girl and that is me in the other photograph. They were taken along time ago when we were both at Bridge Farm, but I expect you know that.'

'I spoke to Mrs Knight the other day, do you remember her? She worked at Bridge Farm but was called Tully then, she married the dairyman Ron Knight,'

'Oh yes! I remember Tully, she liked a good gossip then and I don't suppose she has changed. I last saw her when the farm was sold, she brought me a box of bits and pieces that I had left behind. What did she tell you?'

'Not a lot really, just that you had been adopted by Farmer Harris, that you married his daughter Edith but she thought you were in love with Grace. I'm so glad the photo is of my Great Aunt, I felt it must be her but couldn't quite link the lovely girl in the photo with the Aunt Grace I knew.'

Delving into her rucksack again Sarah brought out a photo that she had taken of Aunt Grace a few years before she died.

'You see what I mean? She was eighty eight.' Alan took the photo and gave a deep sigh.

'I'm afraid anno domini plays awful tricks on us, but I can still see the Grace I knew behind the faded hair and the lines on the face. Sarah would you mind if I kept this?'

'Of course you can keep it, but please do tell me about Grace I was very fond of her and we became very close. I didn't really get to know her until I was fourteen, she looked after me a lot after my father died. What I can't understand is why Grace hid a photo of herself, and I'm more puzzled now because apparently you hid a photo of yourself in a drawer in Grace's room. There must have been a good reason.' Sarah looked at Alan, his face had taken on a blank look and she wondered if she had said too much.

'Alan, if you really don't want to tell me I will understand but ... '

'You don't need to 'but' me' barked Alan, 'I've been a

victim of nosy parkers all my life, I know the difference. You loved Grace and so did I, you don't want to know just out of curiosity but out of love as well, and that makes a difference. I will tell you our story, it's for another good reason though.'

'What's that?'

'My dear girl, don't you know how like Grace you are? When I opened the door to you I had quite a shock. I can tell you now that it is a nice shock' and he chuckled,' after all Troy took to you straight away, so why shouldn't I?' Sarah was really surprised, Mrs Knight had said he was cantankerous, everyone at Bridge Farm had decided he was a recluse and had implied he wouldn't talk to her but here he was laughing and agreeing to tell her about Grace.

9

'Before I tell you about Grace let me tell you something about myself, it will put you in the picture and help me to get the story straight.'

'You were quite right, I was adopted by Farmer Harris and his wife, I really can't remember much about my own mother and father, my mother died from TB when I was about four years old and my father died when I was six. Farmer and Mrs Harris - I called them Ma and Pa - brought me up as one of their own, which was the best thing that could have happened to me in the circumstances. They let me keep my own name and did not touch any of the money, little as it was, that my father left me. You see my father had died as a result of an accident on the farm and Farmer Harris felt responsible.'

'I enjoyed school and did extremely well, almost without effort, and at eighteen won a scholarship to study English and History at London University. Pa was very proud of me, but I was concerned about whether he could afford the extra expense and it was then he told me that my father had left a small legacy that I could use, so I would not be beholden to him.'

'While I was at University I became interested in photography, and joined the Photographic Society. We had great times, we would go for long walks through the streets of London taking photographs of everything, shops, streets, people, the river - trying to get a feel of 'Life'. We developed our photos in the University dark room being very critical of each others work, but at the same time constructive, learning from each other about light and shade, movement and stillness. I think we learnt more that way than if we had done a course. Sometimes I think I still hear their voices when I'm out with my camera, it can be quite eerie at times.'

'I would go back to Bridge Farm during every vacation, it was like drawing breath after a swim, the air was so different, the speed at which people lived was so much slower and the food was much better. It was in 1910 during one of my vacations, that I became conscious of the fact that Edith had grown up. She had always been there but I had thought of her as my sister, I suddenly realised that she wasn't my sister and that she was a lovely girl. We started going out together and we fell in love. Pa told me that there was something really wrong with her and it was likely that she would become an invalid. This did not stop me loving her and in 1911   with her father's blessing we became engaged.'

'Whilst I was at university I had edited the students' paper and found I had a flair for finding the right articles and an aptitude for writing, so when a newspaper in London advertised for a journalist I applied and got the job. A bonus for me was that they wanted me to use my photographic skills too.'

'In 1912 Edith suddenly got worse and needed a lot of help, that's when Grace came along, she was the daughter of one of Pa's friends and had worked in a hospital since she left school at fourteen. She had decided that hospital life was not for her, but she did like to look after people and was looking for a job. She was the perfect person for Edith, they were the same age and had similar interests. Grace was a very happy girl and this rubbed off on Edith, so when she was going through a bad patch, instead of getting really depressed as she had done previously, she was able to cope in a positive way.'

'I would come back to the farm as often as I could, usually during the week as my work did not recognise weekends. I did, however, manage the occasional weekend and then I would take Edith and Grace out for a drive in my ramshackle car. We had great times, we would find somewhere pleasant to stop so that Edith could have a rest in an old garden chair that we took along, and we would all enjoy a picnic lunch. Edith liked to have a nap after lunch and Grace and I got into the habit of going off for a short walk so that we wouldn't disturb her with our chatter.'

'It was all quite innocent to begin with but gradually we realised that our feelings were changing and I am afraid that we fell hopelessly in love. I use the word 'hopelessly' deliberately because it was hopeless, I was engaged to Edith and could not hurt her by breaking the engagement. I suppose I wasn't being fair to any of us, but in a strange way I loved them both and I suppose felt that it could continue like that. You will probably think that I wanted the best of both worlds, well perhaps I did, but that is not how it worked out.'

'During some of my visits we stayed around the farm as Edith was too tired to go out. As before, while she was resting after lunch Grace and I would go for a walk, usually down Shore Road and it was during one of those walks that we took the photos. It was a particularly lovely September day, almost like today in fact, we had walked down to the shore and talked about the future, dreaming as lovers do knowing that that is just what it was, a dream! We strolled along with our arms round each other and as we went past these cottages we laughingly decided that this was where we would live together for ever and ever. Foolish thoughts because we knew in our heart of hearts that nothing could become of it.'

'On the way back we stopped at the bridge and I took the picture of Grace leaning over laughing at me. She said that we should have one of me as well so as to remember the wonderful day, so I posed and Grace took the photo. We decided that we would each keep the photo of ourselves, rather than of each other, as a memento of a wonderful relationship. We would keep the photos hidden, a secret between us, in this way we hoped that no one would know how we felt. When they were developed Grace had gone back to Southampton, so I sent the photo to her with a short letter telling her that I would never forget that day. How my photo came to be hidden in Grace's room at the farm I will tell you later. Grace did know that I couldn't marry her and she appeared to be quite happy with the situation, and in case you are wondering we were never lovers, in those days you didn't just hop in and out of bed if you felt like it.'

10

'In 1913 my work in London made it difficult for me to get down to Tolford as often as I would have liked, something always seemed to be happening on the political front, and the paper wanted to cover as many stories as possible. I wrote to Edith two or three times a week and had frequent letters from her telling me about herself and, of course, Grace. Grace and I had agreed that we would not write to each other and on my part that was a very difficult promise to keep.'

'There were rumblings of war and in June 1914, as a journalist with photographic expertise I was 'invited' - their word not mine - to meet with a gentleman at the War Office. It turned out that he was the Head of the Propaganda Bureau, one of his jobs being to appoint official war photographers and I was offered a post with this select group. It was made clear to me I would be working for the Government and would be in a reserved occupation, this meant that I would not be called up, however, in the event of war I could expect to be sent near to the Front Line and if required behind the enemy lines photographing details of their preparations.'

'At this particular time it was hoped that the assassination of Archduke Ferdinand, the heir to the Hapsburg throne, would not precipitate a war that Britain, and I am sure other countries, did not want. In fact in July 1914 the possibility of Britain joining in a war seemed unlikely and that we would maintain our neutrality. As you know history dictated otherwise and War was declared on 4th August 1914.'

'The Government of the day had very strict propaganda and censorship policies and in the event of war only those designated could take photographs, in fact I believe that if soldiers were found taking photos the penalty could be death! All photographs were subjected to censorship and only those selected were shown to the general public. The Government didn't see how certain photos could raise civilian morale - they were obsessed with secrecy. What would they think about media coverage of the news today?'

'I knew I wouldn't be able to get to Tolford very often, but was able to get down once more before being sent to Belgium. I told Pa, Edith and Grace what I would be doing, but asked them to keep it to themselves. Edith told me afterwards I had got the reputation of being a Conscientious Objector, which in the circumstances was quite funny. To keep in touch was going to be difficult, but I promised to send them a letter or a card when it was safe to do so.'

'The girls were wonderful and sent me off with several pairs of hand knitted socks and mitts as they understood that they were in short supply. They also sent me off with hugs and kisses, and Edith didn't mind Grace hugging me - that, my dear Sarah was the last time I felt Grace's arms round me.'

11

'War is not a pleasant experience and as a photographer I saw the brutal realities, soldiers fighting soldiers, soldiers scared stiff waiting for the next salvo of shells or wave of mustard gas. Civilians looking in disbelief at the ruins of their homes. Refugees fleeing to what they hoped would be safety. Children looking for their parents, parents looking for their children. It's all there in my photographs. I tried to capture the courage and bravery that I saw every day, soldiers hit by bullets being pulled back behind the lines by comrades. Civilians, regardless of their own safety, hiding some of the wounded.'

'As in most situations there were lighter moments. One of my favourite photographs is there on the wall behind you, a British Tommie throwing a little girl up in the air, both of them laughing.'

'I was told later by the Propaganda Bureau that my photos were 'superb' - again, their word not mine - and some were to be included in the official pamphlets that were printed. Apparently many of the photos I took behind enemy lines had helped in the planning of the various offensives.'

'In November 1915 I was able to get home for a few days leave. It was very strange to be back in the calm of the English countryside, knowing that just across the Channel people were fighting for their lives and indeed their very existence. Edith and Grace were still knitting, and the old rapport between the three of us was still there. Edith was going through a bad patch and needed Grace all the time, which was just as well, I don't know what would have happened if Grace and I had re-kindled the spark we had for each other, as it was we could say farewell without a feeling of guilt.'

'It was back to the war zone for me, but I wasn't there for long as I was wounded in my thigh by a piece of stray shrapnel. The doctors did what they could then sent me back to England in a hospital ship. I had several rather unpleasant months in hospital while they tried to save my leg, which fortunately they did and even though I've got a limp I am grateful to them. Pa visited me often during those painful months but it was too far for Edith to travel, and of course, Grace couldn't come.'

'I was invalided out in time for Christmas 1916 and returned to enjoy the peace and quiet of Bridge Farm. It was utter bliss after the noise, filth and smells of the trenches and the painful, sterile and impersonal atmosphere of the hospital. Edith was having a good spell so we were able to enjoy ourselves and spent hours just talking, playing cards or going for short walks. I had been instructed to walk at least half a mile a day until I saw the doctors again in February and we found that this was just about the distance Edith could manage. Grace would occasionally come, but more often it was just Edith and myself, and I realised sadly that no matter how much I loved her the 'affair' between Grace and myself had to come to an end. I didn't have to tell her it was over she could tell by my eyes - if only she could have seen my heart! Poor Grace, I should have spoken to her, but I was afraid that had I done so our feelings would take over again.'

'On 14th April 1917, when I was twentyfour and Edith was twentyone we were married at the local church. It was a simple ceremony attended by most of the village. Edith looked lovely in a cream silk dress that had belonged to her Aunt Maud, she carried a spray of spring flowers and was able to walk down the aisle on her father's arm. Grace was her bridesmaid, she wore a long blue skirt, a simple cream blouse and carried a small posy of primroses. How she managed to cope with the day I shall never know, all I do know is that immediately Edith and I had left for our honeymoon she left Bridge Farm. She told Pa that her mother had been taken ill and needed her, how true that was I don't know. Edith was devastated when she found Grace had gone, she had relied so much on her. I tried to contact her by writing to the Southampton address but the letters were always returned 'Gone away - address not known'. I suppose I could have gone there to see for myself if she really had gone away, but decided I had hurt Grace enough and she probably wanted a life of her own, away from me. God knows how she felt, it was bad for me, but I did have Edith.'

'I was still convalescing and for a short while was able to look after Edith myself, but I knew that this could not last as I would have to go back to the paper in the very near future, so we employed Mary Sutton from the village to care for her. She was a pleasant girl, very reliable and Edith gradually became quite fond of her, which was a big relief to me.'

'November 1917 saw me fit to drive and I started back working with my old newspaper in London. They understood about Edith and I was not given too many commissions for the weekends. We gradually got back into a routine and in our own way were very happy. Edith had always said she wanted a child, the doctors advised against it, but these things happen and in 1918, the year peace was declared, she became pregnant. We were overjoyed, but that was short lived as Edith had a difficult pregnancy followed by a prolonged labour and she died two days after our little girl was born. I was absolutely devastated, the baby was lovely but she had taken Edith's life and I was afraid I might not be able to love her. I called her Grace, it was the first name that came to my mind and I decided that she must take first place in my thoughts and life. I managed to transfer to a job nearer to Telford and Ma and Pa, with Mary's help, offered to care for Grace during the day. Everyone loved her, she was a pretty baby and very contented so this seemed to be a good arrangement and Grace and I stayed at Bridge Farm. The room baby Grace and I had was where the photo was found, everyone called it 'Grace's' room and the name stayed. I put the photo under the lining paper in the top drawer of the chest of drawers, but was in such a state when I left I forgot all about it.'

'The baby was not strong and although everything possible was done she died just before her second birthday. I was inconsolable feeling that it was my fault they had both died - if only Edith hadn't become pregnant.'

'I couldn't stay on at Bridge Farm there were too many bitter-sweet memories, Shore Cottage came on the market so I bought it and moved in. People said I had become a recluse but I still kept my job and returned to London where I had a flat and a good circle of friends. I came to Shore Cottage for weekends and turned one of the upstairs rooms into a darkroom where I worked on my photographic skills. I had several exhibitions and gradually became recognised as a photographer. I was in considerable demand and eventually I only worked on photographic assignments and moved permanently into Shore Cottage.'

12

'So you see my 20's were a sad time and I was very bitter about everything to do with my personal life. I didn't get in touch with Grace after Edith died, as far as I was concerned she went out of my life when she left Bridge Farm without so much as a goodbye. I just decided that if she thought so little of me I didn't want to know her either and stubbornly stuck to my guns.'

'Alan, you must have seen the impossible situation she was in, she couldn't have gone on nursing Edith, the wife of the man she loved, with a clear conscience - surely you realised that?'

'I did deep down, but didn't want to admit it, all I could think of was that our relationship had ended and that was that. Let's face it Sarah, for all I knew she could have met someone else.'

'Well I don't think she did' said Sarah, 'and if it helps she never gave me the impression of being unhappy. You know you really are not being fair, you finished the relationship when you married Edith.'

Alan looked at Sarah and nodded 'You are right of course, but perhaps she was lonely?'

'Perhaps, but she had a close circle of friends.'

'Not quite the same as a loving husband.'

'No, but having heard your story I can only assume that loving you, as you say she did, she didn't feel she could commit herself to anyone else. As I said, she always seemed happy to me, but then I didn't know her until she was in her early seventies, so what happened between 1917 and 1967 we will never know.'

'I sometimes felt I should never have married Edith feeling as I did for Grace, but I had made my promise and no way could I have jilted her. Don't misunderstand me Sarah, Edith and I were happy but there wasn't that special spark that existed between Grace and me.' Alan looked at the photograph and sighed, 'we were so foolish.'

'Grace must have thought you were someone special in her life, you saw how tattered the envelope and photo were, she must have looked at that photograph hundreds of times, in fact it could have been every day.'

'I know you are trying to help, but in some ways that makes things worse, it was really two stubborn people denying their love for each other - she must have known Edith had died, why didn't she get in touch?'

'Perhaps I shouldn't have come, stirring up all your memories.'

'My dear girl, I'm delighted you came, I've kept my story inside me for too long, to share it with someone who also loved Grace is wonderful.' Alan pushed himself out of his chair. 'Now let's have some lunch, then I'd like a rest. We can talk another time, you must have a lot to tell me.'

'Mmn, I'm hungry' said Sarah, 'I've got a pile of sandwiches, we could share them, Joanna made far more than I can eat.'

'And I've got some vegetable soup ready to heat up, followed by sandwiches that will make a good lunch.'

Sarah followed him into the kitchen, everything was immaculate and the kitchen was well lit by the large window that looked out over the estuary and copse. Alan lit the gas under the pan of soup, opened a drawer and took out spoons, knives and paper napkins.

'The bowls and plates are behind you Sarah, we'll eat in here so that you can look out at the view, to the right the roof of Bridge Farm can just be seen. Look after the soup I'll be back in a minute.'

Alan disappeared out of the back door, Sarah gave the soup a stir, laid the table, cut a couple of slices from the loaf Alan had produced, found some butter in the fridge and arranged the sandwiches on a plate. She was beginning to wonder where Alan was when he came in brandishing a bottle of wine.

'Get out the corkscrew Sarah, it's in the drawer behind you, put some glasses on the table and let's celebrate a new friendship, and enjoy our lunch.'

'The soup is delicious - did you make it?'

'Yes, all fresh vegetables straight from the garden, you can't beat freshly picked veg for a good soup.'

Sarah sighed contentedly, finished her soup, put her elbows on the table and leant her chin on her hands. She looked out of the window across to Bridge Farm and again felt a flicker of excitement, a feeling of coming home.

'Bridge Farm is a beautiful house, do you know how old it is?'

'No. but it must be about 400 years old and I believe it was built on the site of an old one, in fact originally I think a monastery stood there. Pa Harris had a lot of papers not only about the house but the whole site, he worked on papers up in the attic but I have no idea where they are now.'

'I wonder if those are the papers Seth is talking about, he

says that there are some boxes in the attic and he is fairly sure that amongst the papers there are some old documents relating to the farm, there could also be old maps and pictures of the village that might be of interest to the local history group he belongs to. It is also possible there are some papers relating to Grace, so he is going to get them down this evening and start sorting out.'

'They probably are the papers. The history of this area is very interesting, did you know the Romans had a settlement here? There was a lot of work done by archaeologists in the upper valley round about 1970.'

'That's interesting' said Sarah excitedly and she told Alan about the project of the lavender farm.

'Babs said that she understood lavender seed had been found by the archaeologists and they want to look into it because they think that 'Roman Lavender' would be a good name to operate under. It was wonderful to hear them talk about it, their enthusiasm was really infectious and I suddenly realised that my life had become rather dull and perhaps now was the time for a change.' She went on to tell him about her proposal to Babs and Ken and how well it had been received. 'I don't know anything about lavender except that it is purple and smells nice, but I just have a feeling that this might be the challenge I need, and I'm sure I must have some skills I can offer. There was a sachet of lavender in the envelope with the photograph, do you think that's significant?'

'It could be, I've got lots of photos that I took during the excavations, they might help in the planning of the lavender farm, I'll look them out for you if you are interested - perhaps the local history group might be interested too.'

'I would love to see them Alan, but don't let's get carried away it was only last night I heard about it and it wasn't until this morning that I floated the idea of becoming a partner and lavender became part of my life. I do find the concept really exciting, but will know more tomorrow when I meet up with Babs and Ken Ashworth. Can I tell them about the photos, I'm sure they would be interested?'

'I have a good feeling about all this' said Alan, 'and of course you can mention the photographs.'

'Perhaps the three of us could come and have a look at them' Sarah said rather tentatively, wondering if he would agree to visitors. Alan looked down at Jason, stroked his head and smiled.

'We'd like that old boy, wouldn't we? I'll get those photos sorted out tomorrow, so you arrange a time Sarah and let me know, I've isolated myself from Bridge Farm for long enough, deliberately avoiding contact because I felt that the ghosts of my past would manifest themselves, but somehow by talking to you the sad memories seem to have been laid to rest and I'll now be able to think of the happy times as well as the sad ones.

Sarah laughed 'We've been talking about the photos giving us all a 'kickstart' in one way or another, it looks as though they are working their magic on you too.'

'Well you never know perhaps Grace intended something like this to happen.' Alan got up from the table and went into the sitting room and settled himself in his chair with the last of the wine to hand and Jason's head on his feet.

'I'll tidy up the kitchen' said Sarah, 'then go for a walk along the shore and get the sea breezes in my hair.'

Sarah wiped the last bowl, tidied the sink and went back into the sitting room. Alan was sitting in his armchair sipping the last of his wine, Troy was dozing, paws on Alan's feet. Sarah smiled at them thinking how contented they looked.

63

'I'm off now Alan, I won't be able to see you tomorrow I have to go home, but we can keep in touch by phone.' She bent over and kissed him, 'I have enjoyed our talk, see you soon.'

'Goodbye dear girl, enjoy the sea and the sun.'

13

Sarah slung her rucksack on her back, put on her boots and shut the front door as quietly as possible. It was still a glorious day even though an east wind had blown up, she hadn't expected it to be quite so chilly and stopped to zip up her fleece.

'Hi there!' A young woman in the end cottage was working in her garden and waved to Sarah. 'How's Alan today?'

'He's fine, I've just had lunch with him - I'm Sarah Bruce and he knew my Great-Aunt, so we've had a great time reminiscing.'

'I expect he enjoyed that. I usually pop in to see him in the morning, but I saw you arrive so left it today, he doesn't get many visitors, seems to prefer his own company. I'm Jonquil Sutton' – she saw Sarah's face and giggled 'I know, isn't it awful? Do call me Jonnie, everyone does.'

'Well Jonnie it is nice to know someone else has suffered with parents dishing out weird names. I was born on St Valentine's Day so no prize for guessing what my second name is.'

'That's almost worse than mine. Are you staying long?'

'Home tomorrow I'm afraid, but I'll be back, in fact I'm wondering whether to move down permanently, I feel so at home here. I'm staying at Bridge Farm and am really enjoying myself. I'm just off for a walk along the shore I reckon this wind will blow all my cobwebs away.'

'Goodbye then, give me a ring next time you're here, perhaps we could go for a walk together. They have my number at Bridge Farm, I go and help out when they are very busy.'

'I'll do that' said Sarah 'It would be nice to have some company, see you soon.' She walked off towards the shore thinking to herself that perhaps she had found another friend, she couldn't remember the last time someone had offered to go for a walk with her and decided that it must be a really different way of life here in the country with the sea on the doorstep. 'If it is' she said to herself 'I want it.'

The sea beckoned and Sarah walked across the road and over the sand-dune, scrunching through the rough grass that held back the sand. The sea was sparkling and gulls were noisy overhead playing with the strong breeze. She was glad she had her wellies on as masses of brown seaweed had been thrown up on the shore and lay glistening in the sunshine, as she walked over it clouds of small black flies rose angrily zooming off to another choice morsel. There wasn't only sea weed, there were plastic beakers, polystyrene take-away cartons, there was a large plastic container that had once held milk and, to her horror, wrapped round a small rock with the hook still attached was some fishing line. Sarah carefully removed the line and hook and wrapped it up in a paper bag she had in her rucksack. 'I'll dispose of that later.'

She walked on along the shore, enjoying the wind, the fresh smell of the sea, the sound of the waves as they shooshed up over the shingle and suddenly thought of two lines from one of Masefield's poems, albeit taken out of context but truly expressing her thoughts at that moment – 'It's a tune for the blood to jig to, and a joy past power of words'.   Again that feeling of contentment drifted over her, she could hardly believe that it was only 48 hours since she had arrived in Tolford.

'Aunt Grace I hope you know what you are doing.' Sarah laughed into the wind and was suddenly conscious of a damp chill in the air, realising she had walked further that she had intended, she turned and walked briskly back towards the cottages and Shore Road not wanting to tackle the road to Bridge Farm in the dusk. It didn't seem so far on the way back and Sarah soon reached the farm to a rapturous welcome from Jason and a wonderful smell of roast pork.

'How did you get on?' Joanna called from the kitchen.

'Fine - I'm just going to tidy up - I'll tell you all about my day later.'

'Don't be long, I need you to do the beans.'

Sarah dashed off loving Joanna's bossiness, it made her feel that she was one of the family, a new experience for her. A quick shower, change of T-shirt , comb through the hair, a dash of lipstick and ten minutes later Sarah arrived back at the kitchen.

'Was that quick enough for you?'

Joanna grinned 'What took you so long? I wasn't serious about the beans, but as you're here ...' and she handed Sarah a vegetable knife and pointed to the large pile of freshly picked runners.

'Now, tell me all about it. Is he as bad as people make out? Has he got two heads? What is he like Sarah?'

Sarah set too with the beans and told Joanna about Alan and how well they had got on.

67

'So you see Joanna it bore out everything Mrs Knight said, my photo was of my Aunt Grace, your photo was Alan Palmer and they were in love, but such a sad story. However, I did not find Alan Palmer cantankerous, in fact he was lovely, we had a very pleasant morning and both enjoyed your sandwiches Joanna, they were washed down with wine though which might have made a difference.'

'Cheeky! You're beginning to feel at home' chuckled Joanna. 'Now let's forget about the big love affair for the time being and concentrate on the dinner, we can carry on when everyone's here, I know the others are interested too.' Joanna turned to the cooker and took out the pork.

'That looks and smells great - and here's the beans done, what now?'

'Put the beans on, stir the gravy, keep an eye on the apple sauce and lay the table, I'll go and ring the bell, back in a few minutes.'

Soon they were all sitting round the table and Seth was carving the joint into succulent pink slices oozing natural juices. Sarah was pleased to see plenty of crackling.

'Sarah had a good day' said Joanna, 'it sounds as though she has made another friend.'

'Well two actually' and Sarah told them about Jonnie.

'Jonnie is a mainstay here in the Summer, does she live next door to Alan?'

'That's right, and I think she keeps an eye on him.'

'That figures! As far as Bridge farm is considered she always seems available when needed and gets on with jobs without needing supervision, in fact Babs and Ken have her in mind for a job on the lavender farm, but she doesn't know that yet. She's another one that keeps herself to herself, perhaps there's a mystery there too Sarah. Something else for you to investigate.'

'You make me sound like a nosey parker, I'm not really, my grandmother would have said 'I'm just interested dear' and I am 'interested' in people, and talking about being interested, Alan was very interested in the lavender farm project. I don't know if you know but he is a brilliant and quite famous photographer, when the archaeologists were working on this site he took lots of photos which he is going to look out and sort through. He wondered if Babs and Ken would like to go down to Shore Cottage and have a look at the ones relating to the fields where the lavender seeds were found. He thought it might help with the planning.'

'You are joking' said Ken 'he barely gives us the time of day when we meet him out with the dog.'

'His life has been a strange one.' Sarah gave them a quick resume of Alan's life as he had told it to her.

'It is a sad story' said Babs 'but he couldn't have just dumped Edith and gone off with Grace - here's something to think about though, would they have been happy had they gone off together?'

'I do think Alan could have contacted Grace after Edith and the baby died' said Ken, 'I think if I had been in his shoes I would have done so.'

'Well' said Seth 'we aren't all the same, thank goodness, and Sarah did say that he himself said it was two stubborn people denying each other, so perhaps he thought Grace would surely have known about Edith and the baby and she could have made contact. We will never know. Don't forget the apple sauce Sarah, Joanna made extra specially for you!'

'It's lovely being spoilt' said Sarah and took a liberal helping. 'Going back to Alan for a moment, he has decided that he has kept away from Bridge Farm for long enough, he feels that most of the ghosts have been laid and I have a feeling that he would like to meet you all. He was also interested in the boxes you have in the attic Seth, it might be that he could help you piece the history of the farm together.'

'Both Alan and Mrs Knight say that Farmer Harris was working on some papers in the attic and nobody knew what they were.'

'Well I shall get the boxes down after dinner and we can have a look, it's the only way to find out. Perhaps you could help me Ken?'

'Sure, it should very interesting, I would like to know all there is to know about this estate.'

'What did we have to talk about, other than the price of milk and when to plant lavender, before Sarah arrived?' said Joanna.

'And what did I think about before I came down here? I'll help you with the boxes Seth, I'm good at unpacking old documents, assuming that's what's in them. You never know it might just be details of the dig, some old newspapers and not much more.'

'Come on Sarah, don't be so pessimistic - we might find another love story.'

'That would be wonderful. Realistically it will probably be details of the number of people working the estate and how much they were paid, together with an inventory of items purchased for the property. With luck there should be some family letters but most of those just might be with your solicitors.'

Joanna opened a drawer and took out a large tablecloth.

'I'll put this on the dining room table so that you can spread out your finds.'

14

Seth pulled down the ladder and clambered into the attic followed by Sarah and Ken. Farmer Harris had installed a couple of electric lights and to Sarah's surprise in addition to the boxes there was a large bare table and a couple of chairs, and at the far end of the attic some furniture that looked as if it had been carefully stored.

Everything was dusty and cobwebby, but the table and chairs had obviously been put there for a purpose, but for what purpose Sarah wondered.

'Seth have you been up here before?'

'Well not for a long time actually, the only excuse I have is that the farm has taken up most of my time and I have kept putting it off. When we moved in we were envisaging piles of rubbish and cobwebs up here, but soon realised that everything was in relatively good order so it was way down on our list of priorities. Seeing it today however, and forgetting the cobwebs, that furniture has been stored very carefully, it is amazingly tidy.'

'I think Joanna might like to have a look at the furniture, it must be old.' Sarah made her way over to the pile carefully negotiating the rafters but still banging her head on the way.

'Ouch! From the way that hurt I reckon these rafters are very old. Hey, this stuff looks similar to the furniture in my room, and look Seth, this looks like a spinet, I'd love to have a closer look at it, it could be Elizabethan it's very similar to one in our local museum.'

'Sarah we have come up here to deal with the boxes, don't get sidetracked.' Ken passed a box to Seth 'I think she is going to be uncontrollable, but at the same time she has a point, we must look at everything up here.'

'Agreed' said Seth 'but boxes first, let's see what's in them, it might not be very interesting.'

'The table and chairs are interesting' said Sarah, 'Alan said that Pa Harris came up here and worked on some papers. Do you think Farmer Harris sat up here and examined the papers relating to Bridge Farm? You know I think this house must have been a Manor House at one time, which would explain the position, the lovely floors and some of the furniture.'

'We can only find out by looking in the boxes, so why don't you go down the ladder and take them from us.' Ken picked up one of the smaller ones and carefully balanced himself at the trapdoor. 'Wait a minute, I think it would be easier and safer if we put some strong string or rope round the boxes before lowering them. Sarah, go and see if Joanna has some in the kitchen. We'll get the boxes ready up here.'

A few minutes later Sarah called up to Ken 'Here's some string and a knife, Joanna hopes it will be strong enough.'

'That's fine' said Ken and quickly ran some string round the small box. 'Are you ready Sarah, first installment.'

The box slid down the ladder and was caught by Sarah. 'Not so fast next time Ken, I think that was heavier than you thought!'

There were four boxes altogether, the last two being

particularly heavy. Soon they were on the table in the dining room, rather dusty but in fairly good condition.

'Judging by the state of the boxes it can't have been all that long ago that they were packed - there's a story in itself' said Ken.

'Joanna has given me the vacuum cleaner, I'll go over them very carefully with the soft brush and get rid of most of the dust.' Sarah worked away and a few minutes later called out. 'Look here's a number 1 and some dates, which I can't quite decipher. This one, number 3 has something written on it, I think it says 'Roman' but there are no dates. Number 4, has 'Monastery 850 -1535 AD' written on it. We are going back into history. Number 2 has some dates on it '1706 – 1900'.'

'Well' said Seth, 'it looks as though someone, I presume Farmer Harris, has done a lot of research and has put it altogether for, as they say, posterity.'

'I don't know why we are surprised, it's not only our generation that has been interested in family and local history.' said Sarah. 'Let's get organised I've got some pads of paper in my room I'll go and get them and we can have a pad for each box, then systematically list all that we find.'

Seth brought out his large penknife, and cut through the thick string on box number one. Inside was a double sheet of newspaper covering the contents, it was dated 1920.

'That newspaper tells me that during the time Farmer Harris lived here someone, presumably him, must have looked at and arranged these documents' said Sarah, 'probably done in the attic which would account for the table and chairs, I wonder if Alan will know?'

'Well here we go' said Seth, 'I'll take them out and you and Ken lay them on the table.'

'Be careful handling them, some of them might be very old.'

'How are you doing?' said Joanna half an hour later.

'Not very well' shouted Sarah, 'I'm afraid some of these documents are really old and fragile, in fact I'm beginning to think we'll need some professional help. There is one document that is reasonably intact that makes interesting reading. Apparently there was a monastery on the land in the 1500's, but in 1535 it was 'dissolved' and the land given to Francis Courtney. What about you Ken, have you found anything exciting?'

'I've just found something written by Farmer Harris, it looks as though he really got stuck into finding out the history of the farm. It's appears to be a chronological list of the families that lived here.'

'Let's have a look' said Sarah. 'This could save us a lot of rather boring research, assuming he has his facts right! Would you let me take a copy back with me, I'll show it to the archivist and she will be able to check.'

'That sounds a very good idea and she might come up with some facts we know nothing about.'

Ken looked up and laughed

'Look at this Sarah it seems to be an invoice for the building of the cottages, it is dated 1640. I bet that interests you?'

'Of course it does! Let me see, that's when Elizabeth Hampton lived here according to Farmer Harris's history, now we are getting somewhere, let's dig a bit deeper, I know there is a story here waiting to be told.'

Ken laughed and told the others that Sarah would never be satisfied until she knew who had lived in the cottage she was planning to rent.

Sarah put her pencil down and closed her notepad 'I don't know about you chaps but I'm ready for my bed, the mysteries can wait until tomorrow so will it be sweet dreams or will the history of Bridge Farm take over? We ought to protect these papers Joanna, do you have another large tablecloth?'

'You go on to bed Sarah, I've got just the cloth for the job.'

Sarah said 'goodnight', stumbled up to her room and was soon in bed.'

'What a day! What will tomorrow bring?'

15

The next morning Sarah woke to a lovely sunny morning, the smell of bacon filtering through to her room. With her stomach grumbling in recognition she had a quick shower, dressed and went down to the kitchen.

'Good morning, this is just as forecast' she said to Joanna, 'it really looks beautiful out there this morning.'

'We'll go and look at the cottages after you've had breakfast, I've arranged for Tony Briggs to meet us here at ten, he lives locally and will tell us what is needed to be done to make them really habitable keeping within the regulations of course. Along with all the other buildings on this site, they are listed buildings so we have to be very careful about what we do. Tony's an expert at restoration, in fact he did the work on Ken and Babs cottage, or rather cottages, as they had two knocked into one, but had to keep the original ambiance of the workers' cottages. He did a superb job, but you will be able to see that for yourself later this morning.'

'They, whoever 'they' are, say that life in the country is slow, I can't say I've found that, at home we would have had to wait several days, if not weeks, for a builder to come round.'

'Not here Sarah, folk need all the work they can get and Tony employs local labour. I hope you like the cottage, and I hope your plans go through, it seems to me that a lot of people will be helped if you do come to Tolford.'

'I'm excited by everything that is happening, but remember until I have spoken to Ken and Babs and the solicitors nothing can be decided. You do realise that if everything goes through and I do like the cottage there will be a time lapse of approximately a year because of probate.'

'The cottages have been empty for at least ten years, I don't think another year will matter. It will give us time to have the necessary work done properly - it's my time for a 'kick-start', planning permission was granted when the other cottages were done and I've been intending to start on these two for a long time. One cottage can be let out for holidays, and if you decide not to have the other one that too can be let out, so don't worry about it. Have you finished your grapefruit? Your bacon and eggs are ready?'

'I'm going to miss this tomorrow' said Sarah tucking in, 'back to cereal and coffee.'

'Hullo Joanna' a deep voice rang out. 'I won't come in I am really muddy.' Jason gave a great 'woof' and dashed towards the door.

'Just take your boots off and come in, have some coffee and meet Sarah, she is just finishing her breakfast.'

'OK! A cup of coffee would be most welcome.' So saying a thickset man in his early thirties crashed into the kitchen, tripping over Jason and upsetting a small vase of flowers on the way. 'I'm sorry Joanna.'

'It's alright Tony, no damage done, just some upset water.'

'You alright old boy, you do get in the way sometimes'

said Tony giving Jason a really rough stroking which the dog obviously thoroughly enjoyed.

'Jason doesn't seem upset' said Sarah as she watched the dog wriggling round Tony's legs.

'No, Tony takes him for lots of walks so there is a good rapport between them. Tony can I introduce Sarah Bruce, why she is here is a long story but she is interested in looking at the cottages next to Ken and Babs with a view to renting one for a while.'

Sarah shook the outstretched hand and found herself looking up into a pair of bright blue eyes in an unshaven face, he did look rather grubby. 'A shave wouldn't have come amiss' she thought, then blushed violently as Tony turned to Joanna and apologised for the stubble.

'I got called out at some unearthly hour this morning to unblock the drain at the pub, some idiot had rammed newspaper down one of the loos, so it was a ramrod job.'

'That's OK Tony, we must keep the pub open. Now what about our cottages?'

'So, you could be interested in moving into one of the cottages?' Tony Briggs smiled as he said it, looking at Sarah rather quizzically.

'Yes! but it does depend on lots of things and there is no way I can move in for about a year.'

'That's no problem, if I remember correctly there is a lot of work to be done, hopefully no massive structural alterations. I can assure you the cottages will be lovely when finished.'

The semi-detached cottages stood just beyond the paved courtyard at the back of the farm house, they looked rather dilapidated, the roofs were minus a few slates and ridge tiles, the front gates were lying on their sides and the paths were overgrown.

'It all looks much worse than I thought,' said Joanna as she pushed past the brambles and opened the front door, 'when you live with something on your doorstep you tend not to notice it, it becomes part of the scenery.'

Inside it lived up to all of Sarah's expectations, it was like a scene from a Hitchcock film, dust and cobwebs were competing with each other, the wooden floor was covered with a film of dirt and there were small footprints that looked as if mice had been having a field day in the cottage. The sun was shining through the windows and Sarah loved the imperfections in the glass. A large fireplace dominated the room, the surround was of dark wood, darkened even more with grime. There were some small figures carved across the front which were difficult to see because of the encrusted dirt, Sarah thought she had seen them somewhere else. In the fireplace a cast iron basket containing a few partially burnt logs covered with soot, twigs and bird droppings, completed the picture. The three beams in the ceiling had their share of cobwebs too and she hoped that they were still strong enough to support the upstairs floor and the roof. A staircase went up from a corner and a door lead through to what was obviously the kitchen.

Tony nodded towards the stairs. 'There are three rooms up there, one can be made into a bathroom, but we won't go up today as I wouldn't like either of you to have an accident on the stairs, some of the treads look very worn.'

Joanna and Sarah agreed, the stairs did look decidedly rotten. Tony started tapping the woodwork and the walls.

'Structurally it really isn't too bad down here, apart from the stairs everything appears to be sound. We must get the chimney sweep in first though, those rooks have really taken over, I bet there are loads of nests up there. Then when my high-powered vacuum has got rid of the cobwebs and dust we will get a better idea of how things look, and what needs to be done.'

'I love the windows, are they really as old as they look?'

'They certainly are Sarah, the cottages were built round about 1640 and must have been well looked after for centuries as they are in a good state of preservation, the thick walls have helped and those beams will, I'm sure, pass the tests I'll make on them - they look good to me.'

They went through to the kitchen, again a haven for spiders and creepy crawlies, the window looked out on to a garden very much in need of tender loving care, but Sarah thought it was wonderful.

'A kitchen not looking out on to houses, I like that.' She smiled up at Tony. 'Can a built-in kitchen be installed without upsetting the listed building status?'

'A great deal can be done as long as the original building is respected.' Tony took out his tape measure and pencil and started to sketch in his notebook.

'Getting in the electrics is the most difficult thing to plan, so Sarah could you look at the rooms and give me a rough idea of where you would like lights, plugs etc.'

'Wait a minute, I haven't decided to move in.'

'I think it is only a matter of time' said Tony, 'anyway you've given me the impression that you are really interested in the restoration, so let's hear from you.'

'I've got a better idea' said Joanna, 'Sarah is due at Ken and Babs shortly, let her have a look at their cottage then come back to you with ideas.' Sarah looked at her watch, the morning had certainly flown by.

'Joanna's right, I must go or I'll miss my lunch, I've been promised soup.'

'That's fine' said Tony, 'I'll carry on here with Joanna, tell her if you have any brilliant ideas.'

'Well the cottage belongs to Joanna, but if it were mine I would definitely keep the fireplace and its surround. As for the range in the kitchen, I would love to keep that as well but I do realise it might have to be sacrificed for central heating and a good cooker. I expect you know better than me what is needed, but I will come back to you with any special requirements.'

'Don't worry Sarah, the cottages will be carefully restored and converted into comfortable homes, remember you will have a choice between two.' Tony grinned at her, 'I really do think you will be moving in, so help Joanna by choosing which one you want and what you want in it.'

'I'll have a look next door after lunch, but this one has a lovely feel to it - I just love those figures carved into the mantelpiece, where have I seen them before?'

'I wondered if you'd notice, they are the same as those carved into the mantelpiece in our dining room at Bridge Farm, Seth made a rough sketch and we have used them on our headed notepaper.'

'Of course Joanna, I saw it on your notepaper in the Hall. Do you know who, or what, they are?'

'We haven't a clue, perhaps Seth will unearth something whilst doing his research.'

'They look like angels to me, if so, that surely is a good omen' said Tony.

'I think you're right. We'll have to have a good look when they've been cleaned up. Perhaps I can have a go at that next time I'm here.'

'There you are Joanna, she will be back,' and Sarah found herself laughing with Joanna and Tony.

'Well, of course! Was there ever any doubt about it?'

'You go and talk to Ken and Babs, decisions can come later.'

16

'Good timing' said Babs as she put the bread in the oven.

'Sorry I'm so late, I got caught up with Tony Briggs in the restoration-stroke-planning of the cottages next door, he is quite sure I'm going to move in even though I've told him that no decisions have been made.'

'That's right, we know that things have to be discussed and we have to make decisions as well. Let's talk about it over our soup. Lunch is nearly ready.'

'Can I have a look round your cottage while you're finishing it off, Joanna said I would get a good idea of what Tony can do to the cottages after seeing yours.'

'Of course! He's a great person to have around, he studied architectural history when he did his degree and is very careful about his planning and loves restoration work.' Babs looked up at Sarah, 'I bet he's given you the impression he's self taught and a jack-of-all-trades.'

Sarah shook her head, 'He didn't succeed I've met types like him before, people who are actually embarrassed by the knowledge they have. I didn't know he had a degree, but I was aware that he knew what he was talking about, he obviously enjoys his work and looking at what he has done here, it shows, he has managed to retain the old but at the same time make a beautiful modern home.'

'He has a thriving business Sarah, he does a lot of work for English Heritage and many of the manor houses round here have benefited from his expertise.'

'And it's still possible for him to come and have a look at Joanna's cottages at a minute's notice.'

'That's our Tony, you'll find he has lots of attributes, one of them being that he is not married.'

'No, but he is looking' said Ken, and laughed at the expression on Sarah's face. 'Don't worry, we aren't match-makers.'

'Given half a chance we might be, it's high time he settled down,' said Babs dishing up the soup. 'Let us settle down, have our lunch and try and sort through our plans such as they are, then we can go out to the farm so that you can put everything in perspective, you have made us sit back and think about what we want to do here Sarah. Originally we had not envisaged taking on a partner but recently we began to think it was the realistic answer to our problems and the more we think about a 'working' partner, the more we like it.'

'Good, I'm glad about that, the idea did come all out of the blue, but sometimes plans are all the better for that. I expect you are interested in how much money I can invest with you, I phoned my solicitor this morning and he is not sure of the final figures but it will be something like £80,000 - it might be less of course, I have to keep enough capital to buy a small property. Does that sum seem realistic to you?'

'It certainly does' and Ken raised his glass of water to Sarah.

'An important factor as far as my solicitor is concerned is

what I will get out of the deal. I would imagine a good plan would be to get our solicitors together so that they can work out the best for us all.'

'That makes sense. Let us know when your man is ready to meet ours and we'll arrange a date. Now another very important factor is where do you, as a working partner, see yourself in all this? We want to build up the business so that we make our own products, creams, soaps, polishes and anything else that uses lavender. We don't know anything about that side of the business, would that interest you?'

'Well it would certainly be a challenge and a change from working in the library and my first job was in a laboratory, though that was a long time ago. My immediate reaction is one of interest, I would want to know a lot more about what would be expected of me, and what about the training? Thinking about it that might not be a problem, I don't have to worry too much about money at the moment, so perhaps I could take time off and go and work on a lavender farm somewhere, there must be one around that would be willing to take a trainee. That would fill in the time between now and probate being granted, then if everything goes through I can move here and try my hand at producing the products wanted and giving a hand where and when needed.'

'That would be brilliant, that would give us time to get our house in order. We went to a lavender farm for several weekends to find out about the types of lavender, how to grow them, when to harvest and the distilling. We found it very useful and everyone was most helpful. The distilling we don't do ourselves at the moment, the equipment needs a special building and we are talking mega bucks. Currently we send our lavender off to a local distillery which works very well. The oil we sell on to manufacturers, but we would like to make our own products so if you were really interested we could start there and get our own distillery when our bank balance gets bigger.'

Ken finished his soup and went on, 'Any money you put in at the moment Sarah would be used for development. We have just planted the sloping field with plants - thousands of them, we had help but at one time we just did not want to see another lavender plant and a machine for planting is top of our list. A laboratory and workshop to make our products is essential, but we want to encourage more visitors, so a tea-room is high on the list of priorities, plus, of course, the inevitable toilets and car park. Somebody once said that if you were involved in anything remotely connected with tourists, a good tea-room and clean toilets will ensure visits. We are busy at the moment converting a small derelict barn into a tea-room and shop, that's one of the things we'll be looking at after lunch. Tony Briggs drew up some plans and put us in touch with a firm specialising in reclaiming old bricks and tiles and the work is going fairly well but an injection of money would really help, we could afford more labour.'

'We must tell you this' said Babs, 'Joanna is so impressed by our barn conversion that she has decided to convert another one into a Farm Shop, we thought this was a super idea, between us we should be able to attract a wide range of customers, what they don't spend in the Lavender Shop they could well spend in the Farm Shop, and vice versa. We hope that Jonnie might join us and manage the shops, but we haven't asked yet, so Mum's the word please.'

'I won't breathe a word, but it really sounds as though you need some staff there is such a lot of work to be done, still the more you can offer the better the business, which means hard work. Incidentally do you have a list of lavender farms that might be interested in a trainee? If so could I have a copy so that I could suss them out during the next week or two.'

'Hold your horses' said Ken. 'To be quite realistic and to bring us down to earth, we must remember that nothing can be decided until our solicitors have got their heads together.'

'I know that Ken, it does seem like jumping the gun, but I am genuinely interested and would be glad to do some preliminary research.'

'Ken, you know if all goes well, and I can't see why it shouldn't, we would welcome Sarah as a partner, so at least we can say that. Sarah what you have done to us all I don't know, but everyone suddenly seems full of enthusiasm, something that had gone out of our lives.'

'Don't thank me' said Sarah with a laugh, 'it's all thanks to Aunt Grace.'

'We mustn't forget Alan either' said Ken. 'We opened the other boxes after you had gone to bed and in 3 & 4 there were all sorts of artefacts! We hope Alan might be able to tell us a bit about them, we are pretty sure that Farmer Harris collected them all, he listed the documents carefully, but there doesn't seem to be any lists for these boxes.'

'Alan's photographs of the archaeological dig might help, do go and see him, you'll really like him. Try and persuade him to come up to the farm, I know he would like that.'

'We'll ask Joanna to invite him for dinner and tell him we have some 'things' we'd like him to look at.'

'That should work I wish I could be there' said Sarah.

'Come on you two we ought to go and look at the farm while it is sunny.' Ken got up from his chair. 'Let's leave the dishes Babs or Sarah will never get home tonight.'

Sarah looked round as they walked over to the farm, the sun was deceptively warm and she was glad she had worn her heavier anorak, she pulled the hood closer to her neck and looked back at the cottages, again she had that strange feeling that she had seen them before. The rooks were busy circling the chimneys looking for suitable nesting sites, she wondered how many nests the chimney sweep would find in the cottage chimney.

The barns looked decidedly dilapidated but Sarah could see the possibilities, the grey stone looked most attractive in the sunshine and when she went into the larger of the barns she was surprised at the beams.

'Those beams are beautiful, they wouldn't come amiss in a church.'

'Tony will be making a feature of those. This barn will be the tea-room and shop, the toilets will be discreetly hidden on the side. As Tony has already drawn up the plans, with your injection of money we should be able to start building.'

Sarah looked at the smaller barn 'Is this where you hope to make the soaps. etc?'

'That's right, a workroom at the back and the packaging will be done at the front, there is also a small space for an office.'

'Let's go and look at the lavender now' said Ken, 'it doesn't look much at present, but it will soon grow away.'

Sarah bent down and rubbed her fingers along some leaves. 'It's a wonderful smell, can I take a couple of sprigs home then I can dream of lavender all night.'

'You're getting as bad as Babs' laughed Ken and picked her a couple of sprigs. 'You'll love it here in the Spring, this bank is massed with snowdrops, followed by primroses and forget-me-nots.'

'It sounds wonderful, but I'm afraid I really do have to be off I must get home before dark and I have to look at the other cottage, but I did have a feel for the one nearest to you - and I loved that fireplace.'

'You noticed the carvings then?' said Ken.

'Yes! I noticed them, they are most intriguing, Tony thinks they represent angels and if so he says they are a good omen.'

'I like that idea, but hopefully some of the documents will tell us the story behind them, if indeed there is a story to tell.'

'I do hope so, I'll keep in touch, it won't be too long before I'm back.'

Babs put her arms round Sarah and gave her a big hug, 'If Joanna can't put you up remember we have a small guest room and would love to have you to stay.'

'Is that a good idea, we could be up all night talking lavender.' Sarah laughed and returned the hug. 'I'll phone you as soon as I've seen my solicitor. Goodbye, and thanks for one of the most exciting weekends I have ever had, it's not only you who are full of enthusiasm I am too - I can hardly wait to hand in my notice.'

17

The documents from Box 1 had been put in neat piles and catalogued by Sarah according to the year and name of the family. During the next few weeks Seth and Joanna tried to piece together the history. They found the detailed chronological history compiled by Farmer Harris to be very helpful, but something was missing, there were no personal remarks or comments.

'He must have written something down somewhere.' Joanna went through some of the papers and documents again but found nothing, she thought this was very strange as Farmer Harris had obviously spent a lot of time on the project and must have been interested. However, together with Sarah's lists, the chronological history and various phone calls they felt they were getting somewhere, but that there must be another box in the attic that they had overlooked.

'I must get up in the attic again Joanna' said Seth, 'there must be something we haven't found. We are getting the facts together but do you wonder what really happened in the past? I do. What was Francis Courtney like when he took over the land in 1535? Why was Elizabeth Hampton's marriage unhappy? I must read the letters she left very carefully, hopefully they will tell us, but they are difficult to decipher, perhaps Sarah can help there - and why was Elizabeth's son a 'ne'er-do-well'? Who was Cedric Lafolley? What about those carvings on the fireplaces in the house and the cottage - that surely must have a meaning.'

'There could be a very rational explanation for that, the carpenter carved the fireplace in the cottage, the family liked the carvings and asked for them to be duplicated in their dining-room.'

'Well' said Seth grinning at Joanna, 'I prefer to think there is a mystery.'

'We will never know all the answers Seth, but I agree it is fascinating trying to find out. Incidentally, we must find a home for the documents, they can't stay in the dining-room we have a lot of B & B bookings next week and will need to use it, suppose we turn the small bedroom upstairs into a temporary 'workshop' and operate from there. You can plug your computer set-up in there, so you won't have a problem with scanning or word processing.'

'That would be fine then we could work on them without interfering with the running of the house.'

'We'll have to work out what to do with the information, is it just for our benefit or should we write it up?'

'Write it up I think' said Seth, 'though goodness knows who would be interested in doing that, perhaps Sarah could help out there.'

'Don't tell her that yet ' laughed Joanna, 'it might put her off coming - assuming she's coming that is. Ken and Babs say that everything is going well, both solicitors have agreed details and they are just waiting for probate, there doesn't seem to be a major problem, she's coming next weekend so she can fill us in on the latest. I must go and get the dinner started, don't forget that Alan and Tony are coming tonight, I hope they both like beef stew.'

'Your beef stew, my potatoes, my onions, my beans and my carrots, come on Joanna that's a meal fit for a king, of course they'll like it.'

'Raspberry and apple crumble and our own cream to follow, I suppose you are right 'fit for a king'. Will you remind Ken that he is picking Alan up at six thirty.'

Joanna looked at the stew, she had got it out of the freezer in the morning and debated about putting it on. She decided 'later' and started preparing the vegetables. The onions made her eyes water even though she was peeling them under running water. 'It doesn't matter what I do' she muttered, 'none of the so-called tricks work. They must all be old wives tales.' For good measure she gave a big sniff and wiped her nose on her tee-shirt 'Where are those tissues? Why don't people leave things where they find them?' She wiped her hands, turned round and spotted the offending box on the dresser 'There you are,' she said triumphantly and jumped as the wind chimes played more loudly than usual at the front door.

'Can I come in?'

'Tony! Of course you can, but dinner won't be ready for ages.'

'I know but I came to see if you needed any help, I've just been up at the cottages and decided it would be silly to go home. Can I have a quick wash first though?'

'Of course, you know where to go, have a shower if you like, the blue towel is a clean one, so just help yourself.'

'Good idea, a shower, will help to get the old grey cells moving around in the brain.'

'Tony disappeared and Joanna sorted out some herbs for

91

the stew, she was a big believer in not using too much salt and had been told that herbs used carefully could compensate the taste buds. She was still not convinced, but went along with the theory.

'That's better Joanna, now what can I do?'

'That was quick Tony. You could scrape the carrots for me, then lay the table we'll eat in here as the dining room table is still covered in papers.'

'That's fine, it is probably exactly what Alan would like, Sarah says he is really looking forward to meeting us all.'

'I see, Sarah said … ' and Joanna looked at Tony who raised his shoulders and laughed.

'Isn't it what you wanted Joanna? A big romance on your doorstep.'

'You are joking, aren't you? You've only known Sarah for about six weeks and for most of that time she has been in Southampton and you've been here.'

'I am teasing you Joanna, but at the same time … ' and Tony left the sentence in the air, knowing it would intrigue Joanna. In fact he had seen Sarah at least once a week but was not prepared to share that fact at the moment.

'You know it really does sound as though Sarah will move here, all the legal work is going through without any hitches and I understand from Babs that the solicitors have reached an agreement regarding an investment in the lavender farm.'

'So Babs was telling me, it all sounds satisfactory and we will really welcome her, when she spent that weekend with us it was as if she belonged I could hardly believe how well she fitted in, as if she had known us for years.'

'I got that feeling too' said Tony, 'and moving down here seems to be what she really wants. She talks about the cottage as though it is hers. When she comes next weekend she wants to work out if her Aunt's antique furniture can fit in and she wants a good look at the fireplaces, she would like to give the one in the cottage a good clean and work out exactly what the carving is and compare it with the one in your dining-room. She is convinced there is a story there.'

'So is Seth, well I hope they are right. Looking at it from a commercial point of view it would be good for my B and B business if there was a story. I'll be very happy for Sarah to have that cottage, she really fell for it, dilapidated state and all. Right Tony, stew is going on, let's have the carrots and what about a glass of wine for the cooks?'

'Good idea, there's an open bottle of red - will that be OK?'

'Fine, open another one and can you put a bottle of white and some more fruit juice in the fridge please. How do you think Alan will re-act to what, for him, is really 'coming home'? Sarah says that he feels he has laid the ghosts, but I wonder, he lived here a long time and had the deaths of two loved ones to cope with.'

'Hopefully he will come back and remember the happy times as well as the sad ones and in doing so help us with our research. He must have been aware that Farmer Harris was working on some papers in the attic, he must have known that some lovely furniture had been stored up there, he knows about the archaeologists working in the fields and has photos, in fact he must have a lot of information he can pass on.'

'You are right of course, but we must tread carefully, remember he is in his nineties - he might not want to be involved.'

'Well that is not the impression Sarah has got, and she has spoken to him several times in the last few weeks, I think he is quite excited at having something to think about and, most important, contact with other people. He has been very lonely for a long time and Sarah has offered him a new lease of life which can only be good for him. I am really looking forward to meeting him.'

'You won't have to wait any longer, here they are.' Joanna could hear Ken shouting in the car park.

'Whatever's going on?' She dashed out to find that it was the dogs causing all the fuss, Alan had brought Troy and Jason couldn't believe his luck, someone to play with, the pair of them had gone berserk and Ken and Alan were trying to control them.

'Let them be for a while' said Joanna, 'at least they're not fighting and they can't do any harm in the car park, we'll get them in in a minute. Hello Alan, I'm Joanna and it is really nice to see you here, do come in - I hope you like stew?'

'Love it, never make it for myself, can't remember the last time I ate it. Thank you so much for asking me here, I should have visited you before this, but I expect Sarah has told you my story, and why I didn't feel I could come.'

'Yes she has, but she said that you felt that she had helped you to lay the ghosts so please enjoy your visit, the first of many I hope. We're eating in the kitchen tonight, you'll understand why when we show you the dining room. Meet Tony Briggs, he does all our restoration work for us and has become a good friend.'

'Sarah mentioned you the other day when she phoned me, said you were going to Southampton for the day.'

Joanna looked up and laughed. 'Your secret's out now Tony.'

'Oh dear! Have I put my foot in it?'

'No, of course you haven't Alan' and Tony laughed. 'It's just that I haven't told Joanna and Co that Sarah and I have been seeing each other, they've been so inquisitive I've kept them guessing. Sarah's coming down next weekend and we would have told them then, it has just been a bit of harmless teasing.'

'That's alright then, but just remember young man that you'll need my seal of approval to become, as we used to say, 'serious'.'

'I'll remember that, but I really am quite a nice person. Have a glass of wine Alan and let's change the subject after all you are re-visiting your old home in the first time for years, how does it feel?'

Joanna glared at Tony, but Alan smiled, took a sip of wine and told them that he was happy to be there, and was looking forward to meeting everyone.

18

'That was a grand meal' said Alan, 'I can't remember when I last sat down with a crowd, I have enjoyed it, those vegetables and the raspberries were superb, home grown I assume?'

'That's right, all organic, there are occasions when we have to deal with slugs but we use beer traps now, so no chemicals even if the packaging says 'bio-degradable'. If you are interested I'll take you round one day so that you can see just how successful organics can be.'

'I'd like that Seth, I was always interested in the farming side of life here and one of my earliest memories is the smell of the cattle shed.'

Joanna laughed. 'That doesn't change, but I expect the husbandry has altered considerably, we don't need so many farm workers, which is good in some ways but bad in others. That's why the cottages Tony is restoring have been empty for so long.'

'Sarah was telling me about them the other day, it seems as though she would like to rent the one nearest to Babs and Ken.'

'Did she tell you why?' said Babs, 'it's because there is a

fireplace with a lovely carved surround and she is convinced a story is lurking there as the carving is apparently the same as the one on the dining room fireplace here.'

'Now that is striking a chord with me, I can remember Pa Harris telling us lots of stories about the history of Bridge Farm.'

'Stories?' said Mollie, 'were there any ghost stories?'

'I believe there was one, it certainly wasn't a frightening one. You know we always thought he had made them up to entertain us, but perhaps he did base his stories on fact. I can vaguely remember him telling us one about fireplaces, hopefully it will come back to me.'

Seth stood up. 'I think it is time we went into the dining-room so that Alan can see what we found in the attic. Did you know that Farmer Harris worked up there?'

'I'll bring the coffee in to you' said Joanna and set the percolator to work.

'Yes, I helped him store some furniture up there ages ago, he was very particular about it said it was quite valuable, but I'm afraid I didn't give it a second look. We knew he was busy up there with a mass of papers, but didn't know what he was doing, he was rather secretive about it so we just left him to it.'

'Well, here are the papers, we've sorted them into date order with the help of Farmer Harris's lists and hope that perhaps you can help us piece together the history of Bridge Farm.'

'I don't really know a lot about it but it wasn't always Bridge Farm,' said Alan 'it was an old manor house and before that a monastery, as I expect you know. The manor had a strange name I can't recall it at the moment, but will think about it. What a lot of papers, are they all dealing with this house?'

'Yes, we hoped you might be able to help with some aspects, for example Sarah said you were around when the archaeologists were excavating the site. There are a lot of artefacts in the other boxes, they might hold clues. Incidentally, was the name you were trying to think of 'Hapstead'?' said Seth.

'Of course it was. I'll do what I can to help you, I'll get out my photos and see if they jog my memory but it is a long time ago since I had anything to do with Bridge Farm. So this is what Pa was working on in the attic?'

'It would seem so' and Babs looked at Alan, 'you don't remember a file or book that he wrote his own ideas in do you?'

'He had a large black folder with masses of papers in it, it was the one he looked at when he told us his stories and I can't see it here.' Alan sat down on one of dining chairs and looked around. 'Do you know I don't think the furniture in this room has changed very much, the curtains and pictures are different, but other wise … ' and he left his sentence unfinished which Seth took to be praise.

'Easily explained' said Seth. 'The furniture came with the house, Dave Harris's wife had died earlier and as they had no family when he died the farm went to a cousin who was not interested in farming or in the house and estate. It was put on the market and we were lucky enough to find the necessary finances to purchase. It was only after we had bought it that we realised all the furniture was included. Everything was in a bit of a sorry state, Mrs Knight had done her best but Farmer Harris had let things slide so when Dave took over there was a lot to be done and I'm afraid that a lot was left undone. We decided that most of the furniture was worth keeping, we got rid of the grot and concentrated on making the most of the 'good' things. This room we are particularly pleased with and your reaction to it is marvellous.'

'I think it's marvellous that you haven't come in and got rid of all the old furniture, now-a-days you could probably only get a table and chairs like this in an antique auction and the starting price would be very high because a lot of the quality items are ending up in America.' Alan reached into his pocket and took out his camera. 'Do you mind if I take some photographs?'

'No! Of course we don't' said Joanna and she giggled, 'I was going to ask you to take some that we could use in our B & B brochure and on our web-site. Cheeky I know, but please do take photos of anything that pleases you.'

It was Alan's turn to laugh 'Sarah told me that I would start to laugh when I came here and she was right. Yes, you can use any photographs you like, as long as I can come to dinner again.'

'Now what can be fairer than that' said Seth.

'The first one I want to take is of the fireplace, especially for Sarah. I'll take several including a close-up of the carvings that I can 'blow-up' for her to look at closely. '

'That's an excellent idea' said Tony, 'then perhaps when Sarah has cleaned up the cottage fireplace you could do the same there, it would be so much easier to compare the two sets of carvings if we could see them side by side.'

'Exactly what I had in mind dear boy' and Alan clicked away with his camera, the occasional grunt indicating his satisfaction.

Seth looked at the first lot of papers. Sarah had agreed the date of 1539 that Farmer Harris had put on his list and had put a little note beside the date 'dissolution of the Monasteries, land given to Francis Courtney.'

'Do you remember Farmer Harris telling you anything about Francis Courtney Alan? He apparently built the manor house in the sixteenth century.'

'Yes, I do remember the name. I believe there had been a monastery here since about 850AD but during the time of the Dissolution of the Monasteries Henry VIII decreed that it should be pulled down and the land to be given to Francis Courtney to build a manor house. Pa used to tell us a story about that period, you know you'll have to have another look in the attic, his large black folder is the missing link in all this. I would think it's up there somewhere.'

'We were so taken up with getting the boxes down and emptied that I must confess we didn't look any further, but I did say to Joanna the other day that another look wouldn't go amiss ' said Seth.

Ken looked at him 'I'll go up there now, if that's alright with you?'

'Can we come too?' asked the twins 'we're good at looking for things.'

'OK, but don't get in the way. Tony could you give them a hand?'

'Of course, I'd like to see the attic anyway, I bet there are some interesting beams up there - and searching for lost treasure is right up my street. '

The twins dashed off to get the ladder down and Ken and Tony went off discussing exactly what they might find, was there a box they had overlooked? Could the furniture be hiding anything?

'There could be some drawers that need to be looked at' said Ken, 'although it does seem that Farmer Harris was thorough in his research.'

'Give me two minutes Ken I've got a couple of torches in the van that are very useful for getting into corners. If anything is hidden we should find it.'

'You know' said Tony as he joined Ken on the landing, 'I

reckon Alan is right, we need to find what he calls the 'black folder'. It looks as though the twins have already put the lights on, so up we go.'

Although he had been told the attic was tidy Tony was surprised at just how tidy. A rough floor had been laid, possibly in the early 1900's giving easy access to most corners Tony's immediate thoughts were that he would like to take some of the floor boards up and have a good look at the structure underneath. The rafters looked to be in a surprisingly good state of repair, even though they were hung with cobwebs that were so thick with dust they looked like curtains. They brushed some cobwebs aside to have a closer look at the furniture which was neatly stacked at the far end. Tony was most intrigued by the spinet it looked really old.

'Everything is certainly dusty but I've never seen such a tidy attic' he told Ken, 'and I've been in a few. I'd like to have a good look at that furniture it has been stored very carefully, some of it looks valuable to me and you could be right there might be something of interest in the drawers. Now everybody let's do some positive thinking, where do you think that black folder could be? Do you think Farmer Harris dropped it up here and it's gone down a crack?'

'I would imagine it to be too large for that Tony. You go and look at the furniture and the twins and I will go and look at the other end of the attic, we haven't been down there yet and it is very gloomy.'

'Mind where you put your feet, remember the floorboards are quite loose. I've found another switch Ken, let's hope it works.' The light came on but it was very feeble, so Tony called down to Seth to see if he had a 100W bulb that they could use.

'Coming up, I didn't know there was another light up here' said Seth as he came into the attic.

Tony put the bulb in and switched on, they were all surprised, there was a lot more furniture than they had first realised, the shadows and cobwebs had hidden it and at first glance it all appeared to be very old.

'Did you say this all came with the house?'

'Yes, we didn't know it was here until recently, we've been using a barn for storing our things as it was easier to get at and I'm afraid we really didn't give this furniture a second thought imagining it was stuff to be thrown out, and we'd do that later, but it looks valuable. I must say I am rather shocked, I feel as if we diddled the previous owners - some of this must be worth a lot of money.'

'Don't worry about it Seth, they didn't want to know and the furniture did come with the house, I am surprised the valuers of the estate hadn't included it. Perhaps they didn't bother with the attic.'

'This spinet is beautiful' said Tony. 'I think Joanna might like it downstairs, it should be moved anyway and I think you ought to have an expert look at it. Let's move it out a little Seth so that we can have a good look.'

Seth took out his handkerchief and dusted the top.

'Look at this' he exclaimed, 'the lid is beautifully painted. I wonder if it still plays?' Seth touched a couple of keys and rather discordant notes were heard. 'Well, that is amazing, I wonder how old it is.'

'It looks late Elizabethan to me, but wait a minute' Tony had lifted the lid and pasted on the underside was a rather tatty piece of paper. 'I can only just make out what it says but it looks as though it was purchased in London in 1623. We are going to have to take our time over this Seth, it looks as though you've got some treasures up here.'

'You lot going to be up there all night?' called Joanna, 'Alan is ready to go home.'

'Coming' said Ken, 'I wish he could get up here, I bet he would remember some of the furniture.'

Alan and Troy were patiently waiting in the kitchen.

'Sorry we've been so long but you should see what we've found. Were you aware of some lovely old furniture being stashed away up there Alan?'

'Ages ago I helped Pa store some furniture up there. Now I think about it some of the stories Pa told us seemed to be based round pieces of furniture - where is that black folder? As I said before it should answer a lot of your questions.'

'Come on, I'll take you and Troy home and leave the others up there, you never know they might find it by the time I get back.'

'I do hope so. Joanna thank you so much for a lovely evening, now that I've met you all I just wish I had knocked on your door before this.'

'I've just had an idea Alan, Jonnie is coming up next week to help with the B & B's and the work in the dairy, why don't you come with her, she always comes in her car so you shouldn't have a problem, then you could spend a bit of time looking at the documents and artefacts. She comes up at about nine o'clock, has lunch here, then leaves at four o'clock.'

'That's a brilliant idea, how about it Alan? We've so many mysteries up here that I'm sure you can help with.'

'Yes, I'll come willingly and by Monday I can have some photographs sorted. Life isn't dull round here is it? I look forward to telling Sarah on Saturday just how much she has done for me. Come on Troy we've got to go home, and once again, thanks Joanna.'

Joanna put her arms round him and gave him a kiss, 'I think you're one of the family now. See you on Monday.'

19

The rain lashed against Sarah's face as she ran from the library to her car, no distance really but she managed to get soaked. It had been her late night and was getting quite dark, she gently swore to herself realising she had left her small torch at home. After several attempts she managed to get the key in the car door. Success at last. Sarah eased herself behind the wheel, found the tissues in the side pocket and mopped at her face thinking to her self that although getting so wet wasn't nice her face was glowing and her skin felt wonderful.

It was Thursday and Bridge Farm, lavender and Tony all seemed a long way away as Sarah started the car and headed for home. The weekend was only twenty four hours away but Sarah was dying to tell them all her news, so it seemed an eternity. She had been to see her solicitor that morning who told her that everything was going through very smoothly, he thought probate would be granted by June. The lavender farm project had been investigated and approved both by him and Ken and Bab's solicitor, so plans could now be put into motion. Sarah had decided not to wait any longer and had her notice ready to hand in on Monday. She had already told her landlord she would be leaving and he'd asked her if she could be out in two weeks. This was not a problem as she had decided to use Aunt Grace's house temporarily, this would give her somewhere not only to live but to store her furniture and the bits and pieces she had accumulated, and she could then decide at leisure what to keep and what to get rid of before moving into the cottage. The three pieces of Aunt Grace's furniture that she wanted to keep needed to be thoroughly examined, would they be right for the cottage? She had contacted a lavender farm in Jersey and they were very happy for her to go there for a month in the New Year to learn about making the lavender products. She couldn't believe everything was working out so well.

Sarah was looking forward to the weekend, and staying at the farm again, she hoped Joanna's breakfasts were still the same. Tony had wanted her to stay with him but she didn't feel that their relationship had developed enough for her to do that, even though they had been seeing quite a lot of each other. Tony had been down to Southampton several times but had never stayed over. She was recovering from a disastrous affair, they had had a wonderful time together and it was only after being together for nearly six months that Sarah discovered he was two-timing her. She was devastated and vowed there and then that she would be very careful in the future, hence her treatment of Tony. She hoped he didn't find her 'cold' because she knew that her feelings were anything but cold, in fact she couldn't remember ever feeling this way before.

The traffic lights changed to red, the rain was still lashing down and the road gleamed under the street lights. Sarah jumped as the car behind bleeped its horn, the lights had gone green and she realised she'd gone into a daydream thinking about Tony. With an apologetic wave of the hand she drove off. The windscreen wipers were having difficulty in keeping up with the rain, street lights reflected on the wet pavement and weird shadows were cast as pedestrians, umbrellas up, hurried homewards.

Just for once her parking space was free, dashing from the car she opened her front door slamming it behind her as she made for the bathroom to grab a towel. The light on the answering machine was blinking, Sarah smiled hoping it would be Tony but it was Alan to say how much he was looking forward to seeing her at the weekend and would she come to lunch on Saturday. He told her he had some excellent pictures of the carvings of the dining room fireplace at Bridge Farm, and reminded her to bring some brushes to clean up the carvings in the cottage as he wanted to photograph those as well.

Sarah smiled and phoned him back to say that she would like to have lunch with him and was most intrigued about his interest in the carvings.

'I'm not going to tell you dear girl until I've photographed the carvings in the cottage.'

'I'll have to get to work on them early then, Tony said he would help, can I bring him to lunch?'

'Yes, of course, see you both at twelve.' Alan rang off leaving her with a lot of unanswered questions.

Sarah put the answer machine off and started to make herself a quick meal.

'Joanna wouldn't approve' she thought to herself as the pizza went into the oven. Knowing that she would be going to Tolford the next evening she decided to get herself organised. Whilst packing her clothes she thought about the carvings, she had a couple of soft toothbrushes and three paintbrushes that had never been used so they went into a pocket of her overnight bag. 'I bet Tony has some other ideas but I will take them anyway.' The phone rang and Sarah jumped, she had been standing beside it.

'Tony! I was just thinking about you.'

'Nice thoughts I hope, do you realise you will be having dinner with us all this time tomorrow?'

'Lovely thought' and Sarah laughed as she told him she was having pizza. 'Incidentally, Alan wants us to have lunch with him on Saturday he has some lovely photos of the carvings in the dining room to show us. I think he knows more about them than he is telling, he is being very secretive.'

'That's fine! I would like to get to know him better. We've been searching in the attic for a black folder he said Farmer Harris had, apparently he used it when he told his stories to the family and Alan is convinced it has a mass of information in it and will answer a lot of our questions. Did you see all that beautiful furniture up there?'

'I remember seeing a spinet that looked really old. I thought it might be Elizabethan.'

'You haven't seen it since it was dusted off, it's lovely with a beautifully painted lid and I think you might be right about the date. There are a lot more antique pieces up there that need to be examined thoroughly. The folder could be in a drawer or perhaps it has slipped down the back of something, anyway, this weekend we are all going up there to have a jolly good search.'

'I'll help. I didn't know about the folder, we must find it, it must be up there somewhere.'

'We've got the twins helping.'

'How much are you paying them?' laughed Sarah.

'Nothing at the moment, they seem to be really interested in the history of the place. Mollie asked Alan if one of his Pa's stories had a ghost in it - she's convinced there's one around - he said that one had been about a ghost, but a 'nice' ghost. I suppose you can have nice ghosts.'

'Why not? I feel the same as Mollie, there seems to be a 'presence' in the entrance hall at the farm, I feel quite a chill in the air when I walk through, but it doesn't frighten me. I can't wait to get back to Tolford and start investigating.'

'Tomorrow will soon be here, it will be lovely to see you again Sarah.'

'It'll be nice to see you too Tony, I'll be at the farm at about five o'clock. See you soon, good night.'

'Goodnight, sleep well.'

'That was good timing' thought Sarah as the timer went off. She decided to eat in front of the telly, poured herself a glass of wine, sat on the settee and started on the pizza. 'I wonder what the ghost ate? I'm going to have find out more, thank goodness I like history.'

20

The afternoon was blustery with more than a hint of rain in the air, but Sarah and Tony decided to have a short walk along the shore keeping to the road as the waves were crashing up to the wall, every so often spilling over splashing anyone or anything in their way.

'This is lovely' and Sarah flung her arms up and did a little twirl, 'it really does wash away worries and all those cobwebs that accumulate in the head.'

'Usually I come down here with Jason, he loves it - chasing the waves, catching stones and digging up goodness knows what rubbish, it was an old sandwich the other day that he thought was real treasure and was miffed when I took it away from him.'

'Talking of treasure, Alan was interesting at lunchtime and weren't those photographs of the fireplace wonderful. You were partly right when you said they were angels, but they are angels with a difference, the two main ones, that's the one in the corner on the left and the one on the corner on the right have different faces. Is this another slant on Aunt Grace's hidden photograph theme that started all this? Perhaps we have a love story here too, but not another unrequited one I hope.'

'We made good progress with cleaning up the cottage fireplace this morning and I think that if we work away at it this weekend Alan could photograph it when he comes up next week. He's coming up every day with Jonnie so that he can look at the records and the artefacts and who knows we might get him up in the attic to look at the furniture.'

'Do be careful Tony, you might get him up there and not be able to get him down, he's no spring chicken.'

'We'll manage don't worry, we are going to treat him like one of us and forget his age, we're doing the same with the twins and they love it.'

The heavens suddenly opened and Sarah and Tony dashed back to Shore Cottage, fortunately they had come the long way round in Tony's van so getting back to Bridge Farm was not going to be a problem.

The side of the van had Tony's logo on it, a neat moulded roundel with 'Tony Briggs - Restoration – ornamental plasterwork a speciality' painted round it.

'Tell me about your work Tony, you obviously love doing it, but what exactly do you do? We've known each other for several weeks now, but don't seem to have got round to talking about you.'

'We have been rather taken up with Aunt Grace and the cottages, one day I will tell you all about my work but it would take too long to tell you today, suffice to say that I go into old properties and assess what there is to be done, sometimes it is renewing old plasterwork and my team are expert at this type of work, in fact we have won awards for some of the restoration work we have done. More often it is a major reconstruction job which entails a lot of research, for example we are currently working on an old theatre so have had to delve into the archives to make sure we will do the restoration correctly. Is that enough for you to be going on with?'

'It sounds fascinating. I'd love to see the theatre.'

'I'd like you to see it. What about your new venture, everything going through smoothly still?'

'It certainly is.' Sarah told him all the details of her visit to the solicitor. 'Probate should be granted by June, that's just over six months away so I have decided to hand my notice in on Monday. Ken will think I'm premature but I need a change anyway and at the moment I do have Aunt Grace's house to live in and some money to pay the bills so it seems the right time to do it. I'll be able to think everything through without the distraction of the library and there will be time to do some research about lavender and what you can do with it. Will I enjoy making lavender products? How much of my stuff should I chuck out and should I keep Aunt Grace's furniture? Next time you are in Southampton perhaps you will give me your judgment, it might not be at all suitable for a cottage.'

'If you really like the furniture you should keep it, but I know what you mean, that cottage is rather special to you isn't it?'

'Yes it is. Do you believe in 'déjà vu'? I just feel that I know that cottage and the people that lived in it, do you think I'm being melodramatic?'

'Not at all darling.'

'What did you say?' Sarah looked up at Tony, 'did you say 'darling'?'

'I'm afraid I did.' Fortunately they had arrived at Bridge Farm, Tony stopped the engine, put his arms round Sarah and hugged her really close.

'You don't mind do you?'

'Mind? Of course I don't.' Sarah put her face up and kissed Tony as she had never kissed anyone before.

'You know I have this feeling of 'déjà vu' again, it really is uncanny.'

'You reckon we've met in an earlier life?'

'Something like that, it really is creepy.'

'Well, before we get too carried away let's join the others in the attic and see if the folder has been discovered yet, Seth said they would all be up there this afternoon.'

'I must go and change into my jeans first, I don't want to get these trousers dusty.' Sarah dashed off to her room still thinking about the kiss and the strange feelings she had. She decided that she needed to know about the carvings on the fireplaces, she felt sure that the story behind them would help her to understand her emotions.

Ken was coming down the ladder and seemed very excited.

'Hi Sarah. Guess what, the twins found the folder, it had fallen off a chest of drawers and slipped behind it getting wedged in the floor boards, we've had to move some of the furniture because pages had fallen out and we need them all. I'm just off to see if Alan will come up and have a look and put them in some sort of order, we can't wait until Monday. Joanna says he can stay for dinner, that'll be the clincher.' He laughed and gave Sarah a big hug and a kiss and disappeared down the hallway.

'I hear the folder has been found' she shouted as she went up the ladder.

'That's right,' and Seth pointed to the table where there was a nondescript, rather tatty black file lying open with most of the papers in small piles beside it.

'This is it?' Sarah pulled a face, it all looked rather

112

disappointing, but as she looked closely at the papers she saw that they were all written in beautiful copperplate handwriting. 'Just look at this writing, isn't it beautiful? Are they the stories that Alan was telling us about?'

'We think so, that's why Ken has gone for him, everything is in such a muddle, the folder had sprung open and the papers were scattered and not numbered, he'll probably be able to put them straight for us reasonably quickly, and I think, will enjoy doing it.'

'Look Tony, here's a drawing of the carvings, but it's mixed up with facts about the Monks, I wouldn't have thought there would be a connection would you? Oh why didn't Farmer Harris number his pages? I suppose he didn't think anyone would want to read his stories. This drawing is interesting though, it shows quite clearly that the faces in the corners are different but have been made to look as if they are the same. In other words, the same hair, the same background and the same expression, but look, the eyes, nose and mouth are different.'

'Perhaps we are closer to the truth than we thought Sarah, I know you won't be happy until you've read the story, if there is one. Come and have a quick look at this furniture. You'll have to get all this valued Seth, it probably needs to be insured, I can give you the address of a chap I work with occasionally, he has a good reputation and would be very interested in all this.'

'I hadn't thought of insurance before, but I'm sure you're right, could you contact him for me?'

'First thing Monday morning. Have you had a good look at the spinet Sarah?'

'I love it, the lid is beautiful.'

'Have you looked inside it seems to be dated 1632, I wonder which of the families that ties in with?'

'The one in the carvings of course' and Sarah laughed up at him as he stood under the rafters looking round at everything. 'You just love this don't you Tony? You want to look more closely at the rafters and the floor.'

'You're not wrong, but that can be done later, at the moment as the folder has been found, we can go back to the cottage and hopefully have the fireplace cleaned off by dinner time.' Sarah left the spinet and turned towards the table, as she did so her jeans caught on one of the chest of drawers and pulled a drawer slightly open. She went to close it and to her amazement saw some rather ancient pieces of lavender and a small note book at the bottom of the drawer.

'Look everyone, some more treasure trove but we must get a tray to put it on in case it starts to disintegrate. Mollie, go and see if Joanna has a small one we could use please.'

'What else are we going to find? We only came to look for a black file, don't tell me we're going to end up with all sorts of information, I can see us being busy every evening during the Winter.'

'I bet there's a secret drawer somewhere Uncle Seth, shall I have a look?'

'What with Mollie and her ghost and you and your secret drawer James I reckon you've been watching too much tele.'

'A chap on the Antiques Roadshow said that it is quite usual to find a secret drawer in an old desk or chest of drawers and that some papers, or love letters even, could remain hidden for years, only to be found when some one was inquisitive enough to poke around. I reckon I'm inquisitive enough, and honestly Uncle Seth I will be careful, I think this furniture is marvellous.'

'Well! OK then, but no forcing things and if you have a problem ask for help.'

'I'll start over at the other side of the attic, so that I won't get in your way.'

'Here's your tray Sarah, Joanna has lined it with some kitchen roll, she thought it would help catch any bits and pieces.'

'Thanks Mollie. That was thoughtful of her, is there a spare piece that we could slip under the notebook to lift it?'

'There's a sheet of file paper over here' said Tony, 'it's stiffer so would be better, if you can wait a minute I'll come and help you.'

'It seems to be a very pretty book.' Mollie shone the torch into the drawer. 'Look Sarah, there's embroidery on the cover.'

'You're right. What fun, at one time young ladies were encouraged to cover little books, such as address books, with their own designs that they had embroidered.'

'How boring' said Mollie.

'Well, not if there was nothing else to do, and I don't think people found it boring because it was the norm. Look closely Mollie, that embroidery is very fine, I think it is a spray of lavender done on grey silk, that must have taken ages to do. We must be really careful we don't want to damage that beautiful work. Are you coming Tony, we can't wait much longer?'

'On my way.' Tony grabbed the sheet of paper and looked into the drawer.

'How pretty. We must be careful, silk usually ages well, but the inside might be brittle. Can you gently lift a corner and I'll slip the paper under it.'

Mollie watched, she was really wanting to help, but knew she had to leave it to Sarah and Tony, she found she was holding her breathe with excitement and then gave a cheer as Tony manipulated the book on to the tray.

'Shall we let Mollie carry the tray down stairs?'

'Why not' and Sarah laughed at Tony as they saw Mollie's face.

'You'll trust me? I'm dying to tell Mum about this - lavender, she'll go mad.'

'Of course we'll trust you, but I'll be behind you and Sarah will be in front so you can concentrate on keeping the tray steady. Get your balance and you'll be alright going down the ladder, Sarah will guide your feet, I'll keep my eye on the tray.'

A few minutes later Mollie ran into the kitchen, Babs was helping Joanna prepare dinner.

'Come and see what we've found, it's beautiful.' She grabbed her mother and beckoned to Joanna. 'Come on it will only take a minute, I helped to rescue it.'

They dashed up to the spare room that Joanna had given them for the finds and found Sarah and Tony drooling over the little notebook.

'You won't believe this Mum it's a little book all about the use of herbs including lavender, so lavender must have been grown here at one time. More research.'

'What a lovely book!' Babs put her hand out only to draw away, 'I don't like to touch it in case I damage it.'

'If everyone agrees, I'll take it into the archive department at the Library and get it photocopied.'

'Good idea Sarah, won't they mind?'

'No. we'll have to pay for it, but it won't break the bank.'

'There's Ken and Alan, I'll tell them to come up, let's hope Alan can help with the black folder I'm dying to know what the stories are. You've got about an hour before dinner.' Joanna disappeared calling out to Ken and Alan and in a few minutes they arrived in the spare room.

'Have a look at this first Alan' and Sarah pulled him towards the little book.

'That is beautiful.' Sarah told him where she had found it, and Alan gave one of his grunts.

'Have you seen it before?' said Sarah excitedly.

'Yes, I have but I can't remember where or when, more important to me at this moment is the black folder it's a little shabbier than I remember, but that is Pa's alright. I see what you mean about everything being in a mess, but I'm sure with a bit of thought it can all be put in order.' Alan sat down at the table and started sorting out the papers.

'Do you need any help Alan, or will it be easier on your own?'

'Easier on my own dear girl, just call me when dinner's ready.'

'We'll do that, Tony and I are going over to the cottage to finish cleaning off the fireplace, Seth is needed in the farm, what about you twins?'

'Could we stay Alan, we won't get in the way' pleaded Mollie, 'you might need someone to move things around for you.'

'Now there's a good idea, but you've got to be quiet.'

'I'll go back to the attic' said Ken, 'do you want to come with me James, you could go on looking for the secret drawer and we can leave Mollie to help Alan.'

'What secret drawer?' asked Alan, looking up from the pile of papers.

'Just one in James's imagination, but we're letting him look, you never know.'

'No you don't' said Alan and bent over the papers again quickly becoming absorbed in his work. Everyone, apart from Mollie, left the room laughing at the way Alan pitched in.

'Why has he kept himself to himself for so long' said Seth, 'we would have loved him to visit, and Jason loves Troy.' The dogs could be heard woofing away in the courtyard, obviously having a lovely time.

DEJA VU

21

'I think this is the first of Pa's stories Mollie, would you like to read it?'

'Yes, I would, isn't his writing lovely?'

'They don't teach children to write like that any more, in fact' said Alan with a sigh, 'they didn't teach us to write like that. Here's the story Mollie, I've put in the page numbers so you shouldn't have a problem. In fact we must get some new files and put the stories in them, but that can be done later.'

'It's half-term next week so I'll get them for you first thing Monday morning Alan, I'll get ten to start with. Have you found the one about the carvings yet?'

'No, in fact I'm beginning to wonder if there was one. Get on with reading that one and I'll go on sorting out.'

Molly picked up the papers and started reading.

Where now? - 1539

The watery sun was breaking through the morning mist and the smoke that hung over the valley, eerily no birds were singing. The smell of burning got stronger as the villagers made their way up the road by the river towards the bridge, they were eager to see exactly how much devastation the King's men had created this Spring morning. Notices had been nailed up in the village telling them that the King had decreed the Monastery of Ponte Verdi would be closed and that the land had been purchased by 'a good Protestant' Sir Francis Courtney. He was to pull the Monastery down and build a small manor house and a farm.

The villagers muttered amongst themselves, they were sorry to see the monks go, they had been good men and had given the village support and help when needed. Brother Erasmus had always been willing to attend the sick and the dying using his herbs to heal and comfort. The monks had also been an important factor in the economy of the village, they were not required to be self sufficient so paid work was available for local craftsmen. They had provided income for the farmers by buying their meat and wheat. The Brothers had grown their own vegetables, herbs and fruit in the walled Monastery garden, there had often been a surplus and this had been given to the villagers. They were going to be missed.

'He's been doing it everywhere' said Paul Butler, 'why he can't leave the poor monks alone beats me.'

'He wants the money, fighting France, falling out with the Pope and living the life he leads must cost a pretty penny' reasoned Martin Fletcher, 'I suppose the sale of this land has gone into his coffers, I wouldn't have thought it would have been a lot, but you never know and I suppose every little counts.'

They reached the bridge and looked across to their right, smoke was rising from behind the cloisters.

'I suppose they've burnt all the books and Bibles' said Paul, 'after all the work that Brother Joseph put into them. I don't suppose they thought of them as valuable.'

'I've heard that all bibles, prayer books and vestments have been destroyed in other monasteries. *It just seems crazy, they were such good people.' Richard Greene wiped his eyes, 'I for one am really sorry to see this happen, they gave me regular work repairing windows and doors and making furniture, and what about our farmers? Who will they sell their meat and wheat to now? Perhaps the new Lord of the Manor will take it.'*

They looked towards the monastery, which seemed as if it had been empty for months instead of hours - the windows were smashed, the lovely colours of the old glass glinted as it lay shattered in the grass. The roof had been torn apart presumably for the lead which would fetch a good price. The main door had gone, was it part of the bonfire? The lawn leading up to the monastery had been the brothers' pride and joy but was now a mess, a quagmire of hoof marks and cart tracks. At the rear the cloisters were in ruins, statues lay smashed on the tiled floor which in places had been ripped up and the tiles thrown on to the cloister garden, breaking shrubs and pitting the narrow grass walks between the beds with shards of pottery.

'*May he rot in Hell.' said Paul as they stumbled over the rubble. The rest muttered in agreement. 'What will happen next? Do any of you know anything about this Francis Courtney, or rather Sir Francis Courtney?'*

'*Never heard of him meself' said Martin 'but I expect we soon will, if he's one of King Henry's men I bet it won't be long before he pays us a visit. Tom Piper you'd be well advised to clean up your inn, he'll be wanting somewhere to stay. Charge him well, at least one of us can benefit from the change.'*

'*Clean up my inn, Martin Fletcher If my inn is clean enough for travellers and pilgrims it's clean enough for the gentry.' said Tom Piper. 'I know what you mean though and it wouldn't hurt to have some rooms ready. I wonder if the bastards left Brother Erasmus's garden in tact, some lavender between the sheets and some rosemary on the floor wouldn't come amiss. I'll go and have a look.'*

Tom sighed as he walked beyond the cloisters and refectory, the buildings had been very attractive and well cared for. The Brothers had been very proud of it and the villagers equally so, accepting the monastery as part of their community. He wondered where they had gone and what the future held for them and for the villagers. Sir Francis was not known to them he could turn out to be a tyrant or a caring Lord of the Manor, or fall somewhere in between not caring about anyone or anything.

'Only time will tell' he muttered to himself as he walked past the bonfire towards the kitchen gardens.

The sun was higher in the sky and the threat of rain had passed, pink clouds skimmed across the sky driven by a mild breeze that gently moved the rosemary and other herbs growing undisturbed in the kitchen garden, snowdrops and primroses flowered brightening up an otherwise sombre scene, but where was the lavender? He looked over the wall and saw that the next field had been well tended and plants were growing away, there were hundreds of them all different shapes and sizes. He went to have a look and to his astonishment discovered it was a field of herbs. He easily recognised rosemary, lavender and fennel, but there were many others that he could not identify.

'What's going on here?' Tom muttered to himself. There were several rows of mature lavender plants so Tom took a few pieces and added a few sprigs of rosemary. He went back to the garden and was delighted to see it look so well, the fruit trees growing up against the walls would soon be in flower, but with no one to look after them he wondered what would happen to them.

'Perhaps the new Lord of the Manor will employ a gardener, that is if he is interested in keeping this good garden going, all that fruit will be welcome in the winter months.'

Clutching the lavender and rosemary he went back to the others.

'The kitchen garden hasn't been touched, perhaps we ought to look after it until Sir Francis comes, I don't mind lending a hand, a few vegetables in payment would be fine.'

'Good idea Tom, we'll do that, then see what Sir Francis wants to do.'

'Did you know Brother Erasmus had planted up a whole field of herbs? It is looking very prosperous, I wonder what he intended doing with it?'

'I've never heard of such a thing' said Martin.

'Brother Erasmus used herbs in healing, perhaps they were growing a lot to sell to other apothecaries. I've also heard that you get a lovely oil from lavender, I expect that's what he had in mind, perhaps making lavender scented soap and perfumes to sell to the landed gentry, and the other herbs could be sold too, everyone uses them in cooking. It would have helped the funds of the Monastery.' Paul looked at the others, 'it could have been a good business for them.'

'What an idea. We'll have to talk to Sir Francis about it when he arrives, he might be interested. I don't know about the rest of you' said Martin, 'but I could down a pint of Tom's best .' The rest agreed and they made their way to the inn.

Mollie gave a big sigh and put the papers back on the table.

'What a sad story Alan, I've heard about the Dissolution of the Monasteries at school but didn't think about the implications for the people living nearby, your Pa must have done a lot of reading.'

'He was always interested in history, so I suppose he did. Did you enjoy the story Mollie?'

'I certainly did. I must go and get a copy of Farmer Harris's *History of Bridge Farm* so that I can get my head round the dates.'

'Do that now Mollie, then come back quickly, I think I've found the story Sarah wants, at least there are more pictures and it looks as though Pa is talking about angels. I'll get everything in order, then we can read it together. Don't say anything to Sarah if you see her, we'll make sure before getting her excited.'

'I just love secrets Alan' and Mollie ran off to get a copy of the *History* from the farm office.

'Everything alright Mollie?' called out Babs.

'Everything's fine, I just want to get a photocopy of Farmer Harris' *History* I've got to get the dates straight in my mind, I can't remember when the Tudors ended and the Stuarts began, let alone any other dates.'

'It sounds as though you are learning something from this exercise' laughed Babs.

'I certainly am, and one of the things is patience. When will dinner be ready?'

'You've got about twenty minutes Mollie, I'll call you.'

'Incidentally Mum, it looks as though the monks that were here in the 1500's planted up a field of herbs that included lavender.'

'You're joking?'

'Well that's in the story that Pa Harris wrote, so we ought to research it further, Alan reckons that most of the stories were based on fact. I expect there is something about it in the papers we are going through. I must dash, Alan has got something exciting to tell me.' Mollie dashed off laughing at the expression on her mother's face.

'You know Alan, I think Mum thought a lavender farm

here was an original idea, I've just told her about the monks in your Pa's story and her face was a study. It looks to me as though we have to sort out herbs, lavender, ghosts and carvings, what a mix, but there must be a connection somewhere.'

'I think we're getting there Mollie, can you give me the dates for someone called Elizabeth Courtney she must have lived sometime around 1650 when the cottages were built.'

'Here we are. It looks as though she inherited the Manor in 1635 when she was thirty nine. This is interesting, Pa Harris reckons she had an affair with a local builder when she was twenty five and had an illegitimate son Bevis, there's a note beside the entry 'see letters'. Uncle Seth was talking about some letters that he wanted to read, it must the ones. This is getting very exciting Alan.'

'It's you that's getting excited Mollie, however the dates do tie up and we do have some letters but let's look at this story first before drawing any conclusions. Do you see what it's called?'

''Angel carvings', Tony was right then when he said the carvings looked like angels, let's see what your Pa made of it all.'

'There are some drawings here of angels perhaps they're the designs for the fireplace, and some lovely swags of fruit and flowers, including, would you believe it Mollie, lavender.'

'They're lovely drawings' said Mollie 'let's read the story and see where they fit in.'

Angel carvings – 1623

Walter Tanner gave the final touch to the carvings on the fireplace and laughed to himself wondering what Elizabeth Courtney would say when she saw them. In the top corners he had carved angels looking towards each other, however they were not identical, and daringly Walter had tried to capture a likeness to Elizabeth in the left hand one and a likeness to himself in the other. Walter and Elizabeth had been having an affair for a couple of years unbeknown to her father who would not have approved of Walter, a builder, as a suitable partner for his beloved Elizabeth, Sir William Courtney wanted to arrange a marriage between his daughter and the local silversmith John Hampton, a wealthy man with some standing in the community. Elizabeth was holding out against it, John was much older, was not a handsome man and, worst of all in Elizabeth's opinion, he had bad breath.

'Walter don't go I want to talk to you' Elizabeth called out from the hallway. She ran into the sitting room and flung her arms round Walter. 'Such news, you won't believe it.'

'I've got to know what it is first, but don't you think you should be careful, your father could come in.'

'That's the news, he has gone to London for a few days and left Mrs Howard in charge, so we will be able to see more of each other.'

'That's wonderful, you can come down to the cottage on the pretext that you want to check on what I've done, in fact I want you to do that because I have something to show you, in fact I've something to show you here.' Walter turned Elizabeth round so that she faced the fireplace.

'Notice anything my darling? Something strange perhaps?'

'Something strange? Well you've carved angels in the corners, lovely swags of fruit and flowers going down the sides and in the middle of the fireplace there is something I'm not sure about.'

'It's a lover's knot, tying two people together, like you and me, now look closely at the angels.'

'Oh! Walter, how clever, the left hand one is me and the right hand one is you, the noses and hair are different, but no one would realize that without examining the fireplace very closely. That is lovely, I can sit here in the evening and look at you, I can even give the carving a kiss when no one's looking. You really are a clever man.' Elizabeth turned and gave him a hug.

'I'm glad you like it, have you time to come to the cottage I want to show you something there.'

'Let me tell Mrs Howard where I'm going and I'll be with you.' Elizabeth ran off down the hall calling out to Mrs Howard on her way, Walter laughed at her exuberance and hoped that it would be with her for ever and said a little prayer. 'May the Angels always be with her, she is so wonderful.'

'Come on Walter, let's go, I'm dying to see what it is you have to show me.' They walked up to the cottages, past the farm and the outbuildings, the farm dogs marked their progress with incessant barking, the hens clucked round their feet asking for corn and the geese waddled up honking loudly.

'Go away you noisy creatures' and Walter picked up a stick and pushed the geese away. 'You know I'm having one of the cottages don't you Elizabeth?'

'Father mentioned it the other day, he says he is asking you to be responsible for all the building and repair work on the Manor and the farm, and therefore, you should live on the site.'

'Well I've chosen my cottage and I want you to see it.'

'Why? I know what the cottages look like, I helped to plan them.'

'You didn't plan everything my dear, come and see.' Walter took her arm and they walked up the gravel path to the door of the second cottage. As the door opened Elizabeth could see that

Walter had already taken up residence, the floor was shiningly clean, the windows sparkled, a table and settle were in front of the fireplace where logs were smouldering away and a faint smell of lavender permeated the room, Elizabeth noticed that there were some bundles of lavender hanging by the fireplace and wondered where they had come from. Everything gave the impression that someone had been living there for sometime.

'Walter, this is lovely, you have worked hard, but what is it you especially want me to see?'

'Look at the fireplace, what do you see?'

'What do I see? Two angels similar to those on the fireplace in the Manor, what fun! What happens if my father notices?'

'I have made subtle differences, so hope he won't, I can't imagine him coming here and sitting down for any length of time. So you see I'll be able to think of you all the time too.'

'Walter' Elizabeth flung her arms round him and he pulled her towards the settle.

'I wonder if father would consider us getting married?' murmured Elizabeth sometime later as she lay in his arms revelling in the feelings that were going through her.

'Not likely at all, we will just have to see each other when we can' and Walter put his arms round her. 'Let's make the most of this afternoon, I don't have any work that needs doing today.'

'Wonderful' and Elizabeth snuggled up to him. 'It would be lovely if we could live in this cottage forever and bring up a large family, how many do you think Walter?'

'Six to start with my darling, but we must be careful, children born out of wedlock can have a stigma attached to them.'

'We'll be alright, don't let's worry about something that will never happen.' That, however, is where Elizabeth was wrong, she soon discovered that she was pregnant and knowing that her Father would be furious she went to him and said that she was prepared to marry John Hampton.

The wedding was arranged quickly, Sir William did not want his wayward daughter changing her mind again. Elizabeth was glad of it and went along with all the arrangements. It was decided that the happily married couple would live in the Manor, there was plenty of room and Sir William felt that his daughter would look after him better than any housekeeper. To show his pleasure he purchased a spinet for Elizabeth as a wedding present, she had always been interested in music and had often said how she would love one. It turned out to be her salvation, and later when things became difficult she would go into the sitting room and play her music, sitting there with her eyes half closed looking at the carvings on the fireplace letting the problems wash over her, afterwards she felt able to cope with her life.

Elizabeth, of course, neglected to tell John Hampton that she was pregnant and it was quite a surprise to him when after a couple of months Elizabeth told him that he would be a father. He was delighted and bragged about his manhood to his friends in the local hostelry.

Bevis was born 'prematurely' in 1624, but Walter was not fooled he knew it was his, Elizabeth, however, would not see him, in fact went out of her way to avoid him and did not let the baby out of her sight so he didn't get to see Bevis until he was about four and running round the estate causing all sorts of mayhem.

Elizabeth was desperately unhappy, Bevis was a very difficult child to bring up and in his teens seemed to be even more difficult, causing problems with the workers on the farm and the local girls. John Hampton did not help her with him and as the years went by she realized he was not a pleasant man, he almost ignored her, and he treated the workers on the estate like dirt. Elizabeth smiled grimly to herself, it was almost as if Bevis had inherited his traits. It was obvious to her that John had a couple of mistresses, one in the village and one in London, so when she inherited the

Manor in 1635 at the age of thirty nine she decided they would have separate apartments. John was only too happy to agree. It was at this time that she started writing to Walter telling him that he was her one and only love. Walter wrote back and soon they began to see each other again and write regularly, but they knew they could never be together as man and wife.

Elizabeth started to sleepwalk, she would make her way to the hallway then to the sitting room where she would sit at the spinet and play a few notes then go to the fireplace and stroke the angels. Mrs Howard had been retained as Housekeeper and was aware of all that was going on and was most concerned about Elizabeth, fearing for her mental state. She occupied the room next to Elizabeth and, being a light sleeper, always woke when Elizabeth started to sleepwalk. She would follow her to the sitting room, wait until she had played the spinet, and stroked the angels, then would carefully guide Elizabeth back to her room and settle her knowing that having walked once during the night she would go into a deep sleep, waking very refreshed in the morning with no knowledge of the walk.

John Hampton became seriously ill and died in August 1650. Elizabeth felt that she could breathe again and shocked the local people and estate workers by only wearing the widow's weeds for a month, after which she went to London and bought some very colourful clothes as if determined to make a new life for herself. Walter waited patiently, hoping that she would marry him. Letters were still being written and it was obvious that Elizabeth really did care, however before they could marry Walter was killed in a terrible accident on one of his sites. Elizabeth was distraught, but with Mrs Howard's help she carried on with her life at the Manor, trying to involve Bevis in the day-to-day running of the estate. Bevis did not really want to know, all he was interested in was the fact when his mother died he would inherit a prosperous estate and a goodly sum of money. Elizabeth died in 1688 aged ninety two years and Bevis inherited.

'Dinner's ready' Joanna shouted from the kitchen.

'Another sad story Alan, shall we tell Sarah about it over dinner, or let her read the story that Pa Harris wrote?'

'Let her read the story my dear, you know I think she is going to feel that she has been here before, after all she and Tony might be thinking of living in the cottage and Tony could be called a builder as was Walter, and she says that she can feel 'a presence' in the hall, which ties in with Pa's story of Elizabeth sleepwalking.'

'There's the spinet too Alan, the one in the attic must have belonged to Elizabeth, the dates all fit in nicely.'

'I hadn't forgotten Mollie, but we must get it authenticated by the experts before jumping to conclusions.'

'Dinner you two, hurry up or it will all be gone.'

22

After dinner they all went up to the 'operations' room as they now called the spare room. Alan handed Sarah the story of the carvings and Mollie watched as she read. Eventually Sarah put the papers down on the table.

'Well, what do you think Sarah?'

'What do I think? You know Mollie, I almost want to cry, it is as if Aunt Grace and Alan were following along as 'unhappy lovers' in the wake of Elizabeth and Walter. Instead of carvings there were photographs. As for the 'ghost' or 'presence' that we have felt in the hall, that must be Elizabeth, and surely we can establish that the spinet belonged to her. She must have been very unhappy to sleepwalk I do hope that the mould gets broken, I don't think the Manor could take another unhappy affair.'

'Sarah don't you see all it needs is for a happy couple to settle in the cottage to break the spell, if that is what it is, and then the 'ghost' will stop walking too, and if it is Elizabeth she will be able to rest in peace.' Mollie looked up at Sarah and said very solemnly, 'perhaps that is why you and Tony are here, that's what Alan said anyway.'

'Mollie you are incorrigible' said Alan rather gruffly, 'what's more Grace and I were very happy but we never did live in the cottage so I suppose that doesn't count.'

'Well, you didn't live happily ever after did you? I don't mean to upset you Alan,' and Mollie gave him a quick hug 'but you did say to me that Sarah felt she had been here before, and Tony is a builder as was Walter. You must see what I'm getting at.'

'Only too well my dear, and you are not upsetting me, it was all a long time ago, if Sarah and Tony can bring happiness and peace to Bridge Farm, I'm all for it.'

Sarah and Tony looked at each other and laughed. 'What a responsibility' said Sarah and, feeling slightly embarrassed decided to change the subject.

'Seth are you getting anywhere with those letters?'

'It's slow work Sarah there seem to be two sets, written at different times so that should be interesting. One lot of letters has lavender between them I think they were written by Agnes Lafolley, have you got a date for her Mollie?'

'There's an Agnes Morey, but wait a minute she married a Lafolley, so that must be her.'

'Yes Mollie, but give me some dates please.'

'Sorry Uncle Seth.' Molly turned over the pages of the history. 'Here we are, according to Pa Harris she lived from 1744 until 1815. It looks as though she inherited the Manor in 1788 when she was forty four. Perhaps she grew lavender too if she put it between her letters.'

'Lavender?' said Babs as she came into the room.

'Yes, lavender keeps cropping up Babs,' and Seth told her about the letters and the stories. 'We really have to examine the work carried on at the Manor, it seems that the lavender planted by Brother Erasmus was part of a herb farm, later developed into big business by Sir Francis Courtney, then, for some reason or other, it folded but it looks as though herbs, lavender in particular, were around in the mid 1700's. I'm sure the information will be somewhere in all those documents, although Pa mentioned lavender I can't remember it interesting him very much.'

'Perhaps he just was not very interested in it.'

'You could be right Mollie, and it is just waiting to be resurrected by us.' Babs gulped, 'I can hardly believe this, I was under the impression that it was only the Romans that planted lavender here, but obviously I was wrong. As you say Seth we must look into the history of the Manor more closely, if we are planting on the site of an old herb garden or field we could use that background in our publicity material, and perhaps we should rethink the name 'Roman Lavender', we might come up with something that has a better ring to it. What do you think Sarah?'

'I think it's a good job I've handed my notice in' said Sarah. 'My little inner voice must have been telling me that there was a lot of research to do here. I'm particularly interested in that little grey book, I wonder who wrote it and what sort of information it contains, we should know next week when I've had it photocopied, I really do not want it touched until then, it is very fragile. Babs, could I take you up on your offer of a room, not immediately, in about three weeks time when I've finished at the library and moved into Aunt Grace's house. It looks as though I might be needed here to help with the research and the cottage is nowhere near finished.'

'Of course you can, we can work together then and try and get our plans sorted as well as the history of Bridge Farm. What about the weekends?'

'Just at the moment I've rather a lot to do in Southampton,

I must get everything cleared up there. Tony, as you're coming down next Saturday to look at my furniture perhaps you could bring the photocopies back. If it's alright with everyone I'll keep copies for myself so that I can study them and check things with the archive people. There must be some information about Hapstead Manor, perhaps I'll be able to find out when it became Bridge Farm.'

'Yes, of course you can keep a set of photocopies,' Seth looked round, 'is there anything else we should think about before Alan goes home?'

'You were going to ask Alan about the furniture' said Joanna. 'Did you say you helped Farmer Harris store it in the attic Alan?'

Before Alan could answer James shouted out from the attic.

'Dad bring everyone up to see what I've found.'

'Not more excitement' said Ken. 'Can you make it up the ladder Alan?'

'You're not leaving me behind. Give me a push Ken, I'll make it, I've wanted to go up all day.'

When everyone got into the attic they saw that James had laid out some plans on the table.

'Don't touch' said James 'the paper is very fragile.'

'I'm glad you've been listening to me, we don't want finger marks on them. This is another photocopying job' said Sarah, 'then we can all handle the copies and try and make sense of the plans. They look very interesting, what do you think they're of James?'

'A field, looking at the pictures I think it must be for herbs, but I can't see the date.'

Sarah and Seth bent over the plans and shone a torch on them, they were very faded, it looked as though a darkish brown ink had been used on dark cream paper. There were lots of rectangles all the same size, but within each rectangle was a number, they were definitely not buildings. There were some buildings on the left hand side albeit crudely drawn, and down the right hand side of the plans were sketches of what seemed to be herbs, including lavender. Sarah called to Babs to have a look. She studied them for a few minutes and could hardly believe what she saw.

'They're herbs alright, but look each sketch is numbered, are they the numbers that appear in the rectangles? If so these are plans of a very large herb garden, or even farm.'

'Don't get too excited Babs, there might be another explanation, let me get them all photocopied then you can have a really good look, and hopefully we can get the date, it is very faint. James is right they should not be handled too much. Some more photocopies for you to bring back Tony.' Sarah carefully rolled up the plans and wrapped a piece of clean paper round them. 'I must get the grey book now before I forget it.'

'I'll get it Sarah, I'll put it in an envelope' and James dashed off.

'That boy has really got interested in all this,' said Seth 'but he didn't say where he found the plans.'

'I think he said in an old desk. I remember putting one up here, goodness knows how old it was.' Alan frowned trying to remember!

'Here you are Sarah' said James giving her a small package that contained the grey book.

'Where did you find the plans James?'

'In this old desk Dad, they were rolled up and pushed right to the back of the top drawer.'

'Alan, do you think when you are here next week we

could come up here so that you can have a good look at the furniture, we think it is all very old and you might remember something Farmer Harris told you about it.'

'Of course, I'd like to have a good look at it, though I don't promise that I shall remember anything. Can you help me down the ladder, it is time I was getting home.'

A few minutes later they were all at the bottom of the ladder Alan laughing at the fact that at his age he was able to get up and down there without too much help.

'We've cleaned the fireplace in the cottage Alan' said Tony, 'when do you want to take the photographs?'

'Tomorrow morning would be fine old boy, the light should be just right, it will only take a few minutes.'

'Jonnie will be picking you up so see you at nine thirty then.'

'You haven't shown us the other photos yet Alan, why is that?' asked Sarah.

'You'll see when I've developed the photos from the cottage, it should bear out what Pa said about the carvings, but I just want to make sure.'

'Phone me and let me know what you find please, because I can't come back for a few weeks.'

'Of course dear girl, I might send some copies down with Tony, I daresay you'll see him most weekends.'

'That would be lovely, please do that and look after yourself while I'm gone.'

23

Back in Southampton Sarah was glad she had put on her new coat, the north-easterly wind was howling round the library building and though she had her collar pulled up it seemed to be finding its way inside her clothes. She unlocked the staff door to the library and was greeted with the usual smell from the toilets just inside. They were blessed with a cleaning lady who liberally used lavatory cleaners, so the whole corridor up to the reference library had the same pungent smell.

'Something I won't miss' thought Sarah. She went through to her office and was pleased to find it reasonably warm for a Monday morning. There was a pile of papers needing attention on her desk, but she decided that first she must see Tim, the Chief Librarian, and hand in her notice.

'This is something of a shock Sarah' said Tim, 'but I suppose we couldn't keep you forever, you know you are in direct line for promotion don't you?'

When Sarah explained her reasons for leaving he could hardly believe it.

'Sarah you are a born librarian, do you really know what you are doing?'

'Not really, but that doesn't matter, I feel I need a change and as I now have some money to invest this lavender farm project seems exactly right.'

'Well, if that's how you feel of course I'll accept your resignation and wish you all the best with your new venture.'

'Thanks Tim, I will keep in touch because there is a lot of research that needs to be done in connection with the history of the farm. It seems that it was built as a Manor house in the mid fifteen hundreds, and we would like to find out as much as we can about it, so you will see me around as I'll be using the Archive Department quite a lot.'

'That sounds interesting, you know we'll help as much as we can. I'll get an advert in for your post this week, I don't want to be too long without a senior member of staff, and do keep me posted how everything is going.'

'At the moment two things are definitely happening, first of all I'm moving into my Great Aunt's house this weekend, that's why I've asked for Friday off. Secondly, in the New Year I'm going to the lavender farm on Jersey to learn about lavender products and how to make them.'

'We will all expect free samples when you get going Sarah, you do realise that don't you?'

'All I can say is, I will expect all of you to be my first buyers when I invite you to the official opening of the shop.' Tim laughed, and said he would look forward to receiving the invitation.

Sarah closed the door quietly behind her and wiped a tear from her eye, she was pleased to be embarking on a new phase of her life but at the same time slightly sad at leaving the old life behind. She had a feeling that Tim was not convinced that she would be able to change her direction career-wise, and her immediate thought was 'I'll show him'.

Her next stop was the Archive Department. She gave Mary, the archivist, a brief resume of what she had been up to, starting with the photograph.

'I did wonder why you were disappearing into the country so often, what fun to be involved with working out the story behind all the enigmas you have come across.'

'It is fun, and all the people I've come into contact with are wonderfully friendly and have made me very welcome and not because I've got some money to invest, that came along later.'

'I almost envy you' said Mary, 'but let me see what photocopies you need.'

'There's this little grey book for a start, then some plans and some drawings.'

Mary took one look at the little grey book. 'Sarah, this is beautiful, let me get some gloves.'

'As it is so fragile we haven't touched it, but I can assure you we wanted to.'

'I'm glad you didn't, this really does need to be handled with gloves.' As Mary turned the pages Sarah could see that each page was immaculately written in very small handwriting and every so often there was a little sketch and between some of the pages were dried lavender seed heads.

'We'll need to get rid of the lavender before we photocopy' said Mary, 'would you like us to record between which pages the lavender was found?'

'That would be interesting, something I hadn't thought about.'

'It's all part of our job Sarah, every detail has significance. What are you going to do with the book, it is a museum piece.'

'We haven't even thought that far, but we will be very

careful with it. Seth, the farmer who owns Bridge Farm is very interested in local history, so I should imagine it will end up in the local museum. Could you do three 'blow ups' please Mary and these are the plans, they might not look very interesting to you, but I can assure you to everyone at Bridge Farm they are. Can I have three copies of those as well please. Now, these drawings are rather special, I think they were done in the 1630's and are of particular interest in establishing part of the history at Bridge Farm, or Hapstead Manor as it was known in those days and I think they relate to carvings on the fireplaces in the Manor and the cottage I'm hoping to rent. Can I again have three copies of each drawing plus a 'blow-up' of the two I've marked.'

'Fine leave them with me, I'll get them done as soon as possible. Did you say 'Hapstead Manor' Sarah, because I've just had quite a lot of papers sent to me and Hapstead Manor is mentioned in them. I put them on one side because it doesn't come within our County, so you could have a look at them before I send them off to West Sussex.'

'Brilliant. I can't believe that all this is happening, we would certainly be interested in anything to do with the Manor. Our research at Bridge Farm has only just started, and Seth said the other day that as we were uncovering so much information it looked as though we would all be busy during the Winter evenings getting everything sorted.'

'It looks as though he was right.' Mary gave Sarah a hug, 'I'm going to miss you, but all the best with your new project.'

'You'll probably get fed up with me coming in to do some research and I'm sure there will be more photocopying to be done.'

Sarah returned to her office, dealt with the paper work then went to relieve Susan at the library counter.

She was greeted with 'I hear you're leaving us.'

'News travels fast' laughed Sarah, 'I suppose Tim has told you.'

'Yes, in case any of us think of applying for your job. We are going to miss you Sarah, but what are you going to do?'

'I'm investing in a lavender farm and, hopefully, I'll be involved with using the lavender to produce oil, soap, creams and anything else that lavender can be used for. I'm going off to Jersey in the New Year to learn about it.'

'That will be a change from working here, are you sure about this?'

'As sure as I'll ever be, now go and get your coffee and don't worry about me, I've thought it through very carefully.'

Sarah was very busy for the next quarter of an hour, it was Pension Day when many pensioners called in, saving the bus fare. She was keeping her eye on an elderly gentleman who was going through the newspapers, Susan had told her he had been in there for at least an hour. He seemed harmless enough and Sarah assumed he was there to keep warm. She began to wonder whether she would miss the contact with the public, but then realised that working on the lavender farm and having a lot to do with the shop she would still be in contact with people.

That evening she went back to her flat and started to sort out her belongings. She had a pile of throwables waiting to be bagged up, but had got to the stage of having to decide whether to throw certain things out or not, should she really keep the cushion that an aunt had given her many years ago? She decided not to keep it and that seemed to settle her decision making, anything that was not going to be useful in the cottage would have to go. When there was a large pile of things to discard Sarah stopped so that she could bag up the useful-to-somebody-else articles, then the grot in other bags. In the middle of this Tony rang.

'Well, did you hand in your notice?'

'I did, and very strange it felt, but I know I have done the right thing. I'm busy clearing things out at the moment, it really is amazing how much rubbish one accumulates. The removal people are coming on Friday to move me, are you still coming down this weekend? You know I'll be at Aunt Grace's house.'

'Would I miss out on a weekend with you? I know you will have moved but can I stay with you if I promise to take you out for dinner?'

'You can stay if you like but everything will probably be at sixes and sevens, at least there's a spare room and I have put the heating on so it should be warm. It really is a cold house.'

'I wasn't really thinking about the spare room and the heating keeping me warm, but if that's what you want it's OK by me. I did promise to look at your Aunt Grace's furniture.'

'The more I look at it the more I think that at least three pieces are right for the cottage, there is a rather nice chest of drawers, I believe the correct description is commode, and two chairs - carvers with rush seats. There is also a good table but it might be too big and a sideboard that would fit in a baronial hall.'

'Perhaps Joanna could use the sideboard in Bridge Farm. Let's think about it it on Saturday.'

24

Friday was a very strange day for Sarah, it started with a van from the Red Cross arriving to pick up anything they thought would be useful. She was surprised at the things they took, saucepans that seemed destined for the local dump and a chair that needed re-springing.

'We've got a chap that does that Miss Bruce, he makes them as good as new.'

'I wish I'd had his phone number' said Sarah, 'I liked that chair, I hope the next owner enjoys it as much.'

'Are all these bags to go?'

'Yes, the black ones contain items that I think will be useful, the white contain what I would call rags, but I believe you get money for those.'

'It's nice to have it sorted, you'd be surprised at the junk we have to go through to get the good items out. We have a dealer in rags, so none of this will be wasted. Here's your removal men, I'd better be going.'

With all the unwanted items out of the flat Sarah felt she could cope with the removal men. Everything went very smoothly, as most of the furniture was built-in there wasn't a lot of big stuff to be moved, and by four o'clock Sarah was sitting in the kitchen in her Aunt's house enjoying a cup of tea with everything fairly tidy. She had decided not to undo her boxes of books and had left her summer clothes in suitcases and had put them in the small bedroom, she felt she really would be moving into the cottage at Bridge Farm early in the year so it would be a waste of time unpacking.

'Tony will have a surprise, I think he is expecting me to be in a muddle.' Sarah found that little chuckle coming again, she had made Tony's bed up in the spare room, but she did wonder if it would be used. Her phone rang and Tony was at the other end.

'I'm on my way Sarah, I'll be with you at about six thirty. Have you had a good day?'

'A brilliant day thanks Tony, everything has gone like clockwork. I've booked a table in a pub just down the road for dinner, I've been told that the food is good. There is room for you to park in my driveway, I've put my car in the garage. Do you know how to find me?'

'Yes, I've just checked it out on a road map. See you soon darling.'

Sarah smiled as she put the phone down, 'darling' sounded so natural coming from Tony and she began to think strange thoughts. It was the photos and the carvings that kept surfacing. The story of Elizabeth was so sad but at the same time very romantic. Sarah was longing to look at the photocopies of the sketches and to see the photographs that Alan had taken, she was sure they would bear out the story that Pa Harris had told. As for the photographs of Grace and Alan, she already knew the real story behind them, and that too was romantic. Sarah couldn't get away from the feeling that there was a purpose behind her finding Bridge Farm, she felt that she had been there before and was beginning to wonder if she really had been Elizabeth in an earlier life and Tony had been Walter.

'That is absolutely impossible, pull yourself together Sarah, you are letting your imagination run away with you.' At the same time Sarah did have a strange feeling about it, she had felt that she had been in the cottage before, she felt that she had known Tony before, and the estuary had been in her dreams long before visiting Tolford. She began to think that Alan and Mollie might be right, all that was required to break the 'spell' was a happy couple to settle in the cottage, could that be her and Tony? Looking at her watch Sarah decided it was time to go and freshen up. After her shower she decided that she had been hallucinating earlier, and of course she had never been to Tolford before.

It had suddenly got dark and chilly, so Sarah put the lights on, pulled the curtains and lit the fire wanting it to be welcoming for Tony. She got out the photocopies that Mary had done and spread them out on the table, sorting out the ones for Seth and Babs and putting them on one side, she kept a copy of each for herself to look at during the coming week. The grey book looked fascinating but at the moment she was only interested in the pictures of the carvings. The 'blow-ups' of the sketches had come out well and Sarah could see how clever Walter had been in his designs it was literally just the faces that were different and someone looking at it quickly would not appreciate the significance. Hopefully somewhere in the archives there was a picture of Elizabeth but it was too much to hope that there was a picture of Walter. Would Alan's photographs show they had been faithfully copied?

The doorbell rang, then rang again.

'I'm coming' said Sarah 'give me a minute.'

She unlocked the front door. 'Come in Tony' but it wasn't Tony, it was someone from a mail order firm touting for business.

'I'm sorry, but I don't buy anything from the door.' With that Sarah shut the door and drew breath.

'Phew! If I feel like that when I think it is Tony, what am I going to feel like when it is him?' She gave a little giggle, 'Joanna would have something to say about this.' Again the doorbell rang, this time the visitor did not take their finger off the bell. Sarah dashed to the front door a little wary of assuming it was Tony. She had no need to worry, it was him with a large bunch of petrol station flowers.

'They're lovely Tony, thankyou.'

'What about a kiss then?' Sarah was only too happy to oblige.

'Come on in Tony, I've lit the fire, these November evenings are really cold. We have a few moments before we go to the 'Apple Tree', isn't that a nice name for a pub? Apparently they have a huge Bramley apple tree in the back garden.'

'This is very comfortable, you must have worked hard today to get everything in order.'

'There wasn't a lot to bring really, and the removal men insisted on getting me straight before they left. Tony have you brought Alan's photos of the carvings? I've had copies made of the sketches they're on the table over there.'

'Alan gave me this package for you, so I imagine that it is the photos.' Sarah grabbed the jiffy-bag and ripped it open. The photographs were beautiful, Alan had done a lovely job and had enlarged them so that the details could be clearly seen, the angel's faces had been carefully carved, the one on the right was slightly different from the one on the left, the hair was shorter and not so wavy, the nose was longer and there was no necklace. The swags of fruit and flowers on the dining room fireplace were some of the best that Sarah had ever seen, but on the cottage fireplace Walter had used lavender as his main motif. 'Lavender again' thought Sarah. Comparing them with the photocopies of the sketches Sarah could immediately see it was clear that Walter had kept to his original ideas.

'That Tony was definitely a labour of love, Walter seems to have caught such happy expressions on their faces. You know I still have this strange feeling that I've seen all this before.'

'Well think about this, wouldn't it be wonderful if somewhere we could find a portrait of Elizabeth. Her father obviously doted on her so he could well have had an artist paint her. Think about it Sarah, if you feel you've been here before perhaps you can remember something that we have overlooked.'

'I've thought exactly the same, but can only imagine it hanging on a wall somewhere.'

'Not necessarily Sarah, the Manor changed hands a few times, then became a farm, so there could a picture stashed away somewhere.'

'Something else for James to look for' laughed Sarah, 'if it's around I bet he finds it, but I will give it some thought as well. Let's leave all this and go to the pub.'

A log fire burned away in the Apple Tree's hearth throwing out a very welcome heat. Sarah and Tony settled themselves and looked around, trails of hops drifted along the beams, brass plates and copper pans glowed in the firelight, the floor was the original stone flags and Tony remarked on them as so often they were being ripped up and replaced with garish carpet. Tony went to the bar and ordered the meal, the landlord was a young man immaculately turned out, black trousers, white shirt and a red scarf tied round his neck. He answered all of

Tony's questions. The steak was good and well hung. The plaice was fresh, it had been caught early in the morning and rushed into the pubs that specialised in fish, the Apple Tree being one of them.

'I did enjoy that' said Tony, 'I hesitated about the steak, sometimes it leaves a lot to be desired, but that was lovely, and the apple crumble was melt in the mouth.'

'My plaice was good too, it really tasted fresh such a change from frozen meals. Let's go home and you can have a look at the furniture while I make some coffee.'

Tony had a look at the furniture and quickly made up his mind, he was surprised at the quality of the commode and table then realised there was no reason why Aunt Grace shouldn't have been interested in antique furniture.

'I would keep the commode Sarah, but I'm not sure about anything else, I'll measure up the table and chairs and see if they will fit in, as for the sideboard, well I think the saleroom is the best place for that I don't think Joanna has room for it.'

'Tony, it was Aunt Grace's pride and joy.'

'So it might have been, but it will not fit in with either your cottage or the farm.'

'Oh well! Let's get rid of it.'

25

At Bridge Farm Babs and Ken were busy planning the next major step in the development of the Lavender Farm, Christmas was coming and they wanted to have a pattern of work established before being distracted by the festivities.

Babs looked up from her notebook. 'We must ask Alan if he has any information about the lavender that was found when the excavations were being done, he'll probably know if there was any evidence of it being grown here in the 1550's and later?'

'Well, the archaeologists were really looking for Roman remains, artefacts, etc., but at the same time as professionals if they had found things relating to later periods I would think that they would have recorded that information too so you could be right' said Ken, 'Alan might have info that would help, he did say he had a lot of photos.'

'Don't forget he is up here this week, looking at all the papers and artefacts to try and sort them out. Incidentally, Jonnie is up here too, do you think we ought to bring her in on our plans and offer her the job of managing the shops?'

'The sooner we do involve Jonnie the better, then no one

will drop a clanger. Perhaps she could help with the weeding too, we must get on top of that soon.' Ken added another note to his growing list of things-to-do. 'Actually Babs, I'll give Jonnie a ring and ask her to come and see us during a lunch break.'

'Good idea! Changing the subject - shall we ask Sarah here for Christmas?'

Ken laughed 'She and Tony might have other plans.'

'I don't think so, she is recovering from an unhappy affair and wants to play this one cool.'

'Then do ask her, probably Joanna will ask us all down there for Christmas Day, she usually does and I bet she'll include Alan and Tony and probably Jonnie.'

'We mustn't bank on it, but I expect you are right, Joanna really does love a party. Right now I'm going to see Alan, perhaps his photos could help and he could have come up with some info already. He might know what Sarah has found in the grey book, she said the photocopies would be ready by Saturday, I'm dying to see them I'm sure there's a lot of interesting facts there. See you at lunch time.'

Babs stopped to look at the lavender on her way down to Bridge Farm, it looked good, it wasn't growing too fast and even though there were no flower heads she loved the colour of the field, a soft grey against the dark background of the hawthorn hedge which had been clipped in the autumn so the bare branches looked black and stark in the cold November weather. Babs knew that as soon as Spring came the bareness would be covered with the pink of new growth. Even in its bare state the birds seemed very happy so hopefully it was going to be good for nesting. A hawk was stationary in the air above and Babs gave a sharp intake of breath as it dived down and went off with its spoils. She walked over to the field and rubbed some lavender through her fingers, she had done that hundreds of times but was always amazed at how strong the fragrance was, she knew that it took a lot of lavender to make a small amount of oil and hoped they had planted enough acreage, perhaps they should seriously think about buying the extra bit? Sarah could probably help out with this problem after her work experience on Jersey, hopefully she would get some facts and figures that would bear out those they already had. Hopefully too she would learn about what could easily be made on site now, and what equipment would be needed for future development.

Grey clouds were looming up over the farm and the sun rapidly disappeared, a chilly breeze sprang up and Babs shivered as she ran towards Bridge Farm, the dogs came out to greet her, Troy seemed to be really at home and Jason obviously loved having a playmate.

'Jason, Troy come here.' Joanna's voice rang out from the depths of the farmhouse. 'Sorry Babs, I thought it was one of our deliveries arriving, I didn't want the dogs being a nuisance. They do love each other don't they?'

'They certainly do. I've just come along to see if Alan has come up with anything relating to lavender.'

'You haven't? I can't imagine why' said Joanna drifting off into one of her laughs.

'Don't be sarky Joanna, you should be pleased that we have an interest in the history of Bridge Farm, or should we be calling it Hapstead Manor?'

'Bridge Farm will do for me, my mother always used to say 'let the dead past bury its dead', I believe in that up to a point, because of course I'm interested in the history of our farm, and of course I'm interested in the lavender aspect of it, but we have to move on and Bridge Farm has a good ring to it.' Joanna gave Babs a quick hug. 'Go and see Alan, but he's only been here a day so you might be disappointed.'

'I know, but at least he'll know I'm interested in what he finds. See you later.'

Alan was sitting at the table, surrounded by documents, he was busily reading one but looked up as she went in.

'Hello Alan, I've come to have a look at your photographs and to see how you are getting on.'

'The photographs, my dear, are I'm afraid still being sorted, so I've left them at home and will only bring them up when I've finished and got them in order. These papers are all fascinating stuff though, can you believe it they are talking about lavender here, but I want to sort everything out chronologically and by subject before going into things in detail. Sarah has started on it but there's a long way to go.'

'Talking about lavender? What's the date Alan?'

'It looks like 1790.'

'I think that ties in with the little grey book.'

'I hadn't thought about that, but you could be right. I wonder what Sarah has discovered having had it photocopied. Tony has the photocopies, he phoned about half an hour ago, I'm expecting him any minute so you won't have to wait long Babs,' Alan looked up at her and laughed 'it's the waiting game my dear, be patient instant answers aren't always possible.'

'I think we're kindred spirits Alan, you're just as impatient as me. You know this brilliant idea of a lavender farm that I had doesn't seem to be so new after all, I don't know whether to be pleased or sorry.'

'With all the stories we're turning up I should be pleased, think of the publicity aspect.'

'I have, but all I can see is an awful lot of work getting it together.'

'Don't forget you'll have Sarah, she should be good at that and I think she would enjoy it. Here's another bit about lavender. Don't touch, I'll get all the documents sorted, then we can look at the specifics. If we aren't methodical we will have a real muddle here.'

'I'll be good. Here's Tony now. What goodies have you got for us Tony?'

'Lots, there's the batch of copies for you Alan, plus the originals, Sarah says can you be particularly careful with the grey book it is very delicate, she wondered if Seth would put it in the farm safe, it could be very valuable.'

'I'll ask him this afternoon, it certainly looks as if it needs special treatment.' The archivist had put it in a plastic bag and Alan and Babs had a good look at it.

'It's lovely, that embroidery is so fine and it is lavender' said Babs, 'if it is 1790 or there-abouts how did they manage when they didn't have electricity or spectacles to help them? Did Sarah do a copy for me?'

'Yes, she knew you would want one, so here you are plus a plan of the estate.'

'Brilliant, I'm off Alan I don't have to be patient any longer. I'll take these up to the attic and look at them with Mollie.' Babs clutched the photocopies to her chest and disappeared.

'This lavender theme is getting to all of us' said Tony, 'what do you make of it Alan?'

'I just think lavender has been grown here since the Roman times, and hopefully these documents I'm turning up will give us the history.'

'Sarah thinks that the grey book is another link in the history.'

'She could be right, it could have been written by Agnes Lafolley which means it will be dated circa 1790.'

'Is there a story about it?'

'Mollie is looking through the stories at the moment, we hope there's one about Agnes, some of the letters were written to her before she was married, they had lavender between them which hints at romance, so it will be interesting to find out if it was Matthew that sent them, or was there someone else in her life? If the grey book was written by her we could have an interesting slice of local history based on Hapstead Manor. Hopefully Pa came up with a story but as I said before he never really mentioned lavender to us, so if there is a story it will probably deal with another aspect of life in the late18th century. Seth is going to examine the letters this week, and although they are faded the writing is still very crisp, he hopes he can make sense of them, if not a visit to the local archivist will be on the agenda.'

'It's all happening then, do let me know if you want me to help out Alan, I haven't a lot of spare time but do ask I'll always say if I can't do it.'

'There is something you can do Tony and that is help me look at the furniture in the loft, first of all I need someone to help me up there and secondly someone who knows a little about antiques.'

'That I would love to do. I was talking to James the other day and he has found it all fascinating, can we involve him too? He could help in moving the furniture around if nothing else.'

Alan smiled, 'He has already asked me if he can help, he has got so interested it might be the way his career goes so we must encourage him. I watched him the other day and he certainly has a feel for the old, I saw him stroking the patina on one of the commodes, something you expect from an older person.'

'That's interesting, I'm thinking about taking on an apprentice soon, he might well fit the bill, if he's interested that is, I don't work with furniture but perhaps he would like the idea of restoration work.'

'That's an excellent idea Tony let's sow the seed.'

'In the meantime I'll go and see how Mollie is getting on, is she in the attic?'

'Yes, she needs room to spread the papers and I'm taking up all the room here.'

'I'll have a quick look at the furniture while I'm up there and take some photos. Do you know if Seth contacted the chap about the spinet?'

'He's coming today, so we'll know a bit more about it, then a decision will have to made, should Joanna keep it or should it be sold to a museum?'

'I would like to see Joanna keep it but only if it gets played regularly.' Tony laughed 'I'm getting as bad as Sarah, but I feel that spinet needs to be in Bridge Farm, it is a part of its romantic history.'

Alan smiled ruefully. 'You know Tony, Grace and I never realised how much history the farm had, in fact Edith didn't either, I can only think that in those days folk weren't so interested in local history as they are today. I didn't ask that much about the furniture that was stored in the attic, but know now that up there we probably have a treasure trove.'

'You do realise that the story of you, Edith and Grace is part of the history and should be recounted for posterity as they say.' Tony laughed at the expression on Alan's face. 'I mean it Alan, ask Sarah to write it up, I'm sure she would look on it as a labour of love.'

'Well. we'll see' and Alan reverted to his grumpy mood, which Tony knew was just to cover up his embarrassment.

'I'll see you later' and he put his hand on Alan's shoulder, 'it's great having you here, Sarah finding the photograph of Grace really started something, we've become quite an extended family. I wonder if between us we can lay the ghosts and revive the past with the lavender farm.'

26

Mollie was busily sorting out papers when Tony eventually got into the attic.

'Anything more about lavender Mollie?' asked Tony 'I bet your Mum has given you strict instructions to pass any info on to her.'

'That's where you are wrong Tony' and Mollie giggled, 'Mum is being incredibly patient, which is quite unlike her, but apparently Alan told her that all the information must be sorted and dated, then we should have all the info about specific subjects in one place, and she is going along with that.'

'Has she found anything out by looking at the grey book? I know she has only just had the photocopies, but she might have thought of something.'

'She has just brought the copies up to me and said she will study them thoroughly later. There was a note from Sarah to say that the book was dated 1792, if so it was probably written by Agnes Lafolley nee Morey, but that has to be confirmed. I have had a quick look and it is really strange Tony, it seems to be pages of recipes and remedies using herbs, the sort of thing that is coming into vogue now with homeopathy and a wider use in cooking. Whoever wrote the book and did those delightful drawings did it because they were interested in herbs and wanted to use them. I could see myself finding the herbs in the field and wanting to know more about them and what were they used for, couldn't you?'

'Yes! I could. You have given this a lot of thought Mollie and I think you might be right, it certainly makes sense, I shall be interested to hear what Sarah thinks, perhaps you would like to give her a ring and have a chat about it. Here's her number.' Tony scribbled the number down and gave it to her. 'She'd love to hear from you I know.'

'She's coming to stay with us soon, did you know?'

'I hoped she would stay with me, but she wants some 'quality time' as she calls it so I'm quite happy at her staying with you, it will give Sarah and your parents time to talk about the plans for the lavender farm.'

'You'll be able to see her Tony, we won't keep her imprisoned.' Mollie laughed at him. 'What it is to be in love'

'Don't be cheeky, Alan wouldn't approve and might stop you working up here' teased Tony.

'I wasn't really being cheeky, I think it's lovely that you and Sarah are becoming 'good friends' shall we say? You know life was very dull round here before Sarah came on the scene, she only came with a photograph, she must feel excited too at all the developments.'

'Well she has handed in her notice and is getting herself ready to go to Jersey in the New Year. I've got to get her cottage finished because I don't think it will be long before she moves in. Have you seen the fireplace since we cleaned it?'

'I'm going up there with Mum this afternoon, she hasn't

seen it yet either, but she says from the photographs it looks good.'

'Now Mollie, have you found a story, or anything relating to Agnes Lafolley?'

'I think I have, some of these pages are not written in story form, they must be Pa Harris's notes. On these' said Mollie, pushing some rather crumpled sheets of paper towards Tony, 'it looks as though he is trying to work out the history of the late eighteenth century, which would include Agnes.'

'This is just what Alan is looking for and by the time we have details of the letters from Seth we should have a good idea of what was going on at Hapstead Manor in the eighteenth century. All we need now is some material dealing with the later period. You are doing a good job, can I help you get the pages in date order?'

'I think this is a one person job Tony, thanks all the same,'

'I'll go and look at the furniture then.' Tony went off to the far end of the attic, he had brought his camera with him and set about photographing those pieces he thought 'interesting'. There were two commodes, a beautiful glass-fronted bookcase, he did wonder how that had survived in the attic, two small tables and two large wooden chairs with rush seats that looked liked carvers and Tony thought they went with the furniture in the dining room at Bridge Farm. At the other end of the attic were two folding tables, a carved head and foot for a double bed, two small finely made chairs with tapestry seats, albeit very faded, and a lovely chest that had possibly been a blanket box, when Tony lifted the lid he could smell camphor and lavender. Photographs taken Tony told Mollie he was going back to see Alan but if she found any stories about furniture he would be interested in them.

'They've all got to go to Alan first Tony, but I'll make a note then you can easily track them down.'

'Good, I believe he said that one or two of the stories were based round furniture.'

'Yes he did, but I'm wondering how you could come up with a story based round that chest for example.'

'Well it could just be who gave it to whom, and why, perhaps even who made it. I think it's a marriage chest, a place where the bride-to-be stored the linens and other furnishings for the new home, or even her trousseau.'

'Tony' shrieked Mollie, 'you're not trying to say that there might be another unhappy romance here are you?'

'That had not occurred to me Mollie, but that might be the case, of course, it could be a happy one.'

'Not at Hapstead, I'm sure they have all been unhappy romances, weddings, affairs, what ever until now...'

'I know' said Tony interrupting 'until Sarah and I live happily ever after in the cottage. Believe that if you like but there must have been at least one happy marriage and I shall look for it.'

'I'm just looking at Pa Harris' history, you know it could have been Agnes Lafolley, it looks as if she had a stable relationship with Matthew, they were married for thirty six years and had a son. I wonder if it's their love letters that Seth is going through, Mum reckons that they are business letters, but I'm not so sure. You know Tony, if she wrote the grey book, which I'm sure she did, and made the recipes before writing them up she must have been very industrious and I would think was a very intelligent lady, talented too if she did that embroidery, come to think about it she might have done the tapestry work on those chair seats. Let's hope Uncle Seth comes up with the answers it would be marvellous if some of those letters were Agnes and Matthew's love letters.'

'Now you are looking for a happy marriage. There are a lot of questions however, I'll have a word with Sarah and see if she can come here sooner I think she could be well employed with this research work.'

'That would be great, I'm sure she'll come if she can, I've got to go back to school next week, so I won't be able to do too much.'

'You'll be missed Mollie, but check up on what's been going on when you get home in the evening. You could perhaps use some of this information in one of your school projects, like the grey book in an Art project.'

'I wonder if that's possible? I must talk it over with my teacher, but a plan would be good to show her, could you help me there Tony?'

'Of course I can. You must think about the embroidery aspect, stitches etc., then look at the book, try and find out the type of paper that was used, you never know it might have been home-made. Then the little drawings, what sort of ink? There are lots of arty-crafty aspects to examine, you should come up with plenty of material. Get some ideas down on paper and I'll sit with you and help knock a plan into shape.'

'Tony you're wonderful, this just what I've been looking for, I do hope Miss Oswald likes the idea. I shall tell her you are advising me, she will approve of that because she says we ought to involve older people in our projects.'

'Don't forget to phone Sarah, you can ask her if she could come down earlier, tell her how much stuff is being found and that Alan and Seth could probably do with help.'

'Will do Tony, must dash lunch will be ready and Mum likes us to be on time.'

Tony made his way back to see Alan, only to find that he had gone to lunch. There was a note from Joanna on the table saying that Tony would be welcome too. Tony made his way to the kitchen hoping that it was going to be leek and potato soup, one of Joanna's specialities, it was a bitterly cold day and that would be particularly welcome. He was not disappointed, the lovely warm smell of cooked leeks and hot bread reached him in the corridor, he felt an ominous rumbling in his tummy and realised just how hungry he was.

'This is lovely Joanna, I would have been going home to stale bread, cheese and water.'

'My heart bleeds for you, but if you think I believe that for one minute you are mistaken.' Joanna ladled a generous helping of soup into a bowl and told Tony to help himself to bread. Tony was not disappointed, the soup was delicious. He listened to the general conversations going on round the table, Joanna and Seth were gently teasing Alan, who seemed to be enjoying it. Jonnie was laughing with them and obviously enjoying herself. He thought how lucky he was to have found such good friends, friends who gave him work that he was really interested in and enjoyed, then as a bonus there was all this interest in the history of Bridge Farm, and of course, there was Sarah.

27

Sarah wrapped herself up in her dressing gown made a mug of hot chocolate and sat in front of the fire shivering slightly. She had had a meal at the pub and hadn't been home very long, but a cold night was forecast and as she found Aunt Grace's house rather chilly, even with the central heating on, she had lit the fire. The hot chocolate helped, but all Sarah could think of was spending the New Year in Jersey, hopefully it would be warmer. Currently she was finding life a bit hectic, there seemed to be a lot of clearing up to do at the library before she left and in addition to her normal duties Tim had asked her to make a list of all the work she was responsible for. She had also been given photocopies of the papers the archivist had promised her and found she had almost got to the point where work was impinging on her interest in Bridge Farm.

The photocopies of the documents about Hapstead Manor that Mary had found were lying on the coffee table and Sarah knew it was going to take her a while to decipher them even though Mary had run through them with her. Sarah's initial reaction was that they weren't telling her anything new, but Mary had told her that what they would do was to verify some of the facts that they already had. Sarah had decided to sit down and make notes of the relevant bits then call Seth and Alan, after all they were involved with the history more than she was.

The note taking didn't take her as long as she had thought, she found that once she had got her eye in as far as the writing and the usage of English was concerned she could decipher the documents relatively easily. Deciding it was a bit late to call Alan she phoned Bridge Farm.

'Hello Seth, Sarah here.'

'Sarah! Good to hear from you, we were talking about you over dinner wondering how you were getting on.'

'Very well actually, Mary our archivist has found some documents relating to Hapstead Manor and has given me photocopies, one of them is dealing with the transfer of the land from the monks to Francis Courtney...'

'You're joking!'

'No I'm not, this states that the land was actually given to Francis Courtney for services rendered, he was to pull down the monastery, build a small manor house and farm. That seems to tie in with Pa Harris's stories.'

'I found that some of the papers at this end deal with the building of the manor in the 1540's as you said I probably would, they included old invoices for the work done and details of some of the furniture purchased. One item is for a headboard and foot for a large bed, and it looks as though they are in the attic. The valuer came today and he put a date of circa 1550 on them and is coming back with a price. He loved the spinet incidentally, but I'll tell you about that later. What else have you come up with?'

'Mary told me that these documents should verify what we already know, and one of the documents proves that the estate was sold to John Herbert in 1706.'

'Brilliant, we really are getting loose ends tied up, what else Sarah, I'm getting quite excited about all of this.'

Sarah laughed. 'Calm down Seth, or I won't tell you the next bit, which you will not believe.'

'Carry on, you've really got my interest now.'

'In 1771, Cedric Morey the current owner asked for permission to use one of his fields for the growing of herbs.'

'Do you mean lavender? I wonder why he had to have permission?' asked Seth.

'I imagine lavender would have been included but looking at the grey book I would think many different types of herbs were planted, therefore he may have had to ask permission to change the use of a field from grazing to arable. Interesting isn't it?'

'It certainly is. You are probably right, I assume he was sold the land on the condition that he used it for agricultural purposes, and therefore the herb farm had to be approved, possibly by the King.'

'What ever is Babs going to say now?' and Sarah laughed at the thought. 'You do realise that this ties in with the little grey book that was written by Agnes Lafolley, Cedric Morey's daughter, I have really studied it and it is very 'erudite' for the sake of another word. She knew her herbs, and in particular lavender. She has details of when to plant, how to look after it and then recipes for using the oil.'

'Will you be able to use those recipes Sarah?'

'I would think so Seth, perhaps we could use the name *Agnes Lafolley* as a trade name - *Agnes Lafolley's Lavender Water* has quite a ring to it.' Sarah found herself laughing again. 'Tell Babs, I bet she'll like that.'

'I'm sure she will, and I reckon she'll be glad to have you on board if you can come up with ideas like that. Sarah, I must go. I'm hoping to look at the letters tomorrow evening, if I find anything surprising I'll give you a ring. Goodnight, sleep well.'

'Goodnight Seth, I'll try and give Alan a ring tomorrow at lunch time. Love to everyone.'

Sarah put some more coal on the fire, pulled her dressing gown tightly round her and curled herself up in the armchair. It was 10.00 o'clock, time to phone Tony, she had promised that she would do that every night so that they could say 'Goodnight'. There was no answer, Sarah felt quite deflated and wondered where on earth he could be, she decided not to panic, if there was anything wrong Joanna would have phoned. The fire started to blaze up the chimney, so Sarah gave it a poke and turned the draught down, the fire settled into a warm pleasant glow and Sarah found herself drifting off with the smell of lavender in her nostrils. She dozed off and drifted in and out of sleep dreaming about Hapstead Manor and lavender.

28

Sarah suddenly woke and for a moment she wondered where she was, the phone was ringing, but it was Mollie not Tony.

'Hi there Sarah. Won't be long before you are back at Bridge Farm, I'm really looking forward to it, life has been quite dull since you left, that's why I've phoned you actually, I wondered whether you could come down earlier than planned, there are so many things cropping up we need help with. Tony suggested I asked you. What did you make of the little grey book? I haven't looked at it very closely but it seems to be very much in line with the herbal thinking of today.'

'I do agree with you. You know I keep saying that I feel I've been to Bridge Farm before, well this evening I've had really strange dreams about Hapstead Manor, I must check the facts with Seth and Alan, but according to my dreams lavender played a very important part in the history. I've got the day off work tomorrow so I'll get all my thoughts down on paper and check them with Alan's archives, I'm sure there are some true facts there.'

'Do you really think you've been here before?'

'Yes, Mollie I do, it is very strange, it all seems so real, I feel that I know the cottages, I know the estuary, and the herb fields and lavender keep coming into my mind, in fact sometimes I wake up smelling lavender and there is none around, now that is strange, and remember there was a sachet of lavender with Aunt Grace's photograph, I haven't thought much about that until now but there must have been lavender at Bridge Farm when she was here.'

Mollie shivered 'Spooky I'd call it and I had forgotten about the lavender sachet, do you still have it?'

'It had lost its smell so I threw it, I rather wish I hadn't now.'

'Perhaps you do have a sixth sense, perhaps you did live here. Do hurry and come back, then we can get lots of questions answered, I'm sure you know a lot of the answers. Tony said you might come earlier if I asked you nicely.'

'I'm still working out my notice Mollie so it'll be two more weeks at least, I'll give your Mum a ring sometime this week and let her know my plans, she said I can stay with you until the cottage is ready and that won't be until I get back from Jersey at the beginning of February. As far as I'm concerned the sooner I'm with you all the happier I'll be, I don't think I have had such lovely friends as those I've made at Bridge Farm.'

'Talking of friends, Tony gave me a message for you, he said that he wouldn't be able to phone you before eleven o'clock, he was working away today and wanted to finish the job. Hope you'll be able to stay awake.' Mollie chuckled 'I'm sure I'd be able to.'

'You are becoming a cheeky brat Mollie, I'll have to sort you out when I come down.'

'It's only because I like you Sarah, it's when I'm not cheeky you have to watch out.'

'That's alright then, and I'll be awake when Tony phones don't worry. I'm going to have another look at the grey book, I think I'll type each of the pages into my word processor and see if I can come up with recipes that we could use at your Mum's lavender farm, *Agnes Lafolley's Lavender Water* has a good ring to it, I tried it out on Seth and he thought Babs would like it, you never know we might have a new name for the farm.'

'Alan said you'd be full of good ideas, and I know Mum is waiting for you to come so that ideas can be bounced around.'

'I seem to have plenty of those at the moment, and hope I'll have some more after my month in Jerey. We must hang up now, I don't want to miss Tony and he could phone earlier.'

'Goodnight Sarah, dream of lavender.' Mollie put the phone down. Sarah was almost sure she could smell lavender. She gave herself a shake, put some more coal on the fire and got out her laptop. She felt she had a really good idea for a recipe book and wanted to work on it while it was fresh in her mind. It was only ten o'clock and her doze had really refreshed her so she started work.

She had brought some reference books on herbs home with her and decided the first step was to check yesterday's herbs with todays. She wanted to base her recipe book round Agnes's but did not want to include herbs that either had medicinal qualities or were poisonous.

The phone rang and it was Tony.

29

February

'Jason, drop that you disgusting dog.' Sarah grabbed his collar and pulled him away from a decidedly old bone. 'You dogs do like the nastiest of things.' Jason wagged his tail and as she put his lead on tried to lick her face. 'Get off you revolting dog, you stink, come on let's get you home.'

Sarah had been down to see Alan to tell him about her time in Jersey and to look at the photos he had found, he had decided to keep the photos at his cottage until all the papers had been sorted at Bridge Farm. Sarah had been most impressed by the pictures but they were relatively recent as most of them dealt with the archaeological dig, so it was sensible to keep them separate. There were one or two aerial photos that Sarah had found particularly interesting as they showed quite clearly the outlines of ancient fields and she decided she had to check the dates, were they Roman or Medieval? And how did the fields of yesterday fit in with the fields of today? It was something else to talk over with Babs, they had to make sure that their fields were in the best situation, did the Romans know something they didn't? Sarah knew that Babs and Ken had taken advice about the planting, but it would be fascinating to find out if that advice had survived the centuries.

Christmas seemed a long way away, albeit it was only six weeks. Sarah smiled as she remembered the lovely time she had had with Babs and Co and the wonderful Christmas dinner Joanna had put on, followed by an evening playing games. It had been the first time in her life that she had spent the holiday with a family and she now knew what was meant when folks said that Christmas was a 'family' occasion. The month in Jersey had sped by, that had been a good time too, she had been made very welcome and was allowed the freedom of the farm. She had returned to Bridge Farm feeling a lot more knowledgeable about most aspects of lavender and had been particularly interested in the production of toiletries, candles, etc and had made copious notes. There was still a lot to learn and her job for the weekend was to sit down and make sense of them and list ideas for Babs and Ken.

Probate had still not gone through, but she had been told 'any day now' and she felt that until that happened she would feel very restless. Tony had finished the cottage and Sarah was delighted with it, she had moved in as she had sufficient savings to pay the rent for several weeks but had to count the pennies when it came to luxuries, only one bottle of wine a week and super market bread. She rediscovered meals from her childhood like liver and bacon and cottage pie, finding how nice they were and how cheap.

Shivers ran up Sarah's spine as she looked over the estuary, she felt she remembered small boats coming up to the harbour near the bridge. The foundations of a medieval jetty had been recently uncovered and Sarah wondered how long it had been in use, she had this strange feeling that she had been in one of those boats, but why? The estuary was looking very grey, there weren't many birds about just a few gulls swooping down over the water and crying into the wind as they swept skywards. Small grey green crested waves were coming in from the sea adding to the sombre look. The clouds began to darken and Sarah could feel the first hint of rain so she tugged Jason's lead and started to run up the road.

A flash of lightning and a crack of thunder startled Sarah, she was not expecting a storm.

'Come on Jason, let's get home before we get soaked,' even as she spoke the heavens opened and they arrived at Bridge Farm looking extremely bedraggled.

'For goodness sake' said Joanna rubbing Jason vigorously, 'didn't you see the storm coming Sarah?'

'Actually I was almost on another planet Joanna, the estuary seems such a familiar place to me, I was trying to place it in my memory but did not have much luck apart from the fact that I know I've been in one of the boats that used to use the harbour at the bridge.'

'Mollie said that you felt you had been here before, but we are all a little sceptical you know. Do you believe in reincarnation?'

'I'm not sure about reincarnation, but I do think that a lot of people have a feeling of déjà vu about a place, don't you get it sometimes?'

'I must confess I don't, but that doesn't mean I don't go along with what other people feel. Perhaps some of the documents Seth is looking at will trigger off your memory, it would be amazing if you were right and can come up with different aspects of the history of Bridge Farm. Now go on up to your cottage and get out of those wet things, but come back here for dinner Sarah, I've done enough stew that would feed the five thousand. Tony's coming.'

Sarah laughed 'If Tony's coming then I will. Seriously Joanna, please don't feel you have to feed me, I really can manage.'

'My dear girl we have adopted you so you'll have to put up with me feeding you occasionally. Actually today you can earn your keep by getting back as soon as possible so that you can sort out the cabbage and whisk up the egg whites, I'm doing a lemon meringue pie, but am short of time.'

'Lemon meringue pie. I'll be back before you can blink.'

Sarah raced through the puddles to her cottage, it was still stormy overhead and the flashes of lightning lit up the cottages making them look like something out of a Sherlock Holmes mystery. She had her key in her hand so it was just a matter of seconds before she was inside in the dry. Tony had done a good job with the central heating, everything felt warm and cosy. Sarah pulled off her boots and left them inside the door to dry off. She raced upstairs, stripped off her wet things and gave herself a really hot shower lavishly using the shower gel which Tony had recently given her. She felt like a new woman as she stepped out and towelled herself down. Twenty minutes later she was back at Bridge Farm. She cringed as she opened the door as there was another flash of lightning and crack of thunder overhead.

'We're in for it tonight according to the forecast' said Joanna, 'but let's forget about it, we are snug in here, let's get the dinner ready. I think Seth wants you to go and look at the documents after dinner, he and Mollie have really worked hard and it all seems to be coming together. James has helped too but his main interest has been the furniture in the attic.'

'What's happening about that? Are you keeping the spinet?'

'The spinet turned out to be quite rare, therefore if we kept it the insurance would be astronomical. Tony's friend has taken it to a restorer, then it will go up for auction, we really cannot afford to keep it and we can use the money to refurbish parts of the farm.'

'It's a shame you can't keep it Joanna but I can see how useful the money will be.   When I thought about it and how lovely it would be for the spinet to sit in your lounge, I wondered what the insurance would be and hoped it would be manageable. Do you think that when Elizabeth walks at night she will play a ghostly spinet?'

'Sarah enough of that nonsense, I've never seen nor felt a ghost around Bridge Farm, so no more talk of it.'

'Don't forget that some of us have felt a 'presence' in the hall and music has been heard.'

'You mean there was a draught blowing through the hall at the same time as you went through, and as for the music, well I often hear music in my dreams but I don't associate it with someone from the past.'

'Perhaps you ought to Joanna. '

Joanna laughed 'My dear girl, I always hear *Pink Floyd,* now that couldn't have come from the past could it?'

'Joanna you are not taking this seriously, it is your house we are all interested in.'

'I know, I'm really being the Devil's Advocate. Let's get the history and Pa Harris's stories into perspective, chronological order, whatever you like to think of, then worry about ghosts.'

'But they are part of that history.'

'Convince me. Come on, the lemon meringue needs the egg whites whipped.'

'Trust you to get us back to earth' laughed Sarah.

30

Later that evening Sarah and Tony made their way to the operations room. Seth was collecting some papers he had been copying and was joining them in a few minutes. All the documents dealt with so far were arranged neatly on the table, beside them were some small card box files, the green one listed the documents in chronological order, and the blue one listed them alphabetically according to subject, a card for each subject, so if one wanted to look up herbs the documents relating to herbs that had so far been found could be traced. Sarah was impressed, she felt that even with her library skills she couldn't have done better. She saw Mollie's hand in this, no wonder she had been asking her so many questions about arranging documents.

'Everyone's worked so hard here Tony, it's a brilliant job, now all we have to do is put it together.'

Tony laughed 'That could be your job Sarah, it would keep you busy until the lavender farm became a reality for you.'

'You are joking I know, but I would like to do it, it might lay some of my ghosts, perhaps I'd be able to find out if I did come up the estuary in a boat.'

Tony flung his arms round her. 'My dear girl, of course you came up the estuary in a boat, of course you've seen the fireplaces before, of course you know about lavender, you my darling have been here before and we will find out who you were and when you were here. Now are you happy?'

Sarah smiled 'I don't know that you are taking me seriously, but do I understand you to say that you will help me decipher the history of Bridge Farm, when you have time that is?'

'Yes! That is exactly what I mean. Here's Seth, waving some papers and looking very excited.'

'Look Sarah, Tony, Mollie thinks she has found another of Pa Harris's stories.'

'Another, where did she find that one?'

'Mollie found it muddled up with some papers on the desk. We are only guessing but feel that this was not finished and that's why it wasn't in the file. I've done a photocopy for you to read Sarah, remember we don't think it is complete. We think you will like this one it's about lavender and perhaps you can find the final page, or even work it out using some of your memories to help.'

Sarah and Tony sat down at the table and started reading.

Lavender - 1764

Agnes dried her hands on her apron and smiled at Joan, a young girl from the village on the other side of the estuary. Agnes had been looking for someone to be a general help and Joan Harwood had been recommended by the local priest. Agnes couldn't have wished for any one better, she was reliable, willing and a very happy girl working at times in the Manor and when needed with Agnes in the Apothecary Room, which was in fact an outhouse of the dairy, far enough away from the Manor so that the smells wouldn't drift through, even though they were not unpleasant ones, Cedric Morey did not want his friends to know that they were trying to start up a business at Hapstead, he wanted it to be successful first.

'Keep stirring that pan Joan and don't let it boil. Watch the sand timer, when it has finished turn it over again then when it has run out for the second time the lavender water will be ready for me to add some alcohol. I'll only be in the dairy talking to Master Lafolley.'

'That's fine Mistress Morey, I'll give you a shout when it's ready.'

Agnes disappeared into the dairy and Joan had a quiet smile. Agnes and Matthew Lafolley, the farm overseer, had been seeing a lot of each other lately, it was obvious that feelings were running high and Joan was hoping that a wedding was in the offing, she liked Matthew and felt that he and Agnes were right for each other. The sand timer had nearly reached the end of its run so Joan called out to Agnes who came running because she always felt it was essential to get the alcohol into the brew as soon as possible.

'I hope it will be as good as the last lot.'

'So do I Joan' and Agnes very carefully added the alcohol. 'There is a slight problem we are running out of bottles, I shall have to get some more, can your brother see to that again for me, the last ones were such a beautiful blue I think it helped to sell the lavender water.'

'They came from Bristol, I don't know whether John'll be able to get more of the same but I'll ask him, he's coming to take me out fishing in his boat on Sunday. He got them from his friend Silas Lacey in Chichester who deals in glass, the one who found the flasks, piping and funnels you needed for distillation. Perhaps we ought to place a regular order with him then we'll always have some in stock.'

'Everything we've had from him so far has been of excellent quality but first let's see how well we do with this lot of lavender water and the oil that I hope to make this afternoon. We must work out the quantities we are likely, or even hoping to produce and take it from there, we don't want to order too many bottles and have them standing empty. We'll make that our next job Joan.'

'That makes good sense and I know that if he can get the bottles Silas would be glad of a regular order.'

'We must come up with other things to make as well as the lavender water, how can we use the lavender oil? Soap perhaps? We want to get a really flourishing business going.'

'That'll please Master Morey, he's not too sure about all this, perhaps he doesn't like the idea of you running the business.'

'I know Joan, but he'll think differently when we start making money.'

'If you're distilling today Mistress I'll set the flasks and everything up for you when I've finished with this lavender water.'

Agnes ran her fingers along the lavender that had been cut early in the morning but decided that it was not quite ready for distillation.

'The lavender is not quite dry enough for me to work with this afternoon, I'll do it first thing in the morning, but it would be helpful if you set everything up for me. You seem enjoy working with lavender Joan.'

'It's more interesting than milking cows or cleaning the pigs' laughed Joan, 'the smell is better anyway.'

Agnes joined in with the laugh 'I agree with you there.' As Joan started to set up the flasks Agnes had a good look at them.

'I would like to have a talk with Master Lacey, perhaps he could come and have a look at what we are doing he might have an idea about how he could help us because we are going to need some larger flasks, these hold enough while we are experimenting. But if everything goes well we'll need flasks that can hold ten times the quantity of lavender.'

'Ten times?' Joan looked at Agnes in amazement, 'ten times - are we growing enough for that?'

'Not this year Joan, but remember we planted up some lavenders last year that should provide us with enough flowers next year, and if I'm right we'll have to employ workers for the lavender and herb field, there will be too much for us to do.'

Joan drew a deep breath, 'I told you it was better than milking cows'.

'We will be working as hard I can assure you Joan. One thing we must do is to keep a careful record of our work, how much lavender do we need for an ounce of oil, and how many bottles will that fill? A list of all the things it could be used for would be useful, so get thinking Joan, if you are going to work with lavender and herbs you will have to eat, sleep and dream them. We must get some notebooks and put down all the information we have and the ideas as well, it is so easy to remember one day then forget the next. The other herbs in the field is where we are going to make our money to begin with, we have some regular orders from the local inn and apothecary in the village, but we could sell a lot more, we'll have to come up with recipes using them and sell the recipe along with the herb.'

'If you put an extra penny on the cost of the herb the recipe could go for free.'

'Joan, what did I do before you came along?' and Agnes laughed, 'I'm not sure that is very moral.'

'Whose talking about 'morals', this is business, remember I

was brought up in the timber business and my father knew a few tricks I can tell you, he would approve of this one.'

'So you admit it's a trick. We'll see how things go Joan, but it is a good idea.'

'Mistress Morey, you know that piece of embroidery you showed me, the lavender on grey silk, why don't you cover a book with it and use it for your recipes, the other notebooks would be our working books, but the grey one would be special and you could make it look really nice with some of your little drawings. John could get the books in Chichester when he goes to see Silas.'

'Now that is an idea I will go along with, I think we'll need three fairly big ones plus the special one. Come up to the Manor when you've finished here and we can work out the size of book required. As it happens I finished the embroidery yesterday afternoon and I'm really pleased with it. Did I tell you that the grey silk was a piece of material left over from my mother's wedding dress? I've kept the dress, it really is lovely and has some lavender coloured flowers embroidered on it.'

'Perhaps you'll be able to wear it at your wedding Mistress' said Joan rather daringly.

'There's no talk of a wedding yet Joan, but I have tried it on and it does fit. I'll get it out and when you come up this afternoon you can have a look at it.'

'I'd like that. Are you quite sure it's not lavender that's embroidered on it?'

'I think the flowers were just imaginary ones, I've never seen any like it, but they are beautifully done.' Agnes smiled at Joan, 'I've been told that my mother made the dress, she must have spent hours on it, just for one day.'

'Now that's what I call a real labour of love, I look forward to seeing it. That's everything set up what shall I do now?'

'I think you are right Seth, this story doesn't seemed finished, but how to finish it I don't know.' Sarah put the story down and looked at Tony. 'Are you thinking what I'm thinking?'

'That you were Joan and not Elizabeth?'

'I'm pretty sure I was Elizabeth because of the angel carvings and the music from the spinet, they don't fit in with the story of Agnes and Joan?'

'No, but the cottages and the jetty do' said Seth 'there are some papers here that relate to the cottages, they were rented out to workers on the estate, albeit for a peppercorn rent, but it looks as though Joan Harwood and her husband, she married the stone mason John Archer, lived in the second cottage, the one with the angel carvings on the fireplace. The papers are all sorted so you can look through them.'

'You make it sound so simple Seth, but do you seriously believe that I could have been here before as Joan.'

'Think of the parallels Sarah, you are here to help Babs make oils, perfumes, soaps anything else that can be made from lavender, and what was Joan doing?'

'It sounds as though you are talking of reincarnation Seth.'

'Not quite my dear, but I really do think that you have been here before and Joan seems to be the obvious guise, and her husband was a stone mason.'

'But I heard the spinet, I feet sure I must have been Elizabeth.'

'Joan could easily have been in the Manor after dark, either to talk to Agnes or to leave a message for her, she could have heard the spinet then, several people maintain that they have heard the ghostly spinet music. I think Joan seems to be the most likely candidate, now you'll have to try and find out

184

what sort of life she lead, and do you want to follow in her footsteps? Can you finish that story?'

'Only if she was happy. You know Seth, I feel I could have been here as Elizabeth or Joan. Oh! dear, things are getting complicated.'

Tony chuckled and gave Sarah a big hug. 'Cheer up darling, this is the sort of thing you wanted to hear.'

'I know, but it does seem unreal, you have all teased me about my feelings and now you all seem to be saying there was something in them after all.'

'We only teased you so that you wouldn't build up your hopes, but even though this story bears out some of facts you told us it doesn't necessarily mean that you were Joan, and as for Elizabeth…' Seth smiled at her, 'come on Sarah, we've got the future to think about, let's use the documents and the stories, even though parts of them must be fiction, to build up the history of Bridge Farm and the lavender farm. We could start up an educational centre as well, using the story of Hapstead Manor as the basis.'

'What a super idea Seth, have you mentioned it to Babs and Ken?'

'No, I've only just thought about it, they will be here in a minute so we could suggest it then. If you can help Alan and myself we could get these documents into a semblance of the history of this estate quite quickly, it will be a while before the lavender farm gets going commercially, and it would be ideal to have it done in time for the official opening. It would save time if we worked it all in together.'

'Work what in together?' said Babs as she came into the operations room.

'Babs, it's so exciting' and Sarah told her what had been discussed. 'What do you think? Can we do it?'

'This lavender farm is getting a bit out of hand methinks,' said Babs pursing her lips.

'Come on Babs, don't be miffed, honestly we haven't been talking behind your back, while we were discussing the history of the Farm ideas started to bounce around, you came in at the end. Let's face it, we will be a lavender farm with a difference. How many have a provenance of lavender being grown there for centuries, and you will have plenty of help.'

'We'll have to talk to Ken and perhaps include Jonnie as well, but I can see what you mean. Let's all sleep on it and not get too carried away until we have looked at all the implications, first of all where would we put an educational centre?'

'That's not a problem' said Seth, 'there's the 'big barn' as we call it which is just standing empty, Joanna and I have been talking about converting it into a farming centre for school children, perhaps we could include an historical section and one for the lavender farm.'

'Where would the money come from initially? Who would run it? Oh! I could go on and on, it doesn't mean I don't like the ideas I'm just being cautious.' Babs looked quite distraught. 'All I wanted to do was grow lavender and make some nice smellies.'

'All I wanted to do was find out about Aunt Grace, now Seth thinks I was Joan in an earlier life and I think I was Elizabeth. It looks as though we've both got involved with a lot more than we bargained for Babs. We'll have to help each other adjust to a different way of life.'

'You are quite right Sarah, positive thinking must be our priority.'

'Positive thinking? I'll go along with that and hope I'll be able to invest my money in the enterprise very soon, the last time I talked to my solicitor he said 'a few days', so I'm expecting good news next week. It probably won't be enough, but at least it will keep the Bank Manager off your back, then when I've sold the house there should be another injection of money. In the meantime as I have loads of spare time I'll be happy to work with Seth and Alan, Pa Harris did a good job initially it is now up to us to put it all together. I've also been looking at the grey book and have put it all on to my laptop, I hope that some of the recipes Agnes wrote down can be used and we can publish our own recipe book.'

'Good idea. Mollie said you had wondered about calling the products *Agnes Lafolley's* soap, oil, whatever. Ken and I thought that was a brilliant idea, so work away at it while we get everything sorted out and decide how we are going to manage the farm, a distillery, a shop and, now it seems, an education centre. Tony we would like you to be involved with the renovations because the buildings are listed.'

'I would like that, but as so many ideas are being bounced around it sounds to me as if a meeting is required for us all to sit down and work out a plan of campaign, helping each other as much as possible but not interfering.'

'… not interfering' said Ken as he poked his head round the door, 'nobody interferes here surely, we all work together.'

'Tony thinks we should have a meeting with all concerned to work out what we are doing and where we are going with the lavender farm, there are so many ideas bouncing around it is time we pooled them.'

'Joanna and I have just been talking along the same lines, so go ahead Babs, arrange a date, time and place.'

'We've all be asked for dinner here at Bridge Farm on Wednesday, so how about meeting in here after the meal.'

'That sounds fine' said Seth, 'we will all have finished our day's chores and can think more clearly. OK with you Tony and Sarah?'

'Perfect, stay the night Tony then you won't have the hassle of driving home. What about Alan?'

'I think we'll bring him in when we are talking about the history rather than the business side.' Seth looked round for agreement and everyone nodded. 'Time for bed I think, I for one have an early start.' Seth carefully covered the documents with the cloth, shepherded everyone out, put the light off and locked the door.

31

The storm had passed over and had left a beautiful starlit sky and a brilliant moon lit up the farmhouse and cottages.

'Looks as though we might be in for a touch of frost tonight' said Ken 'let's hope the lavenders will be alright. I don't suppose they mentioned frosts in Jersey Sarah?'

'They did actually, and I asked specifically about this farm, they think you should be frost free, it certainly is not a frost pocket and the field is sheltered by trees. What's more if lavender has been grown here successfully before I can't believe that frost would have been a problem.'

'You're right, I should have thought about that. It will be wonderful to have the history written down, get cracking Sarah.' Babs laughed at the expression on Sarah's face,

'Let her draw breath Ken, she's only just got back.'

'I know that, but if her money is coming through next week she'll officially be on the pay roll as a partner and will be involved with the planning of the lavender farm, and that will be a full time job, so all I'm saying is that hopefully she will have time to spare next week for the history side.'

'There's no problem Ken, I'm really looking forward to

being involved with you and Babs, I've got lots of info from Jersey that I must sort out into some sort of order so that I can pass it on to you, so next week I'll be doing that in the morning then work on the histories in the afternoon and evening, there is such a lot that deals with lavender, we must get it down on paper.'

'Leave some time for me' said Tony, 'or are you thinking about seeing me later in the evening and perhaps for breakfast!'

'Tony!' said Babs 'that's just naughty, but it does sound like a good idea.' Everyone laughed and Sarah made it quite clear to Tony that there would be plenty of time for him.

'It's such a lovely night Tony, I'll walk down to the carpark with you, perhaps we could go via the bridge, it will look lovely in this moonlight.'

'That's fine with me. Goodnight folks, see you soon.' Tony slipped his arm round Sarah and led her down to the bridge. It was very quiet apart from the sound of the water running over the stones, a gentle sound that fitted in with the calm after the storm The ducks were obviously asleep but an owl could be heard in the distance, as could a few splashes from the estuary as the nightlife did its rounds looking for food. A particularly large splash made Sarah jump.

'It's alright darling, just a water rat or something similar, they are out foraging.'

'It only made me jump Tony because everything here is so quiet, this really is beautiful.' Sarah leaned over the bridge to watch the silvered ripples disappearing under the bridge. 'I can understand why Alan and Grace thought of this as a special place, can't you?'

'It is glorious tonight, Joanna would say it was just right for lovers.'

'And Joanna would be right' and Sarah held her face up for a kiss.

'Do I really have to go home tonight?' murmured Tony.

'Yes you do, you have an early start tomorrow and I have a lot I want to do, and some of it I want to get sorted before I go to bed, so 'Goodnight' there will be other nights.'

'I thought you loved me, but if that's how you feel, I'll go,' said Tony heaving a great sigh.

'Don't tease Tony, you know I love you.'

'Well, don't work too hard, I'll give you a ring when I get home. Incidentally Sarah we've got to work out where our home will be, my place or your cottage.'

'What are you talking about?'

'When we get married, of course.'

'...married? Whose talking about getting married?'

'Mollie, Alan, Joanna, Babs and now me.'

Sarah looked at him and smiled. 'Give me time darling, but if we do then home will be the cottage, it's got to be, to sort out the ghosts.'

'You and your ghosts, but will you marry me Sarah, sometime soon?'

'I said give me time, ask me again on Wednesday.'

'Done' said Tony, giving Sarah one last kiss. 'Goodnight, phone you later. Love you.'

Sarah made her way back to the cottage knowing that she had a silly smile on her face, it was rather nice to be taken for granted and she knew that Tony was the right person for her, but she wanted a while to think about marriage, was that the way she wanted to go, or did she just want a 'partner'? Perhaps a partner for a while to see how it worked out.

Soon Sarah was back at the cottage, smiling as she looked at the fireplace.

'Is it up to us to sort out the ghosts? I think you are very nice ghosts, so I'm not worried?' and she gave both angels a little pat.

As it was just about ten thirty Sarah decided she could spend an hour sorting through her Jersey info. She had bought several different coloured files, so it was quite easy to separate the information. She put a sheet of paper in the front of each file and listed the contents putting an asterisk beside the bits that she thought really important. She was quite sure that Babs and Ken were aware of most of the facts that she had obtained, but felt it would be useful for herself to have them in order. The phone rang, it was Tony to say 'Goodnight'. Half an hour later Sarah curled up in her bed with her hot water bottle and a book about the history of lavender, she wanted to work out what the monks could have done at Hapstead, could it possibly have been a business then? So far nothing she had read could support that theory, but Sarah had a feeling that the monks were ahead of their times and that a business was a possibility. Making a note to investigate thoroughly the next morning, she put the books on the floor, put off the light and pulled her duvet up round her shoulders.

32

Sarah woke with the warm winter sun on her face and to the sound of ring doves cooing away on the roof. She wondered to herself what it was they said to each other as it was just 'coo, coo, coo' answered by 'coo, coo, coo'. She got out of bed wrapped herself up in her dressing gown and looked out of the window. The road leading up to the cottages was full of puddles glistening in the pale sunshine where they had been edged with rime from the previous night's frost, some starlings, disregarding the cold, were taking the opportunity for a bath and scattered drops of water everywhere as they shook their feathers. Jason came tearing out of the farmhouse and the birds indignantly flew off, Jason returned to the farm wagging his tail, looking as if he had done a good job.

'It's a wellie boot and warm scarf day today alright.' Sarah couldn't remember the last time wellie boots had been so important to her. A quick shower, it wasn't very warm in the bathroom, but a brisk rub down made her feel good.

After a breakfast of tea, toast and honey Sarah put her laptop in its bag, slung it over her shoulder and made her way down to Bridge Farm. Greeted not only by Jason but Troy as well Sarah realised it wasn't quite so early as she had thought, Alan and Jonnie must have arrived, so it must be gone nine o'clock.

'Hi Joanna! Can I come in?'

'Don't bother to ask Sarah, just come and go as you like, I always said that the farm should be called Piccadilly Circus, there's always been so much coming and going here. Leave your boots in the entrance, that's where we all leave ours.'

'I did think to bring a pair of flatties with me, so as not to damage your lovely floors.'

'They are lovely aren't they? They must have been laid when the manor was built. Alan is up in the operations room already, I expect that's where you want to go.'

'I'm working on the lavender theme this morning, Alan has a lot of information about it but I want to try and find out how important it was in the history of the farm. Hopefully Alan has some archaeological data from the dig he photographed, but I think it's going to be a trip into the Archive Office.'

'Good luck Sarah! I'm sure those monks knew what they were doing, and the Romans before them, I bet they started things going.'

Sarah went off to the operations room and found Alan sorting out some rather fragile papers.

'What have you there? They look really old and, therefore, interesting.'

'I found them in an envelope where Pa Harris had obviously put them, on the outside of the envelope in his handwriting was 'Hapstead Manor 1764'.'

'That ties in with Agnes Lafolley and the little grey book.'

'There isn't much on the papers, it just says that Cedric Morey purchased the manor in 1764 and, if you remember, there is the story by Pa called 'Lavender 1764', the one we think you should try and finish, that was mainly about Agnes Lafolley, so we must look at these papers really closely. Now to business, where shall we start Sarah, with the Romans, or later?'

'There was the story about the monks having a field of herbs, including lavender, that will make a good starting point even if lavender was grown by the Romans, we will make life very difficult for ourselves if we go back too far. I think we must keep to the documents we already have and there seems to be plenty of those. Having said that, can you think back to when the archaeologists were working on the site, did they come up with any seeds that have since been identified as to type and date? Perhaps we can ask them.'

'Seeds were certainly found, but at the time I didn't give it much thought, the idea of a lavender farm hadn't been talked about then, also I was very involved with the photographic side of things. I know who to contact though and I'll do that this afternoon.'

'Fine! That should answer some more questions. There are also these aerial photographs I've just been given which show definite outlines of ancient fields, I've brought them along to go in with the rest of the documents, I'm sure they are important, if nothing else we ought to check those outlines with todays layout and see if they overlap.'

'These are interesting Sarah, and you are right we must check with today's fields. As these photos were taken several years ago, it would be a good idea to have them done again so that we could superimpose the new layout on the old, giving us a true feeling of the past and present. Do you know a tame pilot that might do that for us? I don't have any contacts anymore.'

'No, but I reckon Tony does' laughed Sarah, 'he seems to

know everyone.'

Alan laughed 'Well I think it's the job he's doing, he meets up with some very influential people, he doesn't say much about his work but he is very knowledgeable and very skilled. He's working on a theatre at the moment and it is said that it has a ghost.'

'What about our ghost Alan, do you believe in it?'

'I don't really know Sarah, I do feel a chill in the air when I go through the farm from the front door to the kitchen, it faces south so shouldn't be too cold. Is it just the tiled floor, or is there someone there wanting us to know their secret?'

'Of course there is Alan, I'm sure it is Elizabeth' and Sarah smiled up at him, 'just waiting for us to put her rest.'

'Well let's get started on the history of Hapstead and see what else we need to know, then perhaps she will be put to rest.' Alan pointed to a mound of papers on the table. 'Those deal mainly with lavender, perhaps you could start there I'm going to try and decipher some of the letters.'

Sarah plugged her laptop in and started up a new file on *Hapstead* . Alan had left her some space on the table so she started by sorting the papers into date order, some of the dates were difficult to read but with a good table lamp and a magnifying glass Sarah found she could decipher most of them. The older documents were a different kettle of fish, most seemed to be in Latin and in a handwriting that was difficult to decipher, Sarah had never learnt Latin so she decided the only thing to do was to go and visit her friend Mary in the Archives Department.

'These are fascinating Sarah.' Mary put the papers down. 'What do you want me to do, run through them with you now, or translate them thoroughly and put it down on paper.'

'I really don't want to go to those lengths, I think a run

through would be useful, I've brought my laptop so that I can make notes, if I feel we need more information we'll come back to you and get a full translation where we think it is necessary. At the moment we want the basic outlines of the history, with particular reference to lavender.'

'That's fine Sarah, and very sensible because you could find yourself involved in a lot of work if you go into the history in depth.'

'That's right, at the moment it is sufficient for us to know when the various folk were there and did they grow lavender commercially.'

'Hopefully that will be easy to find out, for example we know from these documents about Francis de Courtney that the monks were evicted in 1539, and if you look at this paper dated 1530 the Abbot of Ponte Verdi lists the herbs and remedies the monks were selling.'

'According to Pa Harris Brother Erasmus had a herb garden and an Apothecary room, perhaps he started the herb farm.'

Mary scanned the documents that dealt with the monastery and found that Brother Erasmus was indeed the apothecary.

'How did Pa Harris find out all his facts?' asked Sarah, 'I don't think he knew Latin.'

'Perhaps he did what you have done and went to his local library, they will have a lot more information on Hapstead Manor than we have and as so many of his facts are right he must have had help with the translation. Incidentally his chronological history seems to be accurate, giving you a good basis to work from.'

'So, to get us back on track, herbs were being grown here in 1530, that is definitely authenticated by these documents.'

'Correct and I've jotted down one or two translations for

you.'

'Thanks. Now this lot of papers deals with Sir Francis Courtney.'

'These are fascinating, he had to pull down the monastery and build a manor house and farm, some of these papers actually say how many hours were worked by the builders and various craftsmen that completed what we now know as Hapstead Manor c.1542.'

'Where does Elizabeth Courtney fit in? Are there any papers dealing with her? Pa Harris wrote the lovely story about the angel carvings, he must have found the information somewhere.'

'You left the stories with me the other day and I have enjoyed reading them, incidentally, you could publish them as a small booklet for sale at the lavender farm, at the right price they should sell well. However, although Pa Harris got his basic facts right some of the stories must be figments of his imagination, and the angel carvings might be one of them.'

'They can't be Mary, after all they are there, I'm sure that Walter carved them for her, it would be wonderful if we could prove it.'

'Sarah, if he did it was all done quietly so that her father would not know about their relationship. If there were some letters of this period they might come up with the answer.'

'Alan is looking at letters this afternoon, perhaps there are some that were written by Elizabeth and Walter, wouldn't that be a find especially if they mention the carvings.'

'Don't get too carried away, they might be written by someone else. Now the next lot of papers are dated 1640 and deal with the building of the cottages, but no mention of lavender. Then we come to 1706 when Hapstead was sold to John Herbert, it says here that his occupation was 'farmer', albeit he was lord of the manor. This is the time of the Agricultural Revolution and prior to this date the land had been communal, split into strips and given each year to different serfs, but now the enclosure system had taken over and land was farmed by individuals, this encouraged the experimentation of new types of farming techniques and the use of fertilizers. John Herbert obviously took advantage of this and developed the farming side because there are bills here for the purchase of cattle and grains and also potatoes. Perhaps the aerial photographs will show where the various crops were grown.'

'I can't understand there not being a mention of lavender.'

'Wait a minute, look what I've found stuck to the back of this invoice, it looks like a plan of a garden.'

'However did I miss that' exclaimed Sarah, ' that is lovely. Look there are words in the middle of the beds 'Lav', now that must be lavender, 'Fen' - fennel, 'Rose' - rosemary, 'Dill', well that is obviously dill, Mary this must be a herb garden, or perhaps a knot garden even, they were very popular at that time.'

'You'll have to go to your local archivist and find out a little more about Hapstead, they might even have pictures. You want to talk to Bill Lawrence, I'll give him a ring now if you like and tell him what you are interested in.'

'Yes please, particularly the farming side from the 1700's. Could you ask him if it would be alright for me to go along tomorrow afternoon.'

While Mary made her phone call Sarah looked more closely at the plan, she didn't think the design of the box hedging was elaborate enough for a knot garden, and then looking at the other papers and the chronological history realised that Walter Herbert the farmer never married, did a man design this she wondered? As she looked at it she felt that there was a woman's hand in it. Perhaps he had his sister living with him or even a mistress. Another query for Bill Lawrence, hopefully he would have the answer. Sarah laughed at herself and decided not to get too carried away, she wanted the truth not supposition.

'Bill will be pleased to see you tomorrow, he has a lot of information about Hapstead, including some pictures, he says that they were given to the library in about 1940 by a Mr Harris, he thought they would be safer there during the war.'

'It sounds as though I will have an interesting day. Thanks for all your help Mary, I'll let you know how I get on.'

'Please do, so often we get enquiries, come up with some answers but never hear the final result. Do you want me to go over any of these documents with you again?'

'I think I'm OK thanks I made a lot of notes, I'll go back to the cottage and try and make some sense of them. See you soon.'

33

Jonnie was getting into her car when Sarah arrived back at the farm, she called out and went over to her.

'Where's Alan?'

'He's staying on for dinner, I think Joanna and Seth have adopted him. Actually he wants to go over some of the letters with Seth this evening, I just hope he doesn't try and do too much but, quite frankly, he seems to have a new lease of life since you came on the scene Sarah.'

'I think he realises how stubborn he was in not coming up to Bridge Farm, but now is enjoying the company and the work, he feels useful.'

'That goes for all of us, I must admit I'm looking forward to working in the lavender farm.'

'Hopefully I'll be working along with you soon, I'm still waiting to hear from my solicitor.'

'Joanna's got a registered letter for you, perhaps that will be from them.'

'I'll go and see, but I expect you are right, good news I hope.' Sarah dashed towards the farm, trying not to feel too excited.

'Joanna, I'm home.' Sarah realised what she had said – 'home', 'well it is now' she said to herself feeling a little bit emotional.

'I'm in the kitchen as usual, but only because it's warm, come on through there's a cup of tea waiting.'

'I hope there's a letter too, Jonnie said one had arrived.'

'It looks very official Sarah, I hope it's what you've been waiting for. There's something else waiting for you too, but look at the letter first and drink your tea.'

Sarah opened the envelope and it was indeed from the solicitor, probate had been granted, so the money and the house were now hers to do what she liked with. There was another letter asking her if the house was going on the market, because, if so, he had a buyer with 'cash in the hand' ready to purchase.

Sarah gulped down her tea, gave Joanna a hug. 'This is all I wanted, probate has been granted and, would you believe it, it looks as though he has a buyer for the house and it's not on the market yet. I must go and make some phone calls. Thanks for the tea, see you soon.'

'Wait a minute Sarah, what about this.' 'This' turned out to be a ginger kitten, Joanna picked it up and gave him to Sarah.

'He needs a home, so I thought that you might like him to keep you company, his name is 'Mephistopheles' …'

'You can't call a kitten 'Mephistopheles'.' Joanna laughed at Sarah's indignation.

'You can if you shorten it to 'Meffy'.

'I like that, and I like the kitten.' He had curled up in Sarah's arm and was gently purring.

'Later on he can run around the farmyard without causing any trouble, but you'll have to have him neutered otherwise we could be over populated with cats.'

'He's lovely Joanna, thanks, and I'll make sure he's neutered. Come on Meffy, let's go home before it starts snowing, heavy falls are forecast but apparently won't last long, so we are not in for a big freeze.'

'Come down after dinner Sarah, you don't have far to come so the snow shouldn't be a problem. Seth, Alan and of course Mollie, are looking more closely at some of the letters, you could be interested as the name Elizabeth comes up frequently.'

'I'll come down in time for one of your lovely coffees and fill you in with what I've been told this afternoon, and how Meffy is behaving. Come on Meffy we've got to find you a bed, I've got a cardboard box that I think will be just the right size and an old flanelette blanket that was Aunt Grace's, so you should be alright.' Jason and Troy arrived on the scene as she was crossing the courtyard, and Sarah introduced them to the kitten, the dogs gave him a polite sniff but Meffy lashed out with his tiny claws and spat. 'Now then' said Sarah, 'you have to be friends with these two, they won't hurt you' but Meffy had decided otherwise and his fur was standing up all along his back. 'Early days Meffy, but you must not fight.' Sarah decided she would have to introduce the kitten to the dogs at least once a day and hopefully they would become friends. The dogs galloped off and Sarah made her way up to the cottage, the temperature had dropped and there were slight flurries of snow, she wrapped Meffy in her scarf and ran the last few yards. She was surprised to see a light on, but saw Tony's van outside so realised he had come to fix up her computer for her.

'Hi there Tony, looks as though we're set for snow, but it's lovely and warm in here. Look what I've got.' and Sarah held the kitten out for Tony to see.

'He's nice, a present from Joanna?'

'Yes, now Meffy down you go and try not to wee everywhere.'

'I've got your desk installed together with your computer, printer and scanner, it looks good and doesn't take up as much room as I thought. I'm glad we decided to have the sockets at desk height, it'll make everything much easier for you and we were right to put it against that wall, you have the light coming in at the side during the day and I can fix an overhead light for you for the evenings. You can get on with the lavender story now.'

Sarah put her arms round Tony and gave him a hug. 'It's perfect, and it really doesn't look too out of place in a seventeenth century cottage does it? As for the lavender story, everything is beginning to slot into place. I'm getting a lot of help from the archivists, it really is getting quite exciting.'

'Good, at least you know the right people to ask and your cottage is lovely, your Aunt Grace's furniture is fitting in really well, that commode is something else, you know you'll have to declare it on your insurance policy, it is valued at least £1,000.'

'I know! Thank goodness the chairs weren't valued at that price. Talking about knowing the right people, do you know a pilot who could take some aerial photos of Bridge Farm?' Sarah explained to Tony that they already had some aerial photos but would like to have current ones for comparison.

'I know just the chap, Pete Hoskins he lives in the village at Millfield Cottage and runs a small company specialising in taking folk up on pleasure trips, I could go with him one day and take the photos for you.'

'I told Alan you would know someone' laughed Sarah. 'I'll take you up on your offer? In return would you like to stay to dinner Tony? It's lamb chops tonight, sautéed potatoes, peas and carrots, followed by a lemon torte, washed down with a good red, I'm celebrating, probate has been granted, so now we can get on with our plans. After dinner I'm going down for coffee at the farm, apparently Seth and Alan have discovered interesting facts whilst looking at the letters. I'm sure you would be welcome too.'

'Dinner sounds delicious, I'll be only too happy to help you celebrate, and coffee at Bridge Farm with an input from Alan and Seth will finish the evening off perfectly.' Tony pulled her towards the settee, put his arms round her and kissed her.

'This must be what Elizabeth and Walter did' giggled Sarah, 'just remember I'm not ready for a family yet.'

'Well no! But you did say you would give me an answer to my question, will you marry me Sarah?'

'It is not Wednesday yet so I haven't decided Tony. Do you think it would help if we lived together for a while before taking the plunge.'

'If that's what you'd like when can I move in?' and Tony cuddled her even more closely.

'Let me breathe Tony' and Sarah wriggled out of his arms, sat on the edge of the settee and looked at him.

'You can stay tonight because the weather is so atrocious, but if you are coming on a permanent basis I must have a little time to get sorted, you'll need some space, so what about Saturday?'

'I'll be up for breakfast in the morning, bacon and egg please and plenty of mushrooms. What will you say to having two people to make a fuss of you Meffy?' Meffy had climbed up on to the settee, settled himself on Tony's corduroys and was purring contentedly.

'He'll be in seventh heaven' laughed Sarah.

34

It was a bitterly cold evening as Sarah and Tony made their way down to the farm. A cold wind was blowing up from the estuary and snow was just heavy enough to cause problems. It had been very cold so it had begun to lie and they found it was getting quite slippery underfoot, the sky was black and the farmhouse lights could not be seen. Fortunately Tony had brought his large torch, but even that didn't really cope with the thick flakes as they funnelled towards them. Sarah shivered and stopped to tuck her briefcase with her laptop and documents inside her coat.

'You OK darling? The snow is getting rather thick, let's hope it'll be over soon.' Tony put his arm round her and steered her down the road.

Sarah clutched her briefcase to her.

'I'm fine, it's just that I've got this strange feeling of coming home again, I feel that I've been here in the snow before, it really is strange Tony, but now I'm wondering if I was here as Elizabeth or Joan, in fact my mind is going in circles and I'm beginning to think that perhaps I was Elizabeth, came back as Joan and now I'm here as me. Do you think that is possible Tony?'

'Who knows? If you really have these feelings, and I believe you do, perhaps the letters and other documents will sort your mind out, you might know what is going to be in one of the letters before it is read out to us!'

'Now that is stretching the point a bit far Tony, but you might be right although the information I got from Mary today only verified what we already know.'

'Perhaps Bill Lawrence will come up with some information tomorrow that will trigger a memory.'

'I do hope so, I do have a strong feeling that Elizabeth had her portrait painted, whether it was on canvas or as a miniature I don't know and there could possibly be something in the documents about a sitting, perhaps we've got to do some more searching amongst the furniture in the attic.'

'James is still up there, he might come across a hidden treasure, we have been pulling his leg about it but it would be wonderful if he did find something. Come on Sarah let's go and find the coffee, I'm frozen.'

Sarah and Tony opened the farm door, took off their coats, shook as much of the snow off as possible outside, hung them up, took off their boots and went into the kitchen.

'Hello Joanna' said Tony giving her a big hug and a kiss.

'Get off you stupid man. I've a jug of hot coffee in my hand.'

'Let me take it Joanna, I hope you don't mind me coming along, I'm dying to know what's in those letters and what Sarah found out today.'

'I'm glad you're here, it will save us repeating it all. Jonnie is here as well Sarah, she has got really interested in the history and Seth is hoping to involve her in the research. Has she told you anything about herself? She's been coming here for almost a year and we still do not know anything about her, I find that very strange.'

'I haven't seen much of her Joanna, but I do have the feeling that she has had a big problem to cope with, I'll try and find out tomorrow morning, we are going for a long walk down by the estuary and through the woods, snow permitting.'

'If you do break through I hope she doesn't swear you to secrecy,' said Joanna as she put the mugs on the tray. Tony put his arm round her and told her not to be so nosey.

'She's not being nosey, she's being interested Tony, that's what my Grandmother would have said.'

'I forgot about your Grandmother and her sayings, but hadn't we better get this coffee up to the operations room before it gets cold?'

'Too true. Grab that jug Tony, Sarah get the sugar and I'll find the shortbread.'

The atmosphere in the operations room was electric, Alan and Seth were passing documents to each other, Babs and Ken were looking at some plans, Jonnie was laughing as Mollie danced around saying 'Sarah won't believe this.'

'Sarah won't believe what?' said Sarah as they arrived with the coffee.

'Letters from Walter to Elizabeth written in 1620 onwards, and he talks about the wedding plans, so they must have intended to marry.'

Seth and Alan looked up 'You haven't heard it all folks. Some are apparently copies of letters written by Agnes Lafolley, a century later, to various merchants, including the chap Lacey who dealt with the blue glass bottles that Pa talks about in his Lavender story. She was obviously a very well organised lady. So we agree with Mollie, Pa must have read the letters, the boxes are clearly marked with the dates, but why didn't he tell anyone about them?'

'Perhaps he did' said Sarah, 'he took a lot of papers, and

some artefacts I believe, into the local archive department at the County Library round about 1940, he thought they would be safer there during the war, perhaps he told them about the letters. I'm going in to see Bill Lawrence, the County Archivist, tomorrow afternoon, goodness knows what sort of information he has stored away there, he says he has a lot of information about Hapstead Manor, so perhaps we ought to wait and see what he comes up with before organising ourselves here.'

'That makes sense' said Seth, 'but we do have papers to look at here, if we can understand most of them before anymore arrive it would surely help.'

Jonnie looked up from the letter she was reading 'I think I can help there, I have a degree in English Literature and have a smattering of Old English and can also decipher handwriting going back for several centuries. What if I transcribed them into today's English so that we can all read and understand them? I would be happy to do that.'

Joanna gave one of her laughs. 'What with you and your skills Jonnie and Sarah and her research skills I think we are off to a very good start, in addition there's Alan and his past knowledge of the farm together with Pa Harris's stories and careful sorting of documents into dates.'

'Why haven't you told us about this degree before Jonnie? We were going to ask you to look after shops, I think we are going to have to rethink your role in the lavender farm.' Babs looked quite upset.

'It's alright, really Babs, I don't mind what I do, I just want to be involved.'

'We'll involve you alright' said Ken, 'did you know cleaning the loos was going to be on your schedule as well?'

'Ken, stop teasing, of course it wasn't Jonnie, but we are having a brainstorming session here on Wednesday after dinner, I'm sure ideas will be floated then.'

Tony had poured out the coffee and passed one to Babs.

'You have got such a lot going for you, I almost envy you. She's right folks, ideas are what's needed for the Wednesday session, realistic ones of course.'

'What happened at your old place of work today Sarah?' asked Alan. 'You were going to see if your friend Mary could help with deciphering the papers.'

'Let me tell everyone my news first. Probate has been granted, so it's full steam ahead now.'

Alan grunted and murmured something that sounded like 'About time'.

Ken gave Sarah a hug and a kiss. 'Welcome to the lavender farm, here's hoping all goes better than we are expecting.' Babs blew Sarah a kiss and told her that she knew everything would be alright.

'It looks as though the house might be sold as well, the solicitor has a buyer already, if that is the case it will save a lot of work and time.'

'You can't get much luckier than that' said Tony, 'I just hope she knows what she's letting herself in for working with you two.'

'Get lost' said Babs, 'we have an excellent rapport, and it will continue. Let's get together soon Sarah and get our plans sorted.'

'I know you are all excited and I'm glad you can start planning' said Seth, 'but tonight is 'letter and document' night, and we have to think about the farm, or Hapstead Manor, as well as the lavender theme, but I'm sure they work in together. Let's concentrate on the history of the farm tonight. What goodies did your friend Mary come up with Sarah?'

'What she did was firstly to verify the facts as we already know them, she couldn't fault Pa Harris' *Chronological History*,

210

secondly she picked up on papers that mentioned herbs or lavender and put them on one side, we can have a good look at them later Babs. There seems to be a lack of information about the main farming, but she was sure Bill will have papers dealing with that aspect. I've made notes as to what's required and will put them in some semblance of order tomorrow. There seems to be a gap between 1600 and 1706 when Hapstead was sold to John Herbert but amongst the papers Mary was looking at was a plan of a garden dated 1712 it doesn't look as if it is on the same scale as the monks' herb garden but it will need checking. I'll get blown-up photocopies of it tomorrow. We then come to Agnes Lafolley, but we all know her story, so that takes us up to 1815 and I think that after that the fields were used for other purposes, but again, I expect Bill Lawrence has some of the answers, but it looks to me as though we'll find the history of Bridge Farm clearly defined, it just needs some fine honing and, of course, writing up. That will be quite a job, but I don't mind lending a hand …'

'I'd love to help too it can be worked in with transcribing the letters' said Jonnie, 'so count me in, and I can use a computer. Can I come with you tomorrow Sarah? It doesn't look as though we will be going for our walk.'

'An excellent idea, we can bounce ideas round while we are talking to Bill. We can work on our findings when we get back so that we can tell everyone about them on Wednesday evening. I've got some pizzas in the freezer that will keep the wolf from the door.'

'I love pizzas! Come down to me at about twelve and have lunch, we can have some sandwiches then go on to the County Library afterwards.'

'That sounds like a good arrangement, I don't think I've been out for so many meals in my life as I have since I came here, I am enjoying it. Let's get back to the letters, have you been able read them Seth?'

'Some of them are quite easy to read, but others need a lot of concentration, hopefully Jonnie can help there, but Mollie is being amazing at deciphering some of them and has made lots of notes, so come on Mollie fill us in, you so loved the *Angel Carvings* story you wanted to start there.'

'We only have the letters that were written by Walter, which Elizabeth kept really carefully, wrapping them in soft paper, tying them up with silk thread and putting them in a box with some lavender. The first letters were written in the early 1620's and they really tell of young love and are quite steamy in places, so obviously they were very much in love, but Elizabeth's father dictated that they could not marry, so, when she became pregnant Elizabeth had no alternative but to marry a husband she neither loved nor even cared for. It was in 1650, after John Hampton died that they began to write to each other again, and judging by the tone of Walter's letters Elizabeth must have told him how unhappy she had been to keep the fact that Bevis was his son from him, Elizabeth obviously tells him of the problems with Bevis because in one of the letters, I can't read it all, but he is talking about Elizabeth disowning Bevis and leaving the property to someone else. Apparently, to keep herself busy, she grew lavender in the kitchen garden because in one of the letters Walter says he will come and help her extend it, therefore it must have been an important part of her life, albeit not on such a grand scale as Agnes Lafolley's lavender. He also talks about wedding plans, so they must have intended to marry. Then there is a note in Elizabeth's handwriting to say that Walter died on 2nd April 1652, nothing else, just that bald statement.'

' 'Steamy love letters', perhaps you shouldn't be reading

them at your tender age,' said Tony as he gently pulled her pony-tail.

Mollie pulled away from him 'Just you listen to me Tony Briggs, I think you could learn a lot from reading Walter's letters, have a go and see if Sarah likes them!'

'Tony is doing alright on his own Mollie, thank you very much, I can assure you he needs no encouragement.' She realised what she had said and had the grace to blush, much to everyones amusement. 'Actually it is rather nice being teased, I'm beginning to get used to it.'

Alan looked up from the paper he was reading. 'This is amazing here's another reference to lavender, I find it very strange that Pa didn't make more of it in his stories, you know he told us a lot more than the ones we've found, but I think he concentrated on the furniture, I'm sure he wrote one up about the linen chest that's in the attic, we'll have to move the furniture and see if anything has got lodged underneath.'

'If there is anything there we should find it this week Alan, we are moving the furniture down to one of the barns, its been looked at by an expert and there's a lot of money tied up there, money we can use. It will be collected on Thursday and will end up in the auction rooms as soon as possible.' Everyone groaned and Tony put their feelings across by saying that all appreciated the reasons, but it would have been wonderful if the furniture could have stayed.

'Don't forget, a lot of the furniture in the farm is antique and does come from Hapstead Manor, the furniture in the dining room, our bedroom and Grace's room for example, so we aren't losing everything. Incidentally, the spinet goes up for auction next week, it should do really well.' Joanna looked round at the doleful faces. 'Cheer up everyone, I've decided to keep the linen box, I just love the feel of it and it will fit into our bedroom beautifully. Don't forget the money we raise will all be ploughed back into the farm, so everyone will benefit and it will help with developing the Education Centre, so the lavender farm will benefit too.'

James could be heard calling for Seth.

'I can't open this drawer Uncle Seth, can you come and help, something is jammed and I don't want to force it.'

'I'll go' said Tony, 'I often have to open locked or jammed drawers. I've got some tools in my coat pocket that should help.' A few minutes later he joined James in the attic.

'What have you found my lad, the treasure we've been teasing you about?'

James was standing by a walnut desk holding on to a small drawer just above the kneehole.

'Perhaps it is, I pressed this lever underneath and the drawer opened, I told you there would be a secret drawer.'

'That's obviously why the so-called 'experts' didn't find it then. What have you found James?'

'There's a lot of screwed up paper in here, it could just be rubbish, but I think there's a box causing the jam and it looks as though it's covered in velvet.'

James had managed to get the drawer open a few inches and when Tony shone his torch in he too could see a small box.

'This looks interesting James, but carefully does it. I'm going to slide this flat blade in and see if I can get it over the box, then I'll press down and with you gently pulling on the drawer we should manage it.'

Breathing deeply Tony worked away, removing the blade to wrap it in his handkerchief so that it wouldn't do any damage.

'Are you ready to pull James? I think it's moving. Yes, now can you pull, carefully in case I haven't cleared it all.'

James was beside himself with excitement and pulled as gently as he could, the drawer gradually slid open and inside was a small velvet box and several papers that had caused the problem by getting rucked up under it.

James could hardly believe his eyes, although he had been searching for 'treasure' he hadn't really thought it existed.

'Do we open it now, or wait for the others?'

'Let's take it down to the operations room and surprise everyone, mind you James, it could be empty.'

'No way Tony, it must have something in it.'

The operations room was still buzzing with the information that was being found, but Tony called out from the door for them all to gather round and see what, if anything, was in the box.

'I'd like Joanna to open it' said James.

'I'd love to' and Joanna took the blue velvet case and placed it gently on the table. The case was a bit dusty, but otherwise seemed to be in good repair, very carefully she raised the clasp and opened the box, inside was an exquisite miniature.

'Charles Culpin' gasped Sarah, everyone looked at her.

'What does he have to do with this?'

'Charles Culpin was the artist, I can 'see' him quite clearly, a tall man with greying hair and a very large nose. He painted this miniature of Elizabeth using a portrait that had been painted earlier. Father gave it to my mother and she kept it in a small walnut desk that she used everyday.'

Everyone looked in astonishment at Sarah as she talked about her 'mother and father'. She suddenly realised what she had said and put her hand to her mouth.

'Tony, can this be the proof I've been wanting?'

'All I can say is how did you know it was Charles Culpin that did the painting and how do you know it is Elizabeth if you hadn't been there? These papers that were under the box clearly state that the artist was indeed Charles Culpin and at the request of Sir William Courtney he made a miniature of his daughter Elizabeth copied from the original oil that was painted by his brother Edward Culpin. It says here '… a gift for my dear wife on our anniversary …'. That bears out what you've just said Sarah, and the desk is definitely a ladies desk and it is walnut. It would be wonderful if we could find the original painting, do you by any chance remember how big it was? Do you remember where it was hung?'

'I'm afraid I don't, but I remember the artist, he was tall, like his brother, but his hair was light brown and he had a scar down one side of his face that quite fascinated me, or rather Elizabeth. I am beginning to get confused everything is getting quite eerie, how is it I can remember all these details.'

'Because you were here in another life' said Mollie, 'do you remember hearing the spinet? Have you heard it recently?'

'I have never heard it and haven't been through the front door recently, but when I did I know I found the hallway chilly.'

'Don't forget, the spinet has gone for auction so you may not hear it again' said Joanna.

Sarah looked at her and smiled 'I think we would all have loved it if you could have kept the spinet, but with the spinet sold perhaps Elizabeth will calm down and go to rest.'

'It needs the spinet gone and a happy couple living in the cottage' said the irrepressible Mollie, 'then Elizabeth will stop chilling the hallway. The only thing Auntie Joanna, a ghost might have brought in more customers for your B and B.'

'I think if we get the stories published together with details of the spinet, miniature and whatever else comes up we will have a very interesting history and that should bring in people.

We just have to make the most of it, as Babs does with the lavender aspect.'

'We've obviously got to continue working together' said Babs, 'the stories are so interlinked going separate ways would spoil everything.'

'Who would have thought a few months ago that we would all be so involved' and Alan looked at Sarah, 'If you hadn't found the photograph ...'

'No. I don't go along with that, Seth was going to investigate the boxes soon anyway.'

Seth looked up and smiled. 'That would have been sometime in the future Sarah, it was your interest in the photographs that spurred us on and this is the right time, we badly need the injection of money that will come from the sale of the furniture and by all accounts it should be quite a substantial sum.'

'The next few weeks will be very interesting' and Jonnie put her arms round Alan's shoulders, 'come on Alan it's time for my bed, I expect you are feeling weary too, let's brave the snow.'

'As a matter of fact I'm not tired, I think my adrenalin has taken over, but you are right, we must go, I hope your car can make it home.'

'I looked out just now and it didn't seem too bad, see you at lunch time tomorrow Sarah.'

'Come on Tony we must be off too, there's been enough excitement for one evening.' Sarah shut her laptop, picked up her papers and smiled at everyone. 'It's been a wonderful evening, hopefully we'll have more to tell you after we've seen Bill tomorrow.'

'Goodnight! And go carefully' said Joanna, 'those cobbles can get very slippery when wet.'

35

The lavender fields were looking very sad as Sarah walked down the track towards the bridge. The snow was melting fast, leaving puddles of grey water everywhere, the lavender plants were holding their heads up high but they still looked bedraggled, the hedges had smatterings of snow on them that glistened in the early morning sun, but as Sarah watched the snow slid off the branches with a plop on to the sodden ground. The water flowing under the bridge looked grey and cold reflecting the colour of the sky. Some of the stones shone where they were occasionally touched by the sun as it came out from behind the grey clouds. The ducks had disappeared, obviously taking cover in the undergrowth to keep warm.

Sarah shivered and walked down the road to find the path to the estuary. One look and she decided to wait for everything to dry up as the path looked decidedly lethal where it was so muddy. She had hoped to walk down to the estuary to look for the old jetty the archaeologists had found. The feeling that she had been in a boat on the estuary sometime in the past still lingered, and she wanted to see if the jetty brought back any memories. Joan had told Agnes about her fishing trips with her brother, could it be that she, Sarah, had been Joan as well as Elizabeth, but somehow that did not seem to be the answer, had Elizabeth used the boats? Sarah shivered, but for a different reason this time, she was almost becoming afraid of her thoughts, should she go back and touch the past or leave it to rest, she decided that she had gone too far with her thoughts to leave it and that she had to find out answers for herself. She shivered again, looked at the sky and decided to return to the cottage, collect the papers and sort through the questions she wanted to ask Bill Lawrence.

Tony had gone by the time she got back, he was off to visit a builder friend to see if his firm was interested in helping with the conversion work on the outbuildings at the farm. As the planning had been done sometime earlier and planning permission had been granted, everything should be straight forward, it was now a question of when the work would start. Hopefully there would be no problems financially, Joanna and Babs had made it quite clear to him that everything was ready to go forward, Babs and Ken had had the injection of money from Sarah and Joanna was expecting a good price for the spinet and the rest of the furniture. Tony wanted to be able to tell the meeting on Wednesday when the work would begin.

Meffy greeted Sarah with some plaintive mews. 'Sorry Meff. You've got to see the vet before you can go out to play. Hopefully she will see to you next week, something for you to look forward to.' She picked him up and sat down at her desk with him purring away on her lap.

Sarah went through the papers she had brought up from the farm, which, thanks to Alan and Mollie were in good order. She was again aware that there was a lot of information missing about Hapstead Manor and as Seth wanted to write up the history of the farm it was essential to fill in the gaps, so that went at the top of her list as a main heading with specific items under it, particularly the farming and lavender. What happened between 1600 and 1706? Did Bevis Hampton neglect the farm? Did John Herbert re-establish it as a good working farm? Sarah knew that Bill Lawrence had a lot of information, so she assumed that most of it had come from Farmer Harris at the beginning of the 1939 War when he took some papers and artefacts into the County Library for safe keeping. Sarah was getting a tingling in her fingers, she felt that there was a lot of information available.

Jonnie was waiting at her front gate for Sarah.

'It's alright Sarah, you're not late, I just wanted to see if my snowdrops were beginning to show through they have just come into bud, such a lovely sight at this time of the year.'

'My mother always picked the first ones and put them in a small glass vase that was engraved with my Father's regimental crest. So I get very nostalgic when I see the first snowdrops. I've still got the little vase, perhaps I could pick a few to take back to the cottage with me.'

'Of course you can, hope they'll bring back happy memories.'

'Oh they will! Now what about those sandwiches.'

'They're all ready, and I've got some soup to heat up, it's that sort of day. Come in and take your coat off, sling it over that chair and come into the kitchen the Aga keeps it nice and warm.'

'What made you settle here Jonnie? Job prospects must be pretty low.'

'Indeed they are, however I was hoping that a firm would take me on with a computer link so that I could work from home, but with the developments at Bridge Farm it looks as though everything has worked out nicely. Why did I settle here? Three years ago I had a horrendous time, first of all my husband walked out on me, not for another woman but just because he was 'bored'. Can you imagine how I felt, it had never occurred to me that I was boring. I had a good job with a firm of solicitors dealing mainly with family problems, so when I was confronted with one of my own I was shocked. Just as I was beginning to get over it my parents were involved in a motorway crash and both died from their injuries. Mother had been my mainstay after Geoffrey left me and my immediate reaction was 'what to do now?' My parents were well off so I was left with a substantial sum of money and decided to find somewhere to live and drop out of the rat race for a while, literally to recharge my batteries. When I discovered Shingle Cottage it fitted the bill perfectly. I love it here, there's the shore for a good walk, there is always something happening out at sea, I have Alan to talk to and, of course, the folks at Bridge Farm. Last summer I worked up there helping Joanna with her B and B's and thoroughly enjoyed it, and now you have arrived on the scene and Bridge Farm has really become alive.'

'But what about your qualifications Jonnie, don't you want to use them? Babs was quite shocked when she knew you had degrees, they were going to ask you to manage the lavender farm shop.'

'I know they were, and I would like to use my qualifications but at the moment I am content and that means more to me than a career.'

'In a way we are both at the same crossroad, I decided to pack in my career and invest in the lavender farm, this time next year I hope to be able to say the same as you, that I am content. There will be a lot of work to do at Bridge Farm and I am sure we can both fit in, the Educational Centre, for example, will need a manager, is that up your street?'

Jonnie looked at Sarah and laughed, 'I've been thinking along the same lines and have actually put some ideas down on paper for the meeting, I do feel that it is one area that Joanna and Seth will need help with. Now let's eat, otherwise we will never get to see Bill Lawrence today.'

36

Bill Lawrence was not at all the sort of person Sarah had expected to meet, he was in his early thirties, dressed in jeans, a bright shirt and a black body warmer, his hair was curly and collar length and looked as though it had just been shampooed, he was not the sixty year old Sarah had imagined.

'You must be Sarah' said Bill holding out his hand.

'Thank you so much for taking the time to see us, this is Jonnie Sutton, she helps Joanna with the Bed and Breakfasts at the farm and has become part of the extended family. Along with the rest of us she has got herself involved with the history of Hapstead, so I thought it would be a good idea for her to come along. She has a degree in English Literature, has a 'smattering' of Old English, can decipher handwriting going back for several centuries and is familiar with Latin, and that's for starters.'

'I am so pleased to meet you Jonnie, my Old English leaves a lot to be desired so I might well call on you for some help. As for Hapstead Manor, I have been doing some research on it because we have just been given some more relevant documents so am delighted that you've come along.'

'Then let's hope that your work and the work that is being done at Bridge Farm will complete the history of Hapstead. Until now Joanna and Seth have been very busy keeping the farm going and haven't really had the time to delve into the history, but suddenly there are six of us, plus the twins all willing to lend a hand so things have started to happen. We are particularly interested in any references to lavender because Babs and Ken Ashworth and myself are starting a lavender farm there. Babs originally thought that it was only the Romans that grew some lavender, but some of the documents Seth has found tell us otherwise, as these are mainly in letter format we would like some verification if at all possible.'

'Some of the documents I have do talk about lavender and herbs and as there were quite a few I have put them all on the far table in date order. It will be interesting to see what you make of them, hopefully they will endorse the letters.'

'Let's hope so, positive thinking is what is needed.'

'What do Seth and Joanna intend doing with the history?'

'Well, at the moment they are considering publishing it in pamphlet form to sell in the Lavender Farm.'

'Hmmn! I think it warrants more than that, this really is important local history.'

'I do agree with you, but at the same time who will buy an expensive book about Hapstead when they can buy a nicely produced pamphlet telling them all they want to know? Perhaps there is room for both, but we are already considering publishing Farmer Harris' stories in pamphlet form and thought that the history would be a spinoff.'

'You could be right Sarah, I didn't know about the stories, can you fill me in please.'

Sarah told him about the black folder and the stories, how

the spinet and other furniture was found in the attic and how the miniature was discovered. She asked him if by any chance there had been a portrait with the artefacts Farmer Harris had brought in.

'As a matter of fact there is, quite a small one, the sitter is really lovely, it is amongst the things I want to show you.' Bill took them through to a large workroom, along one side several tables had been set out and covered with sheeting, papers and pictures were laid out in neat rows and on the far table were some artifacts including a portrait. Sarah gasped when she saw it, it was one of Elizabeth and the artist had signed it 'Edward Culpin', bearing out what she had said when she saw the miniature.

'You'll have to know sooner or later Bill, but strange though it may seem I feel I have lived at Hapstead Manor before, this portrait is of Elizabeth Courtney who lived there in the early sixteen hundreds. The miniature that was found was painted by this artist's brother, Charles Culpin and I seem to be able to remember that quite clearly, but I can't remember everything about Elizabeth's life so do wonder what is going on in my mind.'

'This is all very fascinating Sarah, and don't worry about it, many people have a deep seated recollection brought to the surface when confronted with a dress, an item of jewelry or a book. And they come up with facts that they could have only known if they had been there. I admit it is uncanny, but I am sure there is a lot to be said for déjà vu.'

'I wonder why Farmer Harris only brought certain things down to the Archive Department Bill, he left a lot of papers at Bridge Farm, albeit they were the more personal ones like the letters and the stories.'

'We will never know that, perhaps he brought as much he could carry, it could be as simple as that.'

'I wonder why he didn't pay a second visit?'

'We closed for a few months about that time, remember it was wartime and apparently the documents we were holding suddenly had to go somewhere else for safe keeping, it could be he just timed it wrong.'

'That sounds reasonable, but we will never know. Are these documents on loan or were they given to you?'.

'They were on loan, given to us for safe keeping during the war, we have only just looked at them because, as I said, only recently we have had some documents given to us by another Record's Office, how they had them we do not know, but we do want to get it all sorted and into proper order.'

'Those must be the one's Mary was telling me about, everything seems to be getting quite complicated.'

'Let's forget where things came from and just deal with the documents otherwise we won't get anywhere, this is something that happens quite often and we find we just have to stop questioning and sort things out.'

'That's exactly what Seth is doing at Bridge Farm Sarah, so everything should knit together.'

'You are quite right Jonnie, and he is a stickler for order. Bill, I reckon you'll be having a visit from Seth when we tell him all about these documents. Thinking about it, it does seem as though the personal documents were left at Bridge Farm and the main documents regarding purchases and management were left with you. Just looking here I can see reference to work being carried out in 1654, we have nothing like that at the farm. When the two lots of documents get put together it should make very interesting reading.'

'I think we all go along with that and I will certainly be asking Seth if we can meet up, it seems to me that the documents should all be in the same place, perhaps I can persuade Seth to deposit his papers with us for classification and cataloguing, it would make a wonderful local archive and would be easier to use. At present the main gap is the one you are worried about Sarah.'

'You mean from the 1680's until 1706?'

'Exactly, I know it wasn't very long after the Plague but this part of the country was not hit too badly, in fact I have documentation that relates to herbs being produced to sell in London, Hapstead wasn't specifically mentioned, but I will double check, I could have missed something. Elizabeth Hampton could have cashed in on that, she appears to have been quite an astute lady.'

'You know Bill you could have hit the nail on the head, there was obviously money coming into Hapstead, but I wonder how they got herbs into London and money out.' Sarah looked at Jonnie, 'any ideas?'

'Yes, I have, by water down the estuary. We know there was a small jetty by the bridge at Hapstead Manor, they could have used that, taken the produce to London, transferred it to another boat when they were in the Thames, and payment would have been made at the same time. I have a notion that this was legitimate practice during the Plague.'

'That really is good thinking,' and Bill smiled at her 'come and work for me please if you can come up with solutions like that.'

Jonnie listened to Bill as he came up with one or two ways in which she could help him.

'What you are suggesting does not sound like fulltime employment and at present my life is centered around Bridge Farm, there are so many interesting opportunities opening up there, but there is no reason why I can't help on occasions, especially if you need papers deciphered, I'm sure I could find a few hours during the course of a week.'

'Fair enough' said Bill, 'but there was no harm in trying, a few hours if and when will be much appreciated. Perhaps we could have dinner sometime and discuss it?'

'I would like that, here's my phone number' said Jonnie scribbling it down on one of the leaflets lying around. 'Perhaps Sarah and Tony could join us, and we could really get to know each other.'

'Not a good idea if you are going to discuss work' laughed Sarah, 'but another time you could all come up to my cottage for a Cottage Pie.'

'Done' said Bill, 'Cottage Pie it is and I would like to look at your cottage I've been told it has been beautifully restored.'

'It certainly has, Tony Briggs was responsible and I'm thrilled to bits with it, there is a wonderful fireplace which features in one of Farmer Harris's stories, I'll tell you the story when you come for dinner. Ring you next week to make a date.'

'Look at this Sarah.' Jonnie pointed to a rather dilapidated accounts book, 'I think this records Elizabeth Hampton's financial affairs, so must include details of her herb trading, could we borrow this Bill, we will be careful with it, but I think it holds the answers to several of our questions?'

'Yes, you can borrow it. I'll try and see Seth during the week so I could pick it up then.'

Jonnie continued to turn the pages. 'Sarah, there are pages of transactions in here that tie up with the plague years, we must try and track down any references to herbs and lavender at Hapstead Manor during that period. Look, the writing changes in 1688 and after that the entries are few and far between.'

'That's the period when Bevis was the landowner, but you say there aren't many entries.'

'Hardly any, some relate to wages and others to purchases of beer and wine he must have spent most of his inheritance living the good life.'

'Here is another accounts book Jonnie' and Bill handed her one that was in better condition. 'I think you'll find this carries on after Bevis and is quite a good record of John Herbert's land management. It came in the batch we have just received and I have had a good look at it, borrow that as well if you like.'

'Thanks Bill.' Jonnie opened the book and was immediately struck at the neat writing, obviously John Hampton cared about what he was doing. She carefully turned the pages and called out to Sarah to come and have a look.

'He is talking about building cattle sheds here, then two pages later he has recorded buying some 'breeding stock'. A bit before his time I would have thought.'

Bill looked up. 'Actually farmers at this time were beginning to look at selective farming, this is the period of the so-called Agricultural Revolution when the smaller farms were claimed by the wealthy landowners so that more crops could be grown and, as in this case, some of the fields used for more livestock. I have checked the land records and it looks as though John Herbert did just that, increasing the Hapstead estate, albeit just before he died in 1750.'

'What happened to the farmers?' asked Jonnie.

'Surprisingly enough most of them moved to the cities which caused a population explosion within the cities. To supply their needs the farmers had to become more efficient, this resulted in things like the rotation of crops which meant that no field would be left barren, hence the use of the turnip which led to more livestock being produced as they could be fed turnips. This in turn led to selective breeding which it seems fascinated John Herbert.'

'John Herbert was obviously keen on new developments. So he must have become quite wealthy. Let's have a look at the last accounts.' Jonnie flipped the pages and was not surprised to see that each year there was a substantial increase in the Manor's profits.

'John Herbert died in 1750 leaving a very prosperous business to his two sons Walter and Thomas, who efficiently worked the estate until Thomas died in 1764 and it was sold to Cedric Morey, he died in1788 leaving the estate to his daughter Agnes.'

'One of Farmer Harris' stories dated 1764 is about Agnes Morey, later to be Agnes Lafolley, in which it sounds as if she was building up a thriving business dealing in lavender and herbs, hopefully we can find some documentation that will verify this, it will be good publicity for the lavender farm. It also talks about the notebook covered in grey silk being the one she used for her special recipes. If we could find some provenance for that it would be wonderful as we are considering using the name *Agnes Lafolley* for our products.'

'Well Sarah, there are loads of papers here dealing with lavender and herbs, so you can either take them back to Bridge Farm or look at them here, but I think most of your questions will be answered.'

'I would like to look at them here first please Bill, you have more room than Seth has at Bridge Farm, then perhaps I could copy documents that are really relevant to what we are doing, or proposing to do, during the next year.'

'As long as you don't take too long that will be fine.' Bill looked at his watch and made it clear to Sarah and Jonnie that he had other things to do.

Sarah smiled at him. 'We must go now, but thanks for

all your help, do contact Seth he really does have a lot of information. We'll take the accounts books and I'll come back tomorrow morning to look over the lavender documents. You don't need to worry about me taking a long time, we want the information now and ready for print as soon as possible. Thanks once again for all your help and here's to a wonderful history being put together.'

37

'Let me pick up my car Sarah, then I can get home easily after our pizza.'

'That's fine, they've re-graveled the road up to the cottages so do drive carefully. That was an interesting afternoon, and very helpful, I think we have an ally in Bill Lawrence, the fact that he had just received those papers from another office certainly helped, and, of course, now that you are on board …'

'Sarah, that's enough. We have only just met, I do like him, but at the moment on a working basis only, a plus factor is that his mind seems to go along the same lines as mine.'

'Let's hope they aren't parallel and that they might converge.' Sarah laughed at Jonnie's face. 'Let's face it, they probably will, it looks as though we might be seeing quite a lot of him whilst the history is being sorted out, and your expertise will be needed, so you could be meeting up quite a lot and, what's more, if you take on the responsibility of running the Educational Centre you will surely need to call on him a lot.'

'We don't know who is going to be responsible for what at

the moment Sarah, I do like the idea of running an Educational Centre but I can only put forward the ideas that I have and it is for Seth, Joanna, Babs and Ken to decide what they want and what they can afford at the present.'

'I would think it could be worked in with the shop to begin with, I can't imagine dozens of schools or organizations visiting at the start, we will have to build it up gradually and advertise ourselves really widely, but if we don't start it won't develop.'

'That's one of the comments I have in my notes for Wednesday and I'm sure everyone else will have advertising high on their list of priorities. I'm looking forward to our brain-storming session, it should be most constructive.'

'I agree, everyone, even the twins, seems to be excited by it.' Sarah pulled up outside Jonnie's cottage. 'Look there's Alan in his garden, do tell him about our meeting with Bill. See you later Jonnie, just come up when you are ready.' Sarah waved to Alan and drove off wincing at the noise of the gravel on her car, hoping it wasn't taking too much paint off. Arriving at the cottage Sarah could see Meffy sitting on her desk, when he saw the car he stood up and waved his tail in greeting. Sarah dashed inside and scooped him up

'Dinner time Meff,' Sarah looked at the tins, 'do you want chicken or rabbit today? What about chicken, you had rabbit yesterday?' Meffy mewed seemingly in agreement which made Sarah chuckle. Soon Meffy was tucking into his chicken and thoroughly enjoying it if the little purrs were anything to go by.

Sarah switched on her computer and poured herself a sherry, she felt she had earned it. A quick check of the freezer reassured her all was in place for the pizza dinner. She took some crème brulees from the fridge, quickly sugared and grilled them, put flowery table mats with serviettes to match on the kitchen table, brought out her new wine glasses, opened a bottle of red wine, put a bottle of water in the fridge and, most important of all, put out some nuts and nibbles to munch while the pizzas were cooking.

'I hope Jonnie likes pepperoni Meffy' said Sarah as she sat down at her desk with a lapful of cat. She looked at her e-mails, there were three waiting for her, two she immediately deleted as they were from firms touting for business. The third was from Tony saying that his friend Pete Hoskins would take him up for a flight on Sunday and that there was room for Sarah if she would like to go. The e-mail was quickly answered with 'Yes please!' Sarah was beside herself, she had wanted to go up as soon as aerial photographs had been mentioned, but thought the cost would be prohibitive. Pete obviously had two spare seats on his flight and hopefully was doing them a favour.

'Oh! Meffy, life is getting very exciting.' The poor cat got squeezed really hard, but he seemed to enjoy it. The phone rang, it was Babs to see how Sarah and Jonnie had got on. Sarah filled her in very quickly and told her that she and Jonnie were going to try and get all the information sorted for Wednesday, she also told her about the flight and Babs was green with envy.

'Just bring back some really good photos Sarah.'

'There might not be a lot difference from the last ones and they won't exactly have 'lavender' written on them.'

'I know that Sarah, but it would be nice to know where the outlines of past fields are, it might not help us in our planning, but it could be interesting. Ken and I went down to the church today and the vicar was there, we told him what we were doing and he said that he has some Hapstead documents, so we are paying him a visit tomorrow morning to see what he has and how far back they go.'

'Bill Lawrence was saying today that the best thing we can do is to put all the documents in one place to make it easier for historians in the future. Perhaps the vicar will contribute his documents too.'

'We can only ask, but it might be that they are ecclesiastical ones and can't be removed from the church.'

'That's a point. Perhaps we can copy them, that's worth thinking about. Babs, I must go, Jonnie is coming in a moment for a meal and I must light the fire. See you tomorrow.'

Sarah knelt down on the hearth rug and looked at the lovely surround and wondered just how many fires had been lit in the grate, had Elizabeth ever lit a fire for Walter? She put a firelighter in place, heaped it up with coal and lit it.

'Soon have a nice fire going for you Meffy' but he had already settled himself in anticipation. Sarah turned off her computer, drew the curtains and brought in the nuts and nibbles together with the bottle of sherry and some glasses. She was just in time as Jonnie pulled up outside with a loud blast of her horn that started Jason barking and the geese honking.

'You won't be very popular if you sound that horn Jonnie, this is a farm and the animals need peace and quiet.'

'Oh dear! It was an involuntary action, I must stop doing it, I got into the habit when I lived in town, but it is unnecessary here. I hope Joanna and Seth won't be upset. I'm just so excited about all the info we have to share with the others that I feel I'm up on a high. Here are your snowdrops Sarah. Shall I put these accounts books on the table?'

'That's fine Jonnie, the table is very user friendly. Thanks for the snowdrops, on my way home I was thinking that I must look in my garden and in the lavender field, according to Babs there were a lot of Spring flowers round the edges last year, I'm sure she included snowdrops and as they do suddenly appear I could have missed them. Sit yourself down and have a sherry and some nibbles, the pizzas can go on in five minutes.'

'A sherry will be very welcome, I haven't had one for months,' Jonnie filled her glass and took a sip, 'this is nice Sarah, I don't like it too sweet.'

'Tony brought it the other day, he thought we'd like it.'

'Lucky you, when do you see him next?'

'Wednesday evening, he is working up country at the moment and won't be back until then. He's restoring a theatre and is absolutely absorbed in it, he has promised to take me up there to have a look at it, so I'm looking forward to that.'

'It sounds a very exciting project, you must tell me all about it when you come back.'

'I certainly will. Tony now has a reputation for doing excellent restoration work on theatres, he does a lot of research and it really pays off.'

'Well back to today Sarah, although we have been living in the past. These nuts are good,' and Jonnie helped herself to a few more. 'The fire is lovely too and the surround is amazing, I've never looked at it properly before, the faces are beautiful and they do look like angels, I must look at the one at the farm and see if I can spot the differences.'

'They are quite subtle, but they are there and I really can imagine Walter and Elizabeth stroking and even kissing them.'

'Here we go touching the past again. Let's hope we can lay the ghosts for you Sarah, perhaps sorting through these documents will help.'

'I'm not worried by it, I find it fascinating that I seem to know things that happened in the past, the one place I really want to go to is the little harbour, I have this strange feeling about going out in a boat, but the paths are too wet at the moment. This morning when you talked about Elizabeth taking lavender and herbs to London by boat I really did have goose pimples, so perhaps we can go there together when everything dries up and see if anything clicks.'

'I'd like that' said Jonnie, 'Alan has talked about the finds that the archaeologists made whilst excavating, I think he said it goes back to Roman times.'

'Well thankfully my 'feelings' don't go back to Roman times Jonnie, but I am, of course, interested. I'll go and put the pizzas on.' Sarah got up, grabbed a handful of peanuts and went to the kitchen.

'Hope you like pepperoni,' she shouted from the kitchen.

'My favourite! How did you know?'

'Actually Jonnie it happens to be my favourite too. They'll soon be ready.'

Sarah came back and sat on the settee, sipped her sherry and told Jonnie about the proposed trip with Pete Hoskins.

'I'm very excited, let's pray for a nice day. I must look out old aerial photographs so that we can compare them, perhaps you could ask Alan if he has any more. Babs thinks it would be great if we could superimpose transparencies over each other, then changes would be really obvious. I don't think there will be many, but, I do agree, it would be nice to know and it would make an interesting educational tool.'

'Thinking about it, do you know someone who is good with computers? What you are talking about can now be computerised, which would make it really easy for schoolchildren and visitors, including pensioners, to access and see the changes or similarities, it's called 'hand-on experience' and goes down well when advertising a visitor's centre.'

'It's obviously not only me that has the ideas, but we need someone to develop them. Do you think Bill Lawrence could help there?'

'That's a possibility, but I think that's a priority for our Wednesday night discussions, do we want to involve more people? We'll have to put it to the vote.' Jonnie laughed 'I really do think this is all going to be fun, but this evening we really ought to check through the account books that Bill lent us to see if there is any reference to Elizabeth growing and selling lavender during the Plague, and get our thoughts ready for Wednesday night.'

'The pizzas will be ready in a minute so we can do that when we've eaten, I have a feeling that they will tell us a lot.' The timer went in the kitchen. 'Come on Jonnie, the pizzas are ready.'

38

'I'll wash up later' said Sarah as she picked up the older of the two account's books.

'This look interesting, whose are we looking at?'

'Elizabeth Hampton's, 1635 until 1688, the Plague years were 1665 until 1667, so they fall within those dates. Now! Did she trade in herbs?' Jonnie looked down the columns. 'I think she did, look Sarah 1665, these must be entries for lavender, rosemary and thyme.' She pointed to the word 'lav' occurring several times, together with 'ros' and 'thy'. 'I think that even today those are the abbreviations that would be used, so it looks as though Elizabeth did run a business in herbs.'

'It certainly does. There must have been a market for them during the Plague, I've read that the people who stayed in London would wear a bunch of lavender on each wrist as protection against the disease. In addition those who dealt with the corpses, and indeed the grave-robbers, would wash in a solution called *Four Thieves Vinegar* which contained lavender, apparently they rarely contracted the disease. Also rosemary was spread on floors to stop people carrying the disease in from the street. Therefore it could be that Elizabeth cashed in on this and sold her harvest of herbs to merchants in London who then sold them on, but how did she get them there? She wouldn't have been allowed to travel by road so let's have a look and see if there are any entries for use of a boat as you suggested Jonnie.'

They bent over the book, but the writing was so small it was almost indecipherable.

'Can you make this entry out Sarah? I think the name is 'Harwood."

"Harwood'? Why does that strike a chord?'

'Isn't there a Harwood in the Agnes Lafolley story?'

Sarah did a double take. 'You're right, that was the name of Agnes Lafolley's general help and she had a brother John who had fishing boats. I expect the family goes back to the sixteen hundreds and they could have been working with boats then, if so they could have taken Elizabeth and her herbs to London.'

'That must be right Sarah, there are several entries for Harwood, I think the families must have worked together on a slightly risqué business, I wonder who else was involved? Perhaps Elizabeth had local people making up lavender wrist-bands for the residents of London.'

'A cottage industry? I have been thinking along the same lines for our lavender farm, local ladies making lavender sachets for example, perhaps Mrs Knight can help there, but that's for another day. I wonder if Elizabeth is telling me something?'

'Sarah Bruce, you are incorrigible, why should Elizabeth be telling you something that is a perfectly sensible solution to a present day problem?'

'I don't know, it just seems that so many aspects of what we are undertaking at the moment have parallels with the 1600's. Let's look at the Harwood entries in the account's book, when do they start?'

'They start in May 1665 with just lavender.'

'The Plague broke out in London in the Spring of 1665, so that tallies with the entries here. I wonder if the Vicar has the answer, he must have details of births, marriages and deaths, so he would know if the Harwoods were boatmen, it would be on the certificates. I'll talk about this to Babs before she goes to see him.'

'That's an excellent idea, the dates must be there. Do you feel that things are beginning to knit together?'

'It certainly looks like that Jonnie, and perhaps I can find out more tomorrow when I look through the papers that Bill Lawrence has, they must have been growing substantial quantities of lavender here at Hapstead so let's hope some of the papers are invoices or the equivalent of.'

'Don't get in too deep Sarah, the finer research can be done later.'

'I know! We must get the lavender farm up and going together with the shop and café, the trimmings can come later. I'll put my computer on and we can list the topics we've been discussing and put them in some sort of order ready for the meeting.'

'Let's get some thoughts down first Sarah.'

'Right, let's start with these? Leaflet, including name and logo, then pamphlets, the history, educational aids…'

'That's fine' said Jonnie, 'then there's the shop, tearoom and, of course, the toiletries etc that you are going to make, and what about the Cottage Industry we were talking about.'

'Stop' shouted Sarah. 'That's a start, the list can be developed on Wednesday. Suppose you take the topics 'History' and 'Educational Aids', expand them and come up with some ideas to put to the group on Wednesday.'

'Good idea Sarah, then you work on the leaflet and

pamphlet and hopefully come up with a name and a logo. I do like the idea of *The Agnes Lafolley Lavender Farm* but it is a mouthful. I think a logo is going to be really difficult.'

'I do agree, but I'm sure Babs and Ken have ideas, remember Babs wanted to call it *Roman Lavender* , which is really quite a good name, but will it fit in with the history we are uncovering? I'll give them a copy of our ideas so that they can see how we are thinking prior to the meeting, we don't want them to feel we are being too forward. Incidentally I have a lot about the toiletries needed and how to make them, so will bring that along too.'

'I must go, thanks for the pizza and for the evening, I think we have come up with a good basis to work from.'

'Go carefully Jonnie, Goodnight.'

'See you,' and Jonnie went off in a swirl of gravel.

'Well, she'll learn when the paint comes off her car Meffy, I have told her. Come on cat, time for bed.'

39

The weather forecast was not at all inspiring, '... dull, overcast, very cold. Rain spreading from the North ...' Sarah put off the radio, shrugged her shoulders and hoped the rain would stay away until she got back from her shopping, Tony was coming to stay for a few days so she had to get in plenty of food, he had a good appetite.

She began to think about Tony, she had to give him an answer, she had decided several days ago that she really did want to marry him and she hadn't changed her mind. They had a good relationship, their minds worked along the same lines, they enjoyed each others company, and that included bed, what more could she wish for? The next question from Tony would be 'When?' Sarah had a little chuckle and thought that perhaps they ought to ask Mollie. She might come up with a date that was significant in exorcising the ghosts in the Manor.

Putting Tony and wedding plans on one side she sat down at her computer and quickly made a working list of the ideas that she and Jonnie had had, hoping that Babs and Ken would think it a good basis for discussion. She made several copies so that, if approved, they could be passed round and just hoped that she was not encroaching on Babs and Ken's plans. She gave them a ring and asked if she could come round, Babs suggested she came right away as the coffee was ready and they were just about to phone her as they had something important to tell her.

'That sounds ominous.'

'Not at all Sarah, it's something we think you'll like to hear. See you in a minute.'

Sarah picked up her bag, and all the papers she needed, patted Meffy, made sure everything was OK just in case Tony arrived before she had finished her shopping, and checked that she had locked the back door. Satisfied, she pulled the front door behind her, had a quick look at the small front garden and decided that it must get some TLC, there were signs of new growth on one or two of the plants, what they were she didn't know but decided it would be interesting finding out. The garden next door was obviously getting some attention, so she hoped that Ken would advise her as she was a novice when it came to gardening. Babs opened the door with a big grin on her face.

'Come in Sarah, coffee is all ready and we've found some rather nice biscuits.'

'Biscuits, I'm supposed to be on a biscuit free diet, but I suppose one won't hurt.'

'Or even two, you wait until you hear our news.'

'Can I sit down first, I have a feeling I won't be able to take the 'news' standing up.'

'In that big armchair then Sarah and just listen, over to you Ken.'

Ken had a long drink from his mug and Sarah began to feel really edgy and was wondering just what he was going to say.

'We have decided that you must come in as an official working partner, you will be a member of the management team and have specific responsibilities, which we will go into with you later. Your name will appear with ours on all our literature. We have seen our lawyers and they are happy with the arrangement, so if you agree all we need is for you to check things over with us and your solicitor and, hopefully, sign on the dotted line.'

'Ken, I can't believe this, I'm not going to argue because I'm sure I can pull my weight and Aunt Grace would be thrilled if she knew, but are you really sure that my investment is sufficient to make me a 'proper' partner?'

'It's not only your investment Sarah, it's you, we feel that you are right for us, you have lots of ideas and are really interested in the work, but after we have discussed our ideas do talk to your solicitor and make sure that everything is OK for you.'

'I'm sure it will be Babs, but I must check that I can manage the responsibilities you are suggesting. I certainly did not expect this when I phoned you earlier.'

'We'll have a talk about it later, but I'm sure you will find everything satisfactory, we have been very careful in our planning. What was it you wanted to tell us?'

'All I wanted was to come round and tell you what Jonnie and I had 'come up' with as a basis for discussion tonight, we didn't want you to feel that we had gone over your heads and were taking on too much as far as the planning went.' Sarah gave Babs and Ken a copy of the handout.

'This is great, and you haven't taken on too much' said Ken, 'as you say it is a basis to work from and we did need one, we were just going to work out an agenda for this evening, but this is perfect and has saved us a lot of time. I can think of other items to add, like toilets and car park, very mundane things, but essential, and I'm sure there will be others.'

'There we go Sarah' and Babs laughed, 'we obviously complement each other as far as ideas go and it looks as though you could keep us focused, which is what we need. What more can we say but please join us as a partner.'

There was a woof at the front door followed by a knock, the door opened and Joanna came in followed by Jason.

'Hi! Folks, I'm glad you are all here, I couldn't wait until this evening to pass on our good news.'

'Sit down and have some coffee, you look a bit flushed, and you sit down too Jason and behave.'

'Come on Jason' said Sarah, 'come and sit next to me.' The dog went over to her and flopped his head on her lap and gave a big sigh.

'It's a hard life Jason, but you must lie on the rug.' Sarah gave him a gentle push and he stood up, then settled himself on the rug at Sarah's feet.

'Now Joanna, what's your news?'

'We've just heard this morning, the spinet has been sold at auction and has fetched a fabulous price, far more than expected, we are absolutely delighted. The furniture goes under the hammer next week and we've been told it will fetch a good price, so our development can start as soon as possible, hand-in-hand with yours hopefully, which could save us all a lot of money. Has Tony's friend agreed to do the conversion Sarah?'

'We won't know until this evening, Tony is away at present, but will be back for the meeting tonight, he says he will know then. The builder's name is Phil Palmer he and Tony have worked together quite a lot and, I understand from Tony, that he does brilliant work and does not over-price.

That combination seems to be what we are looking for. Tony, Phil and a good price.'

'That's wonderful news Joanna' and Ken gave her a kiss and a hug. 'I'm sure the renovations and building work can be carried out as one project, it does make good sense. We've got some news for you too we are asking Sarah to join us as a fully fledged partner, we feel that she has a lot to offer and her investment was good.'

'My goodness! Two pieces of good news, what will the third be? Seriously Sarah, I hope you do join them, you are so interested in everything connected with Bridge Farm and lavender, and your expertise does seem to complement Babs' and Ken's.'

'That's exactly our feelings' said Babs, 'but we must give her time to think about it.'

'Can you come up with an answer by tonight Sarah?'

'No Joanna, I have to really think about it and talk it over with Babs and Ken so that we all know where we are, then I must talk it through with my solicitor and then, if everything is alright and I'm sure it will be, we can sign on the dotted line. Let's just say for the moment that I am interested in the proposal and there is a very strong chance that I will accept, but even if I don't I would still like to work here because it is anything but dull.'

'Well that sounds promising. Did you get on well with Bill Lawrence yesterday?'

'We certainly did, we will fill everyone in on that tonight, then we won't have to repeat ourselves, however, he is going to be an asset and for those in the romance business Joanna, he and Jonnie could become an item.'

Joanna laughed and shook her head at Sarah

'I just want people to be happy, and sometimes a subtle nudge in the right direction helps.'

'We know all about your 'nudges' Joanna and I don't think they are particularly 'subtle', but I'm sure they are well intentioned,' said Ken attacking another biscuit.

'Look at Sarah and Tony, where would they have been without a nudge?' said Babs.

'Exactly where we are now I expect, and for your information he is coming tonight for a few days, and we are enjoying each other's company very much, so no more questions please Joanna, I promise to keep you up to date.'

'Remember, as Mollie would tell you, we have to have a happily married couple living in this cottage so that the ghost of Elizabeth can be exorcised once and for all, albeit I've never been conscious of her.'

'Are you sure you haven't Joanna, everyone else feels a coldness, perhaps even a presence in your hallway. We have haven't we Ken?'

'Well I do come up in goose bumps sometimes, but Joanna insists it is because it is cold, but I'm not so sure.'

'Of course it's because of the cold, we have a stone floor, thick walls and no windows for the sun to filter through. I do admit that when the spinet went to the auction rooms I seemed to be aware of a sigh, but that could be as a result of all the stories flying around.'

'So, Joanna, you are saying that you never heard the spinet being played at night?'

'That's right, but other people have, including Mollie, she does have rather a fixation as far as Farmer Harris's stories go, but then I do accept the fact that some people have an insight into the past, and you Sarah and Mollie might just have that.'

'You know, I've never thought of Mollie as having thoughts, or of having lived in the past, but you could well be right Joanna, she seems to know what's going to happen in the stories almost before they've been read.'

248

'She goes into the attic every night to see if she can find anymore stories, she's convinced there is one about the linen chest.'

'From something Farmer Harris said it is a possibility, but I would have thought that she and James had looked into every nook and cranny in the attic.' Sarah looked down at Jason and patted his head. 'Come on folks, where haven't we looked?'

'I've just had a thought, Joanna where is the linen chest now?' Ken sat forward onto the edge of his chair. 'Is it still in your bedroom?'

'Yes.' Joanna looked at Ken as if he was mad. 'Why?'

'Have you opened it since you took it there?'

'Ken, are you saying there might be something in it?'

'Have you opened it Joanna?'

'As a matter of fact I haven't, we've only just brought it down from the attic, it never occurred to me to open it, I thought it had already been opened and there was just a smell of lavender in it.'

'That's right' said Sarah, 'it was opened, but nobody really looked in it Joanna, we were so busy with other things we decided that all that was in it was just the smell of lavender.' Sarah turned to Ken 'Are you thinking what I'm thinking, that there might be something in the chest?'

'Exactly! We really were remiss in not examining it properly, but it seemed so ordinary and not worth bothering with and it did seem empty.'

'Perhaps you should open it and prove us wrong Joanna.'

'It is far from ordinary, it matches the furniture in our bedroom perfectly, I'm sure it was made by the same person. First thing I do when I get home is to look on the back, if I can find out who made it who knows what else I might find.'

Joanna almost burst into tears. 'I can't believe I'm getting involved with the past.'

Ken looked at her and laughed, 'Cheer up Joanna, all these stories will be good for business, but how will you be able to know who made it?'

Joanna grinned 'It's not only you who finds out things, on the back of all the furniture in our bedroom a small daisy and the initials HT have been carved, it must be the trademark of the craftsman responsible. I've been intending to find out who 'HT' was, but have never got round to it, if the daisy and initials appear on the back of the linen chest I'll try and persuade Mollie and James to do some research.'

'You'd better go Joanna, don't keep yourself in suspense.'

'There's plenty of time, Mollie and James don't get home until about five o'clock, I'll have the dinner well underway by then and leave myself time for sleuthing. Can you ask the twins to come round please Babs?'

'Of course, and don't worry they'll be there.'

'See you at dinner time, will there be a third piece of good news? Come on Jason, home.' Jason wagged his tail and looked at Sarah, then dashed to the door with a bark.

'That's better Jason, now let's go home. Bye everyone.'

'I hope she does find out something about the linen chest' said Ken, 'whatever happens we will have a lot to talk about tonight, goodness knows when we'll get to bed.'

Sarah looked up. 'One thing I think we should mull over is the name for the lavender farm, *'Roman Lavender'* has a good ring to it, but with all the facts and stories we are coming up with is it appropriate? Jonnie and I have given it some thought and wondered about *'Agnes Lafolley's Lavender'*, but that doesn't seem right either.'

'You're right Sarah, Babs and I were talking this over the

other day and have ruled out '*Roman Lavender*' for the very reasons you have given. Shall we tell her our idea Babs?'

'Well you gave us the idea Sarah when you suggested that the soaps were labeled '*Agnes Lafolley's* soap, and listening to you it seems as though we are thinking along the same lines, we have come up with '*Lafolley's Lavender*', how does that grab you?'

'It's brilliant! I really like it and the alliteration helps to make it snappy. Perhaps the logo can be worked round the two "L's" intertwined with a sprig of lavender.'

'You're earning your place on the Board already' said Ken giving Sarah a big hug. 'Work on that idea and see what you come up with.'

'I'll try and draught something by tonight, it won't be good enough for us to use, but if you like one of the sketches I have a friend who I'm sure would develop the idea, she is a professional designer working with an engineering firm doing their publicity work, so she knows what catches the eye of the public.'

'Things seem to be falling into place Babs it's not always what you know but who you know. We'll look forward to seeing your sketches tonight Sarah, but we must remember the meeting is really about the building works and organizing the running of the Farm Shop, the Lavender Farm and the Educational Centre '

'Point taken Ken, perhaps you and Babs could look at them before dinner, it shouldn't take up too much time. I must go now and give some thought to your offer, contact my solicitor, and do my shopping. Thanks for the coffee and here's to '*Lafolley's Lavender*'.

40

'Hello Geoffrey, Sarah Bruce here, have you got a few minutes? There are a few developments regarding the lavender farm project.' Sarah brought her solicitor up to date with the details, he told her everything sounded good and he would look into the facts and figures, then arrange a meeting with everyone to finalise details.

'That seems alright Meffy.' Sarah went to the kitchen and put away the shopping singing '*Lafolley's Lavender*' to her self over and over again, and decided that she really did like the ring to it. Tony was due at any time, but dinner was already sorted so Sarah didn't have to worry about what to cook but she had promised to go down to Bridge Farm at about five o'clock to help with the last minute vegetable preparations, so hoped Tony would come soon to give them some time together first.

She sat at her desk and doodled but found that designing the logo was going to be more difficult than she had imagined. She could hear the cows lowing in the distance and wondered if Seth and Joanna had a logo, if not perhaps one could be done for them at the same time, something else to talk about.

252

Tony's van drew up outside the cottage and Sarah dashed to the door. 'Well, there's a welcome and no mistake' said Tony giving her a kiss and flinging his bag down in the corner put his arms round her and continued to kiss her. 'Do I take it that you have an answer for me darling?'

'The answer is 'Yes', I would like to marry you.'

'Sarah, that's wonderful, what is Mollie going to say now?'

'I'll tell you that, she'll say 'when?' but I think we should wait a few months before making any plans, there is so much going on with the Lavender Farm, I've just been asked to become a fully fledged partner, and I think I will, provided the conditions are OK, but I'm sure they will be. I would like to get that sorted first and start working on making soaps and other products, then when everything is running smoothly we can concentrate on us. Let's just enjoy being engaged for now and think of the future later.'

'I'm all for that, especially if you are going to become a partner, I think Ken and Babs know what they are doing, but then I'm prejudiced. Congratulations my darling, I'm sure everything will work out beautifully. I have several plans of my own to get sorted too, so I go along with enjoying the present, I think the future will work itself out, but we know what that is going to be, happily married in this cottage with several kids.'

'There isn't room for 'several kids' Tony, so if that's what you want you'll have to give that some thought.'

'I have already, that's one of my plans. The cottage next door is empty and we could do what Babs and Ken have done, and make the two into one good family home.'

'What a great idea Tony, but I'm only renting this one, so we will have to ask Seth and Joanna if they are willing to sell.'

Sarah gave him a big hug, 'I wonder why I haven't thought about that, especially after seeing what you did for Babs and Ken. Can we afford to lay out that sort of money?'

'We are going to have to sit down and work all that out, but I have a nice nest egg, courtesy of my parents, you told me recently that you still have some money left from your Aunt Grace, you should get a good income from the lavender farm and I'm doing very well at the moment.'

'That sounds wonderful, but we must make sure we are not going in over our heads.'

'My dear Sarah, remember, nothing ventured, nothing gained …'

'As, I'm sure your Grandmother used to say, mine would have said the same.'

'Something else in common then, I'll take my bag upstairs and have a shower, I hope the water is hot.'

'Of course it is, I had an excellent plumber. Your towels are the blue ones. I'm just going to put a wash on so if you have any dirty washing throw it down.'

'Will do, and can you put the kettle on please I'm dying for a cup of tea.' Sarah smiled to herself thinking that they could already be married and decided that she must make sure Tony knew how to operate the washing machine and the kettle!

A little while later Sarah called out that tea was ready, she filled her mug and took it over to her desk, a lot of ideas were floating around in her head regarding the logo, but none seemed quite right. Tony clattered down the stairs, grabbed a mug of tea and sat down by Sarah wanting to know what she was doing. Tony pulled a face and grunted.

'I'm sure you are aware that logos are tricky, you need to get over a message as simply as possible, one that visitors, customers, and the public in general will remember. Is there anything on the fireplace that you could use?'

'I've thought about that, Seth and Joanna are already using their fireplace design as a motive on the B&B notepaper and compliment slips. Perhaps if we adapted one of the swags from this fireplace it could tie in with the Bridge Farm theme, after all although separate businesses we are integrated on the Bridge Farm site. I particularly like this one Tony, a little nosegay of lavender, rosemary and thyme, it would be ideal because Babs is talking about developing the herb side. A stylized nosegay behind the double Ls could effective.'

'That's a good start, let's see if anything else inspires us.'

After a few minutes they had four sketches for Babs and Ken to look at and decided that was enough.

'Hello Meffy, where have you been?' said Tony as the cat jumped up on his lap.

'Only in the kitchen I'm afraid, but he is going to the vets tomorrow to be 'seen to' as they say in polite circles.'

'Rather you than me Meffy, but at least you'll be able to go out and play. Has he got used to the dogs yet?'

'Jason was here earlier and he didn't spit at him in fact he just ignored him, so I think he'll come round given time. I have to go to Bridge Farm in a few minutes to help with the vegetables, do you want to come?'

'If you have no objection I'll stay and have a look at the front garden and tidy it up a bit, I've some tools in the van. The gate needs attention too.'

'It does look a mess, and I don't know where to start, so your help would be much appreciated. Don't forget to lock up will you, and come down at about six thirty.'

'Will do, now go woman and let me get on, but first, do you like this?' Tony put his arms round her, took her left hand and put a ring on her third finger.

'Tony, it's amethyst, my favourite stone, it's lovely where did you get it?'

'Where else but from my Grandmother, she left it to me in her will and I just thought with all the lavender connections it was most appropriate, I had no idea it was your favourite stone.'

'It's lovely darling, and what's more, it fits perfectly. Thankyou, you couldn't have chosen better. I can show it off tonight with pride.'

Running down the road she looked at the farm buildings and wondered just how everything would look in twelve months time, most of the buildings had to maintain their original appearance as they were all listed buildings, the barn and the stables having to have a real makeover, and hopefully there would be visitors around. She was going to ask if her laboratory could be given priority as she wanted to experiment with various soaps and essences, she could then work on them while the rest of the restoration work was being done.

Joanna was standing in front of the farm door waving like mad.

'Hurry up Sarah! I've something to show you.'

'Not the linen chest story? I thought you were going to wait for the twins before investigating.'

'No, not the story, but in a drawer in the spare room I found this rather charming lavender bag, it is obviously old and if we can find out when the furniture was made and for whom, we will probably know who made it and be able to date it, which could be a real selling point if you based your lavender bags on this pattern.'

'Jonnie and I were talking about a cottage industry developing from all our ideas, this would be an ideal starter. I will have to go and speak to Mrs Knight and see if she can point me in the right direction for helpers, provided, of course, that it is agreed at the meeting tonight. It's a lovely sachet

Joanna, I think we ought to put it in a plastic bag so that it doesn't disintegrate.'

'Beaten you to it Sarah,' and Joanna waved a bag accompanied by her usual laugh.

'Thanks Joanna. You know, it's a shame but we are going to have to take this lavender bag to pieces to get a good pattern. We must find a firm that can supply us with muslin, or something similar, and the lavender ribbon.' Sarah held the small sachet up to the light and was fascinated by what she saw.

'Look Joanna, there is a faint pattern printed on it, I think it's lavender, perhaps we should think about having material specially printed for us, I'm sure it would pay for itself in the end. Something else for discussion tonight.'

'That is a lovely idea, I'm sure everyone will go along with it.'

'Some of Bill Lawrence's documents may give us the answer as to when it was made and who was responsible, and there might even be details of a cottage industry, or is that wishful thinking? Here are the twins Joanna, go and do your investigating.'

'What investigating?' said Mollie breathlessly, 'Mum said you had a secret mission for us, whatever is it Auntie Joanna?'

'First of all, please forget the 'Auntie' bit and just call me Joanna, you make me feel about a hundred and one.'

'Great' said James 'we always think of you as 'Joanna and Seth' anyway, so it will be much easier for us – Joanna.'

'With respect please James.'

'Of course, Auntie, er Joanna.' Joanna pretended to clip his ear, but gave him a big hug instead, she was very fond of the twins.

'Now come on you two, we've got a mission, there are

some amongst us who think I have been remiss in not opening the linen chest, but I was under the impression that it had already been opened.'

'We opened it but didn't look inside properly because it didn't seem as interesting as the other pieces of furniture.'

'That's what everyone has said but think about it Mollie, it fits in with our bedroom furniture perfectly so it could have been made by the same craftsman, let's go up and I'll show you what I mean.'

Joanna pulled out the tallboy in her bedroom and showed the twins the daisy and the *HT* that were engraved on the back.

'That is nice' said Mollie, 'but we haven't seen it before because this furniture was always in your room, what about the chest? Was it made at the same time?'

'That's what we've got to try and find out, there must be some clues around. Pull the linen chest out James so that we can have a good look. Remember we are looking for a daisy and *HT* , where do you think they might be?'

'I would imagine on the back, so let's look there first.' James moved the chest round so that the light was on its back, but they couldn't see a daisy anywhere. They turned the chest over and looked on the bottom, but there was nothing there either and they drew a blank on the sides as well.

'There's nothing for it Joanna, you are going to have to open it' said Mollie, 'I'm sure the daisy is on the inside of the lid, go on turn the key, or has it stuck?'

'It's fine' and Joanna turned the key and lifted the lid.

'My goodness!' she put her hand to her mouth, there was a package in the bottom with 'Open Carefully' written on it. This reminds me of 'Alice in Wonderland'.'

'Go on Joanna, open it' said Mollie chewing her fingers in excitement.

'First, clear that small table James, and Sarah in the top drawer of the tallboy you will find a small linen tablecloth, let's put that down so that whatever is in here won't get damaged.'

Sarah found the cloth and spread it over the table. 'There, no sooner said than done, now Joanna open the envelope.'

Joanna picked up a pair of scissors from the dressing table and slid them under the flap of the envelope and emptied the contents on to the table. Two envelopes came out, one had 'WITH CARE' written across the top.

'After all the warnings, we'd better be careful' said Joanna, 'remember what happened to Alice.' She gently opened the 'with care' envelope and inside were some rather tattered pieces of paper that appeared to be an invoice. 'This must be what we have to be careful with' said Joanna, working a sheet of paper under the rather crinkly, very dry pieces of paper 'but it doesn't look very interesting.'

'I think this is some of Farmer Harris's handiwork' said Sarah, 'perhaps there's a letter in the other envelope explaining what we have.'

'There you are Mollie' said Joanna passing her the envelope, 'we'll let you open it, but do it carefully in case there are more surprises inside.'

Mollie squealed with pleasure. 'This is exciting, we really weren't expecting to find any more letters, but we were hoping.' She slit the envelope and looked inside, 'I think it is just a letter and some notes.'

'Take them out Mollie' said James, 'we won't know what they are until we have a look.'

A wad of folded papers came out plus what was obviously a letter which Mollie passed to Joanna whilst she and James unfolded the notes. Joanna looked at the signature first and was not surprised to see *David Harris,* known to everyone at the Farm as Farmer Harris.

'You were right Sarah, this is indeed some more info from Farmer Harris, I'll read it aloud so that you all know what it's about.'

'*To whom it may concern … Hopefully you will have found and read the rest of the papers and stories that I left behind, and have been to the Records Office to look at the material I stored there at the beginning of the War in 1939. I was about to give this chest away when I was clearing up prior to leaving the Farm, but before doing so I opened it, something I had done several times before, but his time I discovered the false bottom under which were the remains of the invoice relating to the purchase, and three small lavender bags. The remains of the invoice are in the smaller envelope, they are very fragile but I think you will be able to see that it is made out to Matthew Lafolley and I assume it was done for Agnes Morey, later to become his wife and she of the lavender trade. The lavender bags I left under the false bottom, to raise the false bottom press firmly on the top lefthand corner of the false bottom and that will activate the spring. I have since discovered that the craftsman was Henry Tanner, related to Walter Tanner who was the lover of Elizabeth Hampton, nee Courtney. Incidentally his trademark can be seen on the inside of the lid, top righthand corner. I had to search for a long time before finding it as it is very small. You must be aware this daisy mark appears on most of the bedroom furniture, so I felt it was only right to keep the chest as it seemed to me that it was made from the same wood and was associated with both Elizabeth and Agnes.*

The larger envelope contains some of my notes and I couldn't resist writing a story about the linen chest, so that is there too, I hope whoever finds these envelopes enjoys it, I had great pleasure in writing it, although not strictly accurate I hope it finishes off the story I called 'Lavender – 1764', the one about Agnes Lafolley and Joan, I was never very happy with the ending.'

'Mollie' said Sarah 'how did you know that the daisy would be on the inside of the lid? Are you beginning to have feelings that you too were here before, perhaps as Joan? That you too are 'touching the past'?'

'I think I am, Joan's path does seem to cross mine a great deal and I do have lots of strange feelings, you call it 'déjà vu', in this instance I just knew we would find the daisy on the inside of the lid, although I can't really remember seeing the chest before, that is, in an earlier life. Let's talk about that later, look at these papers from Farmer Harris, show them James.'

James held up some sheets of handwritten paper that were clipped together, the first was a family tree, the next had '*The Linen Chest*' written across it in bold lettering.

'This must be the story he was talking about, it's too long for us to read out to everyone now' said Mollie, 'could we take it and read it before dinner tonight?'

'Of course' said Joanna, 'tuck yourselves away in the sitting room, no one will disturb you. Was there anything else in the envelope?'

James passed her about five pages. 'These notes seem to be mainly about Henry Tanner, probably connected with the family tree, Farmer Harris really did know how to go about researching things. Over to you Joanna, they could be helpful.'

'Thanks James, and we were going to ask you to try and find out who *HT* was. We'll have to find you something else to do.'

'We could put all the stories together to make the booklet you've been talking about, Sarah would help us I'm sure' said Mollie looking at Sarah who nodded.

'Good idea, we'll talk about that this evening, off you go.'

41

The sitting room was quite dark and Mollie shivered.

'I'm sure there's a presence in this room James, I get prickles all up my spine even with the spinet gone.'

'Well, let's try and put the ghosts to rest. Perhaps the story of the chest will help, let's sit on the settee and read it together.'

The linen chest

Agnes Morey took her mother's wedding dress out of the large blanket box that was at the foot of her bed, the dress was wrapped in an old white sheet with a few lavender bags tucked in to keep it fresh and the moths away. She laid it on the bed and folded back the protective covering, again she was struck by the work that had gone into making it and every time she looked at the dress she wondered just how much time her mother had spent doing the embroidery. The end result was beautiful. Joan had suggested earlier that perhaps she could wear it at her own wedding, Agnes liked the idea but although she had been seeing Matthew Lafolley for two years the subject of marriage had not arisen. Giving a little giggle she wondered if she could broach the subject, but decided against it.

Thinking about weddings she thought it was time Joan married Will, her long term boyfriend, a boatman that worked for her brother. It just so happened that one of the cottages on the estate was becoming vacant, it was the one with the beautifully carved fireplace dating back to the 1600's. Legend had it that the carver, Walter Tanner, had fallen in love with Elizabeth Courtney, the daughter of the Lord of the Manor, and had carved a fireplace in the Manor and one in his own cottage especially for her, and that the angels depicted on each of the fireplaces were really likenesses of Elizabeth and Walter. Agnes decided it would be just the place for a couple as much in love as Joan and Will and she would raise the subject when Joan arrived.

Agnes went to a drawer in her tallboy and took out the piece of embroidery she had been doing, Joan was quite right she thought, it would look well as the cover on her recipe book, but as it was rather special she decided to ask Joan if her brother or Will could take her across the estuary to Chichester so that she could choose the note book for herself and ask the stationer if he could get it bound for her. At the same time she could visit Silas Lacey who supplied their glass bottles and had helped with providing the equipment for distillation, the next stage of development would need bigger and better equipment and she wanted to know if he could either help with providing the essentials or by giving the name of someone who could. She also wanted to ask him about the blue glass. Joan called out from the kitchen so Agnes went down to make them a drink before showing her the dress.

Joan bobbed a little curtsey as Agnes entered the kitchen 'I'm quite excited at seeing your mother's dress Mistress.'

'You'll be more excited after hearing what I'm suggesting to you, but let me make us a drink first, then we can talk.'

They sat down at the kitchen table and Agnes told Joan what her thoughts were about her marrying Will and settling into the cottage.

'It'll be easy for Will, he can moor his boat at our harbour overnight, then it's only a few minutes walk to the cottage. It could pay him well as I know there are a few folk round here who would like to go to Chichester in the early morning, but there isn't a boat. Also with the lavender business beginning to take off there will be more work here that I would like you to do as we work so well together. Now, what do you think Joan?'

'I think you've got it all worked out Mistress Agnes, I do like the idea and I know William will as well, we have been talking about getting married but where to live was a problem, no way could we live with either of our parents, so your solution seems perfect, and if you have more work for me then I'm sure we will be able to afford the rent. Your idea of Will offering passage to Chichester to paying customers sounds good too and I'm sure would be workable, but he will have to sort that out with John, as Will does work for him. I'll talk to Will tonight, but it looks as though I'm going to have to think about a wedding dress.'

'Talking of wedding dresses, come upstairs and look at my mother's, every time I look at it I see something different.'

'I've never been upstairs before' whispered Joan 'the staircase is lovely, so beautifully polished,' and she ran her hand lovingly over the banister.

'It's our pride and joy so we do like to keep it looking nice. Now, come and look at the dress.'

Joan had never been in Agnes's bedroom and was surprised to find that although everything was spotlessly clean the furniture was decidedly shabby and the blanket box was falling to bits. She didn't remark on it as she felt it was not her place and looked instead at the dress on the bed.

'What do you think?' said Agnes, 'how many hours do you suppose my mother put in embroidering all the flowers'.

'Goodness knows. It really is beautiful and I think you are right, they are not sprigs of lavender, she must have made them up. The effect is lovely and the grey silk is a perfect background, though it is not a colour I would have thought of in relation to a wedding dress.'

'I must wrap it up again Joan and put it back in this old blanket box which, you must admit, has seen better days.'

'As long as it does its job Mistress it doesn't matter.'

'Quite right Joan, now off you go and talk to Will this evening.'

There was a 'Hullo' from the kitchen and they found Matthew Lafolley standing there with a great big smile on his face.

'Agnes, Joan' and he nodded his head towards them, 'good day to you both.'

'Good Day sir' said Joan giving him one of her little curtsies. 'I'll say goodbye Mistress and thankyou for showing me the dress.' With another little curtsey she left the kitchen and could be heard running down the path.

'What are you doing here Matthew? I thought we were meeting this evening.'

'We are, but there is something I want to show you while we have the daylight. It's a surprise, so no questions. Your Father knows all about it, but more of that later.'

'I don't know that I like surprises, particularly if Father is involved.'

'I think you will like this one, it has given me a lot of pleasure getting it ready for you, and your Father enjoyed being in on the secret. Get a shawl as we are going into the village to Henry Tanner's workshop and I don't want you to get cold.'

'Henry Tanner's, what ever can it be?'

They walked down the path to the village, stopping by the bridge to look at the stream.

'I'm never tired of looking over the bridge Matthew, the water is always so lovely and clear the stones just sparkle even on a dull day. Just look at those ducks, they are coming over thinking we've got some bread. Sorry ducks, not today.' As if they knew the ducks turned and swam back to the bank. The hawthorns were beginning to set their berries on the hedges and the ox-eyed daisies were just starting to droop. There were plenty of alexanders growing there and Agnes decided that she would pick some on her way home for a salad that evening, she had dandelions, chives and parsley in her garden to mix in with it and with the addition of some chopped apple and a few walnuts she decided it would be very tasty.

They soon reached the village and the sun was still just above the horizon.

'Let's hurry Agnes, or it will be too dark.' Matthew started to walk really fast and Agnes had to run to keep up. Henry Tanner was at the door of his workshop obviously waiting for them.

'Come in, Martha has just poured us all a glass of her excellent blackberry cordial.'

Agnes gave a little bob as she took the glass.

'Good Day Mistress Tanner, this is a pleasant surprise, I haven't had blackberry cordial for ages.' She took a sip 'delicious as usual Mistress.'

Matthew and Henry Tanner had disappeared, but soon returned carrying a chest between them.

'Here's your surprise Agnes, a linen chest to replace your Grandmother's old blanket box.' Matthew and Henry Tanner smiled at each other and then laughed at the expression on Agnes's face.

'It is lovely! How did you know my blanket box was falling to pieces Matthew?'

Henry Tanner and his wife took their blackberry cordial and went into the back room of the workshop, leaving Matthew to explain to Agnes.

'Your Father showed it to me when I asked him if I could have his permission to ask you to marry me.'

Agnes gasped 'I can't believe this, but do go on.'

'He asked me where we would live but before I could answer he said we could make the Farm our home as there was plenty of room, and the Farm would be yours one day. I think he had it all worked out because he took me up to see your room, saying that we could have that as our bedroom, albeit that it needed new furniture. That's when I saw the blanket box. Agnes, will you marry me?'

Agnes laughed 'You've been very devious Matthew Lafolley, but of course I'll marry you.' She threw her arms round Matthew and gave him a big hug followed by a long kiss. They stood there laughing and hugging each other.

'I wasn't expecting this when I came out with you today, I must admit it is a lovely surprise.'

'She has said 'Yes' Henry,' said Matthew calling out to the cabinet maker.

'Congratulations to both of you, now Martha and I will raise our glasses to wish you a long and happy life together.' Henry and his wife did just that and Agnes put her arms round Mistress Tanner and thanked her with a kiss.

'What about the rest of the surprise Matthew?' said Henry Tanner with a wink.

'You mean there's more? What an afternoon this is,' Agnes held Matthew's hand and looked into his eyes, 'how many more surprises?'

'Just this one, and I think you'll like it. Come through to the back of the workshop with us.'

Henry and Martha had gone on ahead and were busy taking sacking off some furniture, there was a wardrobe, a tallboy, a small vanity table and a bed. All were very plain and simple but beautifully made.

'I know we haven't had time to discuss anything, but when your Father suggested we lived at the farm I liked the idea, there is plenty of room and it would be convenient for me as I have more and more work to do there, and it could be easier for you with the lavender business to see to. This furniture is for our bedroom, whether at the Farm or not, but it will fit into the room you have now because with your Father's help I measured it up, but we will only stay if you agree.'

'I don't even have to think about it Matthew, it is a good idea, we both get on well with Father and he does need a little bit of looking after now he is getting on in years, and as you say, I do have the lavender business to run. Master Tanner, this furniture is lovely, I will look after it well I promise.'

'My pleasure Mistress Agnes I have enjoyed making it and I have put my mark on each piece, look.' Henry showed her the small daisy with his initials carved on the back of the main pieces. 'I have put it inside the linen chest on the lid, and for fun have put a false bottom in it that can act as a secret hiding place.'

'A secret hiding place. I must go and have a look.' Agnes dashed off and opened the linen chest. 'You've hidden it very well Master Tanner, I can't see any way of raising it.'

'I should hope not' laughed Henry. 'Try pressing gently into the top left hand corner of the bottom and see what happens.'

'Oh my!' Agnes laughed too as the false bottom sprang up leaving a space underneath. 'That is amazing, I must put some lavender sachets in there to keep it smelling nice.'

'Here's something else to keep it nice' said Mistress Tanner, giving Agnes a jar of beeswax.

'Thankyou, I am just running out of beeswax, so accept this with pleasure. Do you have your own bees?'

'Yes we do, and they keep me really busy, at the moment I have more beeswax than I know what to do with.'

'Sell it to me, I'll mix some lavender oil in it and sell it in the lavender shop.'

'Will that work, I'd never have thought of doing that.'

'It really is lovely, I'll bring you down a small phial of lavender oil and you can try it for yourself, and I did mean it, any surplus that you have do sell it to me, I'm trying to build up a little business selling lavender products.'

'You can talk business another day' and Matthew steered Agnes to the front of the workshop. 'We must go Agnes, it will be dark soon and there's no moon tonight to show us the way. Good evening Henry and Martha, thanks for all your help, as you can see Agnes likes her surprises.'

'Indeed I do, and I shall think of the linen chest as an engagement present.'

'An engagement present. I think Farmer Harris has hit the nail on the head, what could be better than a lovely chest for her trousseau or at least for her new bed linen' said Mollie. 'I think Joanna was very clever in thinking that the chest was made at the same time as the furniture, but how did I know that the daisy was on the inside of the lid? It really is creepy.'

James laughed 'It's obvious, when the furniture arrived for Agnes's room Joan had to help with the change over and I can imagine Agnes showing her the chest, the daisy and the false bottom.'

'Of course, you must be right, Joan and Agnes were very close.'

'Remember too that Joan's family ran a firm dealing with boats, some of which came to Bridge Farm, so even before she met Will she was used to going up and down the estuary.'

'Next week, weather permitting, I'm going with Sarah and Jonnie to the old harbour, we want to see if it triggers off any memories. I really do think we are getting to the point where the ghosts are going to be laid, though they haven't frightened anyone,' even as she said it Mollie shivered, 'why do I shiver in here?'

'You shiver my dear sister because it is jolly cold in here. Now come on let's go and get ready for dinner, it's one of Joanna's stews tonight and you know how good they are.'

'What do you think about us getting the booklet of stories together James, do you think we can do it?'

'Of course we can do it, we'll have to edit the stories a little bit, but that won't be difficult and we'll have to find a good photograph or picture for the cover.'

'A good photo of the front of the Farm House could be ideal, especially if it were printed in sepia which would give the impression of age.'

'You know Mollie, you sometimes come up with good ideas, and this is one of them. I think it might mean that we have to get in a professional photographer but the picture could be used for advertising too, if the rest of the gang approve that is.'

'Joanna has just called, so we had better go. I reckon that the meeting tonight is going to be interesting and a long one. Have you made notes of the points we want to raise?'

'I certainly have' said James 'hopefully there be time for us to bring them up?'

42

'Good Heavens! It's time for bed,' said Seth looking at his watch. 'I have an early start tomorrow and didn't realize that it was after ten. Can we just finish by once again congratulating Sarah and Tony on their engagement and say how much we are looking forward to their wedding. I would also like to say how well our meeting went, we came up with some good ideas, managed to get on top of everything and divide the work load fairly. The fact that Tony and his partners can start work next week is a bonus. Goodnight everyone, sleep well.' To a chorus of 'Goodnights' Seth left the room, everyone else was mulling over the meeting and seemed to be happy at the outcome.

'Isn't it great that they are happy to trust us with the booklet of stories?'

'With the proviso that Sarah helps of course.' James looked at Mollie and told her that he thought they were going to be very busy because Joanna wanted the booklet printed as soon as possible.

Joanna heard what he said and told the twins that she was sure they could come up with the booklet sooner than anyone else. Mollie gave her hug. 'I hope we won't disappoint you Joanna, it is quite a responsibility.'

'Now Mollie, you did ask if you could do it, so where's your confidence now?'

'It's disappeared for a few minutes, but we'll be OK once we get started.'

'Come on folks' said Joanna, 'it's time for me to lock up, I've got an early start tomorrow too.'

'Sorry Joanna, we're off now, come on everyone. We've had a super evening Joanna, talk about it tomorrow. I'll come up and see you in the morning Babs, I've got ideas floating around that I need to share. It's very dark tonight Jonnie would you like to stay the night, the bed's made up in the spare room?'

'Yes please Sarah, I wasn't looking forward to the trip home.'

'It's time we went too' said Babs 'so come on twins, hurry up.'

'Night Joanna' chorused everyone, 'see you soon.'

They all walked along the passage to the back door and found it to be very chilly. 'I thought it was the passage to the front door that was cold' said Mollie, 'this one seems colder.'

'You were told earlier that the floors are stone and there are no windows to let in any warmth from outside, so don't go imagining things, accept the facts.'

'But it's a very strange feeling I get and I don't think it will go until Sarah and Tony are married' said the incorrigible Mollie.

'You'll have a while to wait then' said Sarah, 'two years at least.'

'Two years' wailed Mollie, 'two years of feeling chilly every time I come through the Farm door.'

'That's our plan at the moment, it could change. To help you through the two years Mollie, would you like to think about being be my bridesmaid?'

'Would I? Yes please' and Mollie flung her arms round Sarah and gave her a big hug. 'What colour dress are you going to wear, a grey one like Agnes's mother? Or would that really unsettle the ghosts?'

'No problems there Mollie, it won't be grey, we can decide on colours and patterns nearer the date. I don't know about you lot, but I'm ready for my bed it's been a long day. Come on Tony and Jonnie, last one home makes the drinks.'

'Good night everyone.'

To shouts of 'good night' they ran up the road to the cottage and were soon sitting round the fire sipping mint tea. The feeling between them was that they wondered what they had done before they became involved with Bridge Farm, Jonnie was sure she had always been busy and that she had enjoyed her work, Sarah echoed those sentiments, but qualified them by saying that latterly she had felt bored, because she had gone as far as she wanted to in the library and was, therefore, ready for a change. Tony laughed at them and told them he was sure the change would do them good - life wouldn't be dull anymore, and he had to admit that his life had become more exciting and demanding since Sarah had come along with the photograph found in her Aunt Grace's bedroom.

He gave the fire a poke, and cuddled up to Sarah on the settee.

'I'm glad Seth and Joanna agreed to us buying the cottages, I have to see Seth tomorrow to get the details sorted, but I'm sure everything will be OK and we'll be able to start the alterations soon. We should be able to make a really lovely home here, don't you agree Jonnie?'

'I think it's a lovely idea, and it means that the cottages will not be spoilt by someone coming in and altering things. Will it be like Babs and Ken's development?'

'The outside will remain the same, but inside we might have a few ideas of our own, but that won't upset the feel of the cottages. I've got a few plans drawn up Sarah, so we can look at those another day, they are only drafts but it will give us something to work on.'

'Well. I'm for bed, thanks for letting me stay. Everything does seem to be getting sorted out Sarah, and for your ears only, I'm going out to dinner with Bill Lawrence next week.'

Sarah laughed 'I told you he thought you were someone special, keep me posted.' Tony joined in to say that he approved as he had known Bill for a long time, got on well with him and, in a nutshell, found him a really nice guy.

'Nothing is too much trouble for that man Jonnie, he has been very helpful to me when I've needed information about old buildings, if the information is available he finds it. I'm sure you will find him to be a good companion, pleasant, outgoing and caring, what more could you want?'

'It's early days Tony, but he is the only date I've wanted to keep since my divorce. See you in the morning, I think I shall sleep the sleep of the dead tonight.'

Jonnie disappeared upstairs and Tony cuddled Sarah a little closer. 'We'll have to try and involve Bill in some of our work so that he and Jonnie can meet up more often.'

'Are you being a match-maker Tony?'

'Yes! I'm so happy I want everyone else to be. Let's go to bed.'

43

'What are you doing today Jonnie?' asked Sarah as she poured her out another cup of coffee.

'I'm going to see Alan and have a look at his photographs, he wants some help in sorting them. He's promised me lunch, I bet it's vegetable soup.'

Sarah laughed. 'His vegetable soup is good, but I expect it can become a little boring, have you got time to bake some of your bread rolls?'

'I've got the time but not the ingredients. At least I know the soup is nutritious and he does like my company. I've got a bottle of parsnip wine that I won at the local fete, I'll take that along, I hope it doesn't blow our heads off.'

'It could, my Auntie Win used to make wine and her parsnip was lethal, one time the Vicar drank it thinking it was a fruit juice. We heard that he wasn't very well the next day.'

'I'll tell Alan that story, and remind him to be careful. What have you planned for today?'

'Off to see Bill Lawrence and sort out the lavender history, I promised him I wouldn't be long, he wants the space. I will also ask him if he can help with a computer program for us.'

'I'm sure he can Sarah, I expect he already has something that can be developed and we could probably have a link with the Archives Department which would be brilliant, I'm sure he would go along with that.'

'I've got to go and see Babs before I go, she said she had something interesting to tell me and I want to check whether they liked any of the sketches I did for a logo.'

'I'll be off then, it sounds as though you've got a busy day. Thanks for the bed, I think you saved my life.'

'Anytime Jonnie, I won't change the sheets just yet so if you want to stay again please do.'

Jonnie scooped Meffy up and gave him a quick cuddle. 'He is a lovely cat Sarah, I bet he'll make a good mouser.'

'I'm sure he will. Goodbye Jonnie, you can put him out as you go.'

Sarah did a quick tidy up in the kitchen, picked up her laptop and files and went off to see Babs.

She was glad Tony had managed to tidy up the front garden, the weeds had gone albeit there were one or two brown sticks poking up above the soil, Tony had assured her that they would probably be really lovely plants and to leave them for a while until they knew what they were, if they weren't worth keeping they could dig them up later. Somehow Tony had had time to clean off the front gate and rehang it all it needed now was a coat of paint. Sarah decided she could do that.

She gave a little shudder as she went next door, it was a really damp and dismal day, there was no chance of the path to the harbour drying up in the next few days. Sarah had been hoping to get down there on Saturday, Mollie would be free then and also Jonnie, but no way could they venture along the path if it was wet. Heaving a sigh Sarah knocked on Babs' door.

'Come on in Sarah, the coffee is nearly ready you look as though you could do with a cup. Is anything the matter, it's not like you to look depressed?'

'I'm not really, just a bit fed-up, I was hoping the weather would dry up so that we could go down to the harbour and have a look. Not only have I been thinking that it played a part in my past but I have been wondering if we could use it in our enterprises, could we have boats coming over from the other side of the estuary with groups or coach parties wanting to have a look at the farm and the lavender?'

'That's a brilliant idea Sarah. It will cost something to set up, but don't let's be put off by that, it will fit in with the history beautifully. I can imagine parties of schoolchildren really enjoying an approach like that to the Farm, reliving the past.'

'That's what I thought we'll have to work out the logistics and the cost, but it could be a fun entrance rather than coming in through the carpark. Incidentally, as that is the main entrance to Bridge Farm we must have a chat with Seth and Joanna so that we can try and make it more inviting, it shouldn't be difficult, pots of plants at strategic places plus an information kiosk and ticket office. Bill Lawrence has put some really attractive information boards round the village, perhaps we could have two or three relating to the history of the farm and lavender on the path down to the entrance.'

'Another good idea Sarah, but beware of the cost, and as you say we must check with Seth and Joanna.'

'No problem. Perhaps the funding could come out of the Lavender Farm purse?'

'Ken isn't here this morning, he's working in the fields, I'm going to join him after coffee, and will certainly mention your ideas to him, could we come down to you this evening and talk things over? '

'Coffee at seven. I hope to have answers to a lot of our questions today and be able to start putting together a brief history, Bill has all his documents laid out so it shouldn't take me too long to work out, albeit roughly. What was it you wanted to tell me?'

'As you know Ken and I had a meeting with the Vicar and he has uncovered quite a lot of background material as far as dates and names go, info that could help you with the History, indeed it could answer some of the questions.'

'That's marvellous news, some of the names and dates do need checking. Thinking about it I will ask him about re-incarnation as well, I know the Church does not really believe in it but it could be that he has some answers for me.'

'You talk about Mollie being incorrigible, I think you are ten times worse. How could you possibly have been Elizabeth?'

'How is it I know so much about her life?'

'Pa Harris's stories plus a vivid imagination.'

'Babs, have you no soul? I just have such weird feelings about Bridge Farm, and I had them before I read Pa Harris's stories, I must sort myself out and as Mollie says 'lay Elizabeth to rest'.'

'Then go and see the Reverend Green as soon as possible, then we can all rest.' Babs had a little laugh at Sarah's expense, 'we are all with you on this you know that Sarah, but I can't resist being a little sceptical.'

'Fair enough Babs, but I know what I feel and remember, the latter being very spooky. The last laugh will go with me if the chill goes from the corridors at Bridge Farm. I'll give the Reverend a phone call before I go off to see Bill Lawrence and hope to see him tomorrow.'

Sarah's time at the Record's Office flew by, and she was delighted with all the help. She went home with a laptop full of facts and dozens of photocopies. Bill said that they had to file all the papers but if Sarah needed to check up on anything it would be easy to trace.

Back at the cottage Sarah fed Meffy. Tony phoned to say that the traffic was almost at a standstill and he didn't know when he would get home, so Sarah decided that lamb chops would be perfect, she could get them out of the freezer when Tony arrived.

Standing at the sink and looking out at the garden, she noticed there were some snowdrops round the apple tree, and couldn't understand why she hadn't seen them before, perhaps the grass was too long?

She peeled the potatoes and carrots then sat down in front of the fire. Having had lit it as soon as she had come home it was glowing beautifully, sending out a lovely heat. Sarah knelt down and swept up some ash, sat back on her heels and looked at the fireplace. The carvings really were lovely and she couldn't resist stroking the two angels. They had been thinking about a name for the cottage and she wondered if he would go along with 'Angel Cottage'. 'You must admit Meffy, it's different' Sarah said to the cat as he pushed in front of her to put his paws on the hearth.

Tony's car pulled up in the road, so she went into the kitchen to start the dinner. Tony came crashing in looking really excited.

'I've got the aerial photographs Sarah, they look good. You won't believe this but Babs and Ken are following the old lines, I wonder why they did that?'

'Perhaps they have a feeling of having been here before' laughed Sarah, 'tell Babs that and she'll go mad. They are coming down for coffee this evening so you can show them then. I've got the old photos on the table, can you superimpose the new ones?'

'Bob's done better than that, you gave me copies of the old photos and he has already put them, plus the recent ones on a disc so that you can look at them individually or superimpose them. It really is quite brilliant.'

'That's what Jonnie was talking about, something that could be used in the Education Centre. Things do seem to be coming together. Dinner's nearly ready, hope you enjoy it. I think I can hear Babs and Ken coming, can you open the door please.'

'Hi Tony, it's a raw evening out there, nice to see the fire.'

'Come in, make yourselves at home. Would you like a beer?'

'Yes please, I'll get them, are they in the fridge?' Ken went to the kitchen, grabbed a couple of glasses and the beers and went back to the settee.

'Here's some crisps to help it down' said Sarah picking up a couple of packets from the table.

'We're being spoilt Ken, isn't it nice?'

'Sure is! This fire is super and just look at those angels.'

'Tony, talking about the angels, I had a brainwave today, how about calling the cottage 'Angel Cottage'?'

'I'll go along with that, why ever didn't we think of it before?'

'Perhaps it was too obvious' said Babs and looked at Ken, 'we ought to come up with a name for our cottage, I hadn't thought about it before but it would be nice to have a name rather than a number.'

'You've started something now Sarah, give it some thought please.'

'Well, you've got hawthorn hedges all round your fields,

what about 'Hawthorn Cottage?"

Ken looked at Babs and laughed, 'I like it, do you like it Babs?'

'I certainly do, again something so obvious we didn't think of it.'

'To make us look really smart let's have the names carved by the same person, do you know anyone in the village Ken that could do that?'

'I certainly do and I'll see to it tomorrow.'

'I'm sorry we're so late with our meal tonight but Tony got held up in traffic, so while we eat would you two like to look at the photos on the computer, I think you'll find them interesting. You can talk to us while we eat.'

Babs and Ken sat down by the computer and suddenly realized what they were looking at.

'How far back does this go?' asked Ken.

'We are not too sure about that' said Tony, 'but some of the markings that appear on the photos must go back to the 1500's, probably marking out the footings of the monastery. Bob Hoskins is going to ask an expert to look at them and see if we are right. To have it authenticated would be marvellous. There are some strange small square markings at the edge of one of the fields and we wondered if they could possibly be bee-hives.'

'Bee-hives?' questioned Babs. 'We have just ordered some to put at the edge of one of the fields, we need the bees to improve the crop of lavender and hope to have some honey from them, and beeswax for Sarah, but we will have to have help with that. I wonder if it is the same field? This is getting rather creepy Ken we seem to be doing exactly the same things that were being done years ago.'

Sarah laughed 'Not you too Babs. What do you remember

about the past? Have you been here before?'

'I'm not laughing anymore Sarah, as I said to Ken, this is 'creepy'.'

'Now you know how I feel, as you say it is 'creepy', but as far as the fields go, you are good agriculturists/horticulturists and I expect the people before you were as well so it is not surprising that you are following the same lines, even as far as bee-hives go.'

Ken put his arm round Babs. 'There you are my dear. A matter of fact look at the situation and Sarah has come up with a reasonable explanation.'

'I know, but it is still spooky. To go back to the honey problem, do you think it possible for us to have our own honey '*Agnes Lafolley's Honey*' has quite a ring to it.'

'It must be possible, I bet Mrs Knight knows someone who could help with making and bottling the honey' said Sarah, 'I think she knows who does what in the village, I'm going to see her soon to ask her if she knows of any ladies in the village that could help with making lavender sachets, so I could ask her about bee-keeping and honey at the same time.'

'Can I come with you Sarah' said Babs, 'I rather like the sound of Mrs Knight.'

'Of course, she is quite a character and tries to give the impression that she doesn't like visitors, but I think she does and I'm sure that it will please her to help us. I'll let you know when I'm going.'

'Look at this Ken' and Babs pointed to another field, 'it looks like the one next to our property, the one we hope Seth and Joanna will sell to us, there's definitely signs of crops being grown there, but at the moment it is fallow. How can we find out if lavender or herbs were the main crop?'

'Let's go and see Alan, he must have the name of an archaeologist who could take some soil samples and examine them.'

'Good thinking Ken, let's go tomorrow, we want to ask him up for dinner anyway, perhaps Sarah will lend us this disc when he comes, I know he would like to see what has been done.'

'That was a lovely lamb chop' said Tony as he and Sarah came in from the kitchen. 'She's a great cook chaps, you'll have to sample it soon.'

'Did I hear you say that were going to ask Alan up for dinner?' said Sarah. 'As it happens we were too, so why don't we get together, have dinner here, and ask Joanna and Seth too, I have a venison stew in the freezer and you could make the dessert Babs. Then afterwards we can talk about the photos, lavender and the farm.'

'That's a good idea, what about Sunday, I think we are all free then. I bet Alan will have some ideas to offer about presentation etc. Changing the subject, what about the ideas we had this morning for 'tarting' up the entrance, perhaps we could bring it up at the dinner? Ken thinks it might be beyond our means at present.'

Ken shook his head at Babs 'I didn't say 'No' I said 'Maybe'. Sarah, we must cost everything out otherwise we will find ourselves in debt. In principle I like the ideas.'

Tony intervened 'The builders that are coming on Monday have a lot of terra-cotta pots in their yard that they want rid of, i.e. going for nothing. I know that there are at least five really large ones that I am sure would be fine for the carpark, the only problem would be the compost but I expect Seth could solve that problem As for plants, I have a friend who has a nursery and I'm sure he would plant them up as long as we had his name on them, good advertising, hardly any cost to us at all.'

'There you are Ken, it's not what you know, but who. I'm sure Joanna and Seth will come to dinner on Sunday, so we can ask them then, I think they'll like the idea particularly if it doesn't involve spending money or time on it.'

'Phil Palmer and his team are starting work on Monday so there won't be a problem in getting the pots up here and installing them, as long as Joanna and Seth agree.'

'Starting work on Monday?' Sarah looked round and chuckled at the mixed expressions. Ken looked excited, Babs looked apprehensive and Tony looked slightly worried, as for Sarah, she couldn't believe that all this was happening such a relatively short time since Aunt Grace had died and wondered where everything would be in two years time.

TWO YEARS LATER

44

'Wake up' said Sarah stopping the alarm. 'We're not on our honeymoon anymore. We have work to do.'

'Not yet' said Tony nuzzling her, 'I rather like it here.'

'So do I, but we've got to get down to the farm, everything is happening today, the Educational Centre is being opened, Joanna has cooks demonstrating in the Farm shop and the lavender products are on sale for the first time, we must get down there.'

'I know Sarah and bags I the shower first' said Tony falling out of bed.

'Don't be long, I'll get the breakfast underway.' Sarah cut the grapefruit in half and as she did so looked out of the kitchen window. Tony had worked really hard on the garden and it looked lovely in the morning sun. He had designed it round the apple tree using mainly shrubs and had chosen so many different shades of green that it looked like a mosaic. He had put pots containing different shaped and coloured plants at strategic places to give emphasis to the greens. A crazy paving path went down the garden and ended in a summer house. He had plumbed in the electrics so that they could sit there with some light in the evening and use their laptops if necessary.

Sarah gave a sigh, albeit a contented one, and thought how lucky she was. Tony was as romantic a person as she could have wanted to marry. The wedding had been a lovely occasion. She had been delighted with her dress, even though it wasn't the grey silk that Mollie wanted. It was cream taffeta, princess style which suited her beautifully. Her bouquet was of lavender, rosemary, orange blossom and a few dark red roses. She wore her mother's veil which was long and with age had become cream, it had hung in beautiful folds making her feel very special. Mollie, wanting to be different, had chosen a tartan patterned taffeta in purple, mauve, green and black. Sarah had been dubious about it but on the day Mollie looked lovely, the colours combining beautifully with the decor in the church.

She was also pleased with the work that had been done to make the two cottages into one home, Tony and the team had worked hard to get it finished and the end result was almost perfect. There was a smart exterior, both doors had been kept, the stonework had been cleaned and inside they now had a dining room as well as a sitting room. The kitchen in the second cottage had been turned into an office, with room for them both to work. Stairs went up from the dining room and the sitting room making an interesting feature. Upstairs another bathroom had been put in the second cottage and the two bedrooms cleaned out and replastered ready for decorating. It was now up to Sarah and Tony to put their own mark on the cottages, she was looking forward to that and gave a little laugh. 'That's when Elizabeth will be laid to rest. Though Mollie thinks it will be sooner than that.'

'Are you coming Tony? Breakfast will be on the table in a minute.'

'Coming, Can I smell bacon and eggs?'

'This is a one off, it'll be toast and marmalade tomorrow.'

'I'll make the most it then. Two eggs I hope, I'm hungry, I've just been on my honeymoon.'

'Tony, behave yourself, you have one egg, two rashers, some mushrooms and tomatoes, plus some toast and marmalade, that is enough for any man.'

'Well, there you have it, I'm not 'any man', I'm your dearly beloved husband.'

'… and because you are I will make sure that you do not have too much cholesterol inducing foods. I do not want to become a widow.'

'OK Sarah, I give in, one egg please, but two extra mushrooms,' and Tony swept Sarah up into a big hug.

'Give over Tony, breakfast is on the table, eat up your grapefruit and I'll dish up the second course.'

'So, what's happening down at the farm today?'

'Everything you can think of. Joanna and Seth have declared it an Open Day, so I expect all the villagers will come to enjoy the festivities. The local MP is coming at eleven o'clock to open the Education Centre. Jonnie did really well in planning that, the opening coincides with the schools wanting to take the kids out on trips, and the Farm and Lavender Farm are new venues, Joanna told me last night that we have full daytime bookings until the beginning of August and some bookings with the WI and other organizations for the evenings when Seth will talk about the history of the Farm and district. I believe Alan has been asked to help, he will enjoy that, but we must ensure he does not take on too much.'

'This bacon is good, does it come from the Farm Shop?'

'Would I dare buy it from anywhere else!'

Tony piled his toast with marmalade and gave a big sigh.

'I did enjoy that Sarah, can I please have a bacon and egg breakfast occasionally?'

'Yes, of course you can, but not two eggs.' Sarah poured them out another cup of coffee and sat down to eat her toast.

'You know Tony, when we spoke to Joanna last night she sounded really upbeat about the volunteers, they are calling themselves 'Friends of Bridge Farm' and, I understand, have already got a uniform, purple sweatshirts with either the Bridge Farm or Lafolley's Lavender logo on them, together with white T-shirts, again with the logos, they will look really smart.'

'As I don't really work here' said Tony, 'perhaps I ought to invest in a purple sweatshirt.'

'A good idea, perhaps we all ought to have them with our job description under the logo, it would help the schoolchildren during their visits, and we wouldn't be perpetually asked 'What do you do Miss?''

'You see, I do have good ideas at times.'

'It is quite exciting Tony, the villagers have responded so well to the work out here. Mrs Knight had no problem in giving me the names of a dozen ladies who would like to make lavender sachets and help in the shop and the café. The specially printed muslin and the purple velvet ribbon make the finished sachets look almost like Agnes Lafolley's. They go on sale today for the first time. I've had some paper printed with the same pattern for the soaps and toiletries, unfortunately we haven't a large stock to sell, hopefully I'll have some help in the workshop this year so that we can have a good supply by Christmas.'

'Who's talking about Christmas?' called a voice from the door.

'Mollie, come in, how lovely to see you I didn't think you could make it.'

'I wasn't going to miss today if I could help it, so I got my thesis in early and here I am with my Tutor's blessing, she was very interested in the stories. I think it must be today that the warm air blows through the hallway at Bridge Farm, you are back from your honeymoon, and with all that is happening today it augurs well.' Mollie gave Sarah a big hug. 'How was the honeymoon? Idyllic?'

'Absolutely' said Tony and Sarah together, and then burst out laughing.

'What's the joke?' asked Mollie.

'We are constantly doing that, answering a question together.' Sarah and Tony looked at each other and blew a kiss.

'This is seriously romantic stuff. Here's to the laying of Elizabeth's ghost. Have you been down to the harbour yet?'

'About a month ago, and I did get goose bumps as Tony took me down the estuary. I'm sure Elizabeth went down there on the way to London to sell her herbs, I could almost smell them. I didn't feel anything about Joan, so have decided that she did not play a very important part in my life. One piece of disappointing news is that we cannot afford to have the jetty rebuilt at the moment, the Health and Safety people have so many rules and regulations that it is going to cost a lot more than anticipated, but it has been put on hold until we start to make some money with the Lavender farm. We can take the parties down there to see the old jetty, but that is all.'

'That will interest the schoolchildren surely?'

'… and perhaps bring them back when everything is completed.' Tony looked up at Mollie, 'we've got a lot to do, are you coming down to the farm with us?'

'Yes! I'm sure I can lend a hand somewhere.'

'First, please clear up the dishes Tony, I must have a shower and get dressed.' So saying Sarah dashed upstairs.

'I'll help you Tony. Come on I'll wash, you can wipe.'

'What about putting them all in the dishwasher?'

'As a penniless student I'm not used to such luxuries. I'll clear the table, you fill the dishwasher.'

45

Sarah, Tony and Mollie walked down to the Farm looking at the lavender as they went, it was a glorious colour and almost ready for picking.

'I wonder if the Volunteers would help with the picking? It is a pleasant job and we could give them lunch in the café.'

'I'd help if it meant lunch in the café' said Tony, 'Betty Knight's baguettes are wonderful.'

'The café isn't open yet Tony, how do you know that?'

'Before our wedding, Betty and a couple of her cronies were in the kitchen experimenting with fillings, they kindly supplied the builders with lunch at a small charge. It meant that Betty could have some feed-back, excuse the pun, and the builders enjoyed the change from cheese and pickle.'

'I didn't know that, but what a good idea. Baguettes for lunch then?'

'It's very quiet on the farm front today, I can't see Jason and Troy or the geese.' Tony looked round, 'I say, there are people putting bunting up.'

Sarah gasped 'It's the Volunteers Tony, how wonderful, I bet Joanna's pleased.' As she spoke Joanna came to the Farm door.

'What do you think you lot? Have we got people interested in what we are doing or not?'

Mollie ran and gave Joanna a big hug. 'This is super Joanna, what can I do to help?'

'Go and see what your Mum's up to I expect she needs another pair of hands. Before you go, will you all come to dinner tonight, I have lots of cold meat and with salads and baked potatoes, followed by sherry trifle there won't be too much work. Alan will be here, he's staying the night. Jonnie's coming too and she said she could stay with you Sarah, so we will have quite a party.'

'Joanna, I don't know how you do it, but we would love to come it should be a good finish to the Open Day.' Sarah looked at her watch. 'It's nine fifteen already. I must dash and get the shop organised, thankfully I didn't forget the float for the till. The Farm Shop looks amazing Joanna, the vegetables give a lovely splash of colour, the butcher's counter has been beautifully arranged, and as for the smell of the bread and rolls, that's enough to entice customers in. Let's hope we all do well.'

'We've got everything going for us Sarah, the sun is shining, we've lots of helpers and an interesting program of events, so it should be a good day. Betty Knight is here already and has the café open so that if any of the helpers need coffee or tea it will be available. Tony could you go to the carpark to make sure everything is running smoothly. The scouts are in charge and seem to be well organized, we will probably have to use the field next to the park as well, and they already have that marked out with plenty of signs. They will be asking the drivers for donations towards the new scout hut, so I hope everyone is in a generous mood.'

'I'll go along but will keep a low profile, it's good to see young people involved. Later I'll check on the Education Centre to see if Jonnie needs any help. I hope there will be enough seats for everyone.'

'Please do but I think she'll be alright, Bill Lawrence is helping out and he has lent us thirty chairs, so we have about sixty altogether. Also there are two volunteers manning the book stall. That recipe book looks most attractive Sarah, the printers have done a lovely job on the cover. Pa Harris's stories and the History of Bridge Farm have been done in the same format and should sell well.'

'I'm glad you approve of the recipe book, when the printer showed me the proof copy I was really pleased with it. We have all put a lot of effort into getting ready for today, let's enjoy ourselves.'

'I couldn't agree more' said Joanna, 'I'm just on my way to the Education Centre to meet up with Babs and make the final touches for the opening ceremony. Mollie have you seen the café? Your Mum has done a superb job there, the china is lovely with sprays of lavender on the mugs, cups and serviettes. All the décor is in white, blue and green, it looks so fresh and inviting. To finish it off, Betty and her helpers have made lavender sponges and lavender scones which you really ought to sample, they are wonderful.'

'I'll go and have a look then find Mum, I expect she's in the Education Centre already. If you need any help Sarah give me a shout.' Mollie ran off and Sarah went towards the lavender shop, she felt quite a thrill as she unlocked the door and was greeted with the wonderful aroma of lavender. Ruth, one of the volunteers had been helping Sarah get everything ready, with a real flair for displaying items she had made the most of the soaps and oils, giving the impression that they had more than in reality. Ruth had found some Royal

Horticultural posters with herbs on them and had put them on the walls, taking away the bareness. She had displayed some of the books on the shelves in between the soaps which was very effective. The *Agnes Lafolley Recipe Book* was on a shelf with some Bristol blue glass and vases of lavender, Sarah had to agree with Joanna, the cover of the recipe book was superb. Seth had given the original book to the local museum and they were going to do a display of cookery books through the ages, with *Agnes Lafolley's* taking pride of place.

Ruth arrived and seemed to be as excited as Sarah at all the festivities.

'Joanna said we'll be open at ten o'clock. Did you know she had arranged for the Town Band to start everything off? My brother plays the bugle, and he says they are going to start playing in the main road and will march up the lane to the carpark. I think I can hear them tuning up.'

'What fun, but I think it would be a good idea to tell Joanna, I'm sure she would like to know they are on their way. Hurry back Ruth, I've got something to ask you.'

Even as she spoke Sarah could hear the band and found herself getting more excited about the day ahead. Ruth came running back.

'Joanna had just heard them and was pleased they were on time. They are going to play in the courtyard outside the shops and café, and later on will be giving a marching display. What did you want to ask me?'

'At the moment you are working here as a volunteer, how would you like a paid job, it would be part-time to begin with, but hopefully become full-time very soon. I would like you to help with making and packaging the soaps etc, and to help in the shop.'

'I don't even have to think about it Sarah, I would love to

work with you, especially if it involves making the soaps.'

'Yes it would, and distilling the oil, making lavender water and bottles of essence. There will be plenty to do because next year we are hoping for double the crop of lavender. We'll talk it through properly another time, there's a lot to do today.'

'I'll go round with the duster, just to tidy things up. Do you have enough change in the till? If not I'll go and see if the Farm Shop can help.'

'I think we are fine, it is cash only today so we should get quite a lot of change. Listen, it sounds as though the band is in the carpark now. We should soon be getting our first customers.'

Tony came dashing in 'It's all systems go, the band is here and so are the villagers, they followed the band in waving balloons and flags and singing 'Lavender's blue'. Joanna had a volunteer down by the gate selling helium filled balloons and flags with Bridge Farm and Lafolley's Lavender printed on them, they seem to have got the party off to a good start. I'm off now to take some photos. See you soon. Don't forget the MP is officially opening the Education Centre at eleven.'

'You go' said Ruth 'I'll hold the fort.'

'Thanks Ruth, I really would like to be there. Get some good photos Tony.'

46

'Are you ready Sarah? Everyone is going down to Bridge Farm for dinner.'

'I'm ready! What a brilliant day, we have almost sold out, I say 'almost' because I found that Ruth had kept some stock behind so that we would have something to put on the shelves for future customers. She has agreed to work here and I think will be a real asset. Has James come yet? I want to hear from him how you are treating him, not giving him all the grotty jobs I hope.'

'He is doing very well and gives the impression that he likes the work. Here he is, you can ask him yourself.'

'Hi Sarah, how was the honeymoon? I don't think I have to ask, you both look marvellous.'

'The honeymoon was super James, but I want to hear how you are getting on with Tony and his mates.'

'If anyone had told me a year ago that I would be doing plastering and enjoying it I would have laughed, but I am enjoying the work and Tony does take me to different places and explains what has to be done. So, it's great!'

'Good, let me know if he's a pain.'

'Come on you two, dinner beckons, it should be a lovely end to a perfect day. Wasn't the band great?'

'They really got the party going and I loved the balloons and flags.'

'Joanna's got some balloons going down the centre of her table, Mum has provided some lavender serviettes …'

'… and we've provided the wine' said Tony, 'we brought it back from Spain.'

'It should be a good evening then. Joanna said that Alan is staying the night in his old room, I wonder how he'll feel?'

'He has told me several times now that the sad memories have gone and he is happy to be part of the Bridge Farm extended family. He has put a lot of work into the Education Centre and has thoroughly enjoyed himself. His photos that are displayed are superb, we are hoping to have some of them made into postcards for sale soon.'

'Tony took me down to Shore Cottage the other day and I just thought that the wall of black and white photos was beautiful, I didn't realize that he had been a war photographer. He said I can go and see him any time I like and he will show me how to use a camera 'effectively' – that's a lovely word Sarah, and I know exactly what he means so I shall take him up on his offer, it could be that Tony could use a photographer on his sites.'

'You obviously enjoy your work James, and I know Alan will enjoy teaching you. Come on, Joanna is looking for us.'

'What's keeping you?' said Joanna waving a flag. 'This is the party to end a perfect day, if you don't hurry all that lovely Spanish wine will have gone.'

They all laughed and went into Bridge Farm.

'It's still chilly here' said Sarah, 'I think Mollie is going to have a long wait for the warm feel to this hallway.'

'She's been on about that already this evening, so don't you start, we are here to enjoy a good meal and good company and toast the opening of the Education Centre, the Lavender shop and the Farm Shop. We are in the dining room as it is a special occasion.'

There was quite a buzz of conversation going when they went into the dining room the excitement of the day was obviously carrying on. Alan got up and gave Sarah a big hug and a kiss.

'How did you get on dear girl?'

'Really well Alan, the soaps all went and we sold twenty three books. The soap making demonstration went much better than I thought it would, the visitors were really interested in it. What about you, have you enjoyed yourself?'

'I have had a wonderful day! There was so much interest in the exhibits in the Centre, the children loved the computers and spent a long time working out where the lavender farm was now. Bill Lawrence encouraged them to look at other maps and they ended up using new technology and the older methods. I'm now looking forward to one of Joanna's dinners and a good night's sleep in my old room.'

'No problems with that then?'

'I told you that you had helped me lay my unhappy memories to rest, and I meant that. I am looking forward to a night in my old room with some of my good memories.'

'Sit yourselves down, the potatoes are ready, please enjoy your meal.' Joanna put two large salvers of baked potatoes on the table.

Soon the knives and forks were busy and the conversation died away, a true sign that the meal was being enjoyed.

'That meal was amazing' said Ken, 'can I ask you all to raise your glasses to our host and hostess, who, once again have done us proud, Joanna and Seth.'

The glasses clinked and everyone cheered. Seth stood up and thanked everyone for their co-operation in getting the Open Day ready and making it such a success. He then asked Alan if he would propose the toast to the new enterprises. Alan stood up, raised his glass, looked round the table and said 'What a happy place this is, long may it continue. Friends I give you Bridge Farm and Agnes Lafolley's Lavender.' Everyone stood and drank the toast and once again gave a cheer, it was that sort of evening. Then Mollie looked up 'I think there is one more thing we must do, Sarah and Tony please step forward.'

'Mollie, what are you doing?' asked Joanna.

'It will all be clear in a minute. I want Sarah and Tony to kiss the angels on the fireplace, the lefthand one is of Elizabeth, so Tony would you kiss that one please. The righthand one is of Walter, so Sarah would you kiss that one please'

'I hope you know what you are doing' said Joanna.

'I do, believe me Joanna.'

Tony and Sarah kissed the angels as requested by Mollie, everyone in the room was silent, then there was a rush of air, seemingly from the fireplace, that went round the room and out into the hallway.

'I knew I was right' shouted Mollie, 'I bet the hallway is warm now, we have two lovers in the cottage and they know the meaning of the angel faces.'

'Perhaps Elizabeth is at rest now' said Sarah, 'I'm sure I've felt that warm air before, Mollie it's you that's the angel.'

Joanna went out and came back looking dumbfounded. 'You are right Mollie, the hallway is warm. What a perfect end to a perfect day.'

About the Author

The author has written this book to achieve a lifelong ambition, and that is to get a book on library shelves. Books have been her life since the age of six when she was introduced to a public library where the librarian fostered her interests. At the age of seventeen she became an assistant librarian at a University College. The next step was marriage and a family after which she went back to library work, finished her qualifications and eventually became the Tutor Librarian in a College of Further Education. Although now retired, books are still one of her main interests.

Lightning Source UK Ltd.
Milton Keynes UK
31 March 2010

152155UK00002B/2/P

9 781438 974088